O9-BTJ-768

Grammar & Writing
for Standardized Tests
Timed Essay & Multiple Choice

Martin E. Lee

Senior Series Consultant
Beverly Ann Chin
Professor of English
University of Montana

Senior Consultant
Mel Farberman
Director of English Language Arts, K–12
Bay Shore U.F.S.D.
Bay Shore, NY

Sadlier-Oxford
A Division of William H. Sadlier, Inc.

Acknowledgments

The publisher wishes to thank for their comments and suggestions the following teachers, who read portions of this text prior to publication.

Susan Simundson
District Facilitator, English Department
Tamalpais Union High School District
Larkspur, CA

Jackie Kucker
College Counselor
Benjamin Cardozo High School
Bayside, NY

Printed in the United States of America
ISBN: 0-8215-0773-7
3456789/09 08 07 06 05

TABLE OF CONTENTS

ONLINE COMPONENTS
www.writingforstandardizedtests.com

At **www.writingforstandardizedtests.com** you will find the following online components designed to extend and reinforce the instruction provided in the Student Text:

- Two Practice Tests that can be printed out and distributed to students
- Additional practice for Topics 20–32 in the Multiple-Choice section (See page T20.)
- Answer rationales for the multiple-choice items in the Student Text and the online tests

For more information about *Grammar & Writing for Standardized Tests* online components, see page T5.

Introduction

Good writing and grammar skills have always been important to success in school, in college, and in the workplace. Now that these skills are being tested on high-stakes college admissions exams, however, they are more critical than ever. *Grammar & Writing for Standardized Tests* recognizes this fact; it is designed to help students prepare for both the writing and the grammar and usage sections of standardized tests by providing focused instruction, helpful models, and abundant practice in all of the skills most commonly assessed on these tests.

With the introduction of a new writing section to the SAT*, the exam now tests a student's ability to write a timed essay and to complete multiple-choice grammar and usage items in three different formats. The new writing section is worth 800 points, or one-third of the SAT's new maximum score of 2400 points. The ACT*, another high-stakes college admissions exam, has for some time contained a section (called the English Test) that tests grammar and usage skills in formats similar to those of the new SAT. It now also includes an optional timed essay component—called the Writing Test—that is comparable to the new SAT essay.

The PSAT/NMSQT*, a standardized test many students take as practice for the SAT, includes multiple-choice grammar and usage items similar to those on the new SAT. *Grammar & Writing for Standardized Tests* also serves as preparation for this high-stakes exam.

Program Components

The *Grammar & Writing for Standardized Tests* program consists of a Student Text, a Teacher's Edition, and Online Resources that supplement and complement both.

The Student Text is aimed at high school students who will be taking a standardized test. It is clear, concise, and student-friendly, with instruction and practice designed to engage students as well as to effectively prepare them. Key features of the Student Text include:

- A section of topics (lessons) dedicated to the essay-writing process
- A section dedicated to the multiple-choice grammar and usage skills most commonly tested on standardized tests
- Two step-by-step models that illustrate how two student writers proceed from a prompt to a finished essay
- Test-taking tips interspersed throughout the text
- A rubric commonly used for scoring standardized test essays, and three sample essays scored according to the rubric
- Two full-length practice tests

*SAT is a registered trademark of the College Entrance Examination Board, ACT is a trademark of ACT, Inc., and PSAT/NMSQT is a registered trademark of the CEEB and National Merit Scholarship Corporation. None of these were affiliated with the production of, nor endorse, this product.

The Teacher's Edition includes additional information about the *Grammar & Writing for Standardized Tests* program and how it can be implemented into the classroom, with suggested pacing charts, additional writing prompts, and on-page answers to all of the exercise items in the Multiple-Choice section of the Student Text, as well as to selected exercise items in the Essay section.

Online Components for *Grammar & Writing for Standardized Tests* are available at **www.writingforstandardizedtests.com** and are accessible to teachers only. These components include:

- Two Practice Tests in standardized-test format, supplementing the two tests included in the Student Text. These online tests can be printed out in 8½ × 11 in. format and distributed to students for extra practice.

- Additional practice for each of Topics 20–32 in the Multiple-Choice section of the Student Text (which represent the topics most frequently assessed on the SAT and the ACT). These practice sheets, one for each topic, can be printed out and distributed to students to supplement the practice provided in the Student Texts.

- Answer rationales for all of the multiple-choice items in the Student Text—for example, why answer (d) is correct and answers (a), (b), (c), and (e) are not—as well as for the online Practice Tests.

To access any of these components, go to **www.writingforstandardizedtests.com** and use access code: **GNBLBFBFMC**.

Program Overview

In content, organization, and method, *Grammar & Writing for Standardized Tests* directly addresses the challenges posed by the writing and grammar sections of college admission exams: In order to achieve high scores, students must write a well-developed persuasive essay, demonstrate a command of basic grammar and usage, and do both under the trying conditions of a timed test. On the SAT, students will be given 25 minutes to plan and write an essay in response to a prompt, and 35 minutes to complete 49 multiple-choice grammar and usage items; on the ACT, students will have 30 minutes to write an essay (if they choose to do so), and 45 minutes to complete 75 multiple-choice grammar and usage items. *Grammar & Writing for Standardized Tests* has been designed to prepare students for the writing and grammar sections of both of these, the nation's leading college admissions tests.

The Essay

The skills developed in the Essay section of the Student Text focus on the task of responding to a prompt with a well-executed persuasive essay. Though many of these skills apply just as well to other kinds of writing, the instruction and practice provided in *Grammar & Writing for Standardized Tests* are keyed to the demands of writing a *timed* essay.

Because efficient **prewriting** is so important to the development of a successful persuasive essay, the first four topics (pp. 11–24) are dedicated to this task. Students learn to think carefully about what they will write *before* they put pencil to paper. They then learn to improve their **writing** by practicing skills at the paragraph and sentence levels through different types of exercises.

Step-by-Step Models

The Student Text provides two step-by-step models (pp. 73–80) that show how two student writers complete the entire writing process—from prewriting to revising—under the time constraints of a standardized test. Not only do the models break out the essay-writing steps, but they also provide a suggested amount of time to spend on each. They present two different prewriting strategies, and can be used as a guide to illustrate for students how to apply this process to their writing.

Grammar and Usage

As the writing portion of standardized tests assesses grammar and usage skills, so too does *Grammar & Writing for Standardized Tests*. In the Multiple-Choice section of the Student Text, students review and practice—in the same multiple-choice formats as on standardized tests—the skills most commonly assessed.

In addition to focused instruction, the Multiple-Choice topics provide students with guided practice; before they begin each set of multiple-choice items, they are given a sample item, its correct answer, and an explanation for *why* the correct answer is correct.

Test Taking

In addition to providing two step-by-step models, *Grammar & Writing for Standardized Tests* also provides students with instruction in and advice about the framework and conditions of standardized tests. Test-Taking Tips, appearing throughout the Student Text, provide students with additional instruction, suggestions on how to save time, and other helpful pointers. Each Multiple-Choice topic, too, by providing on-page answer ovals, lets students practice filling in their answers as they will have to do on standardized test answer sheets.

How to Use This Book

The *Grammar & Writing for Standardized Tests* program is designed to be flexible and easy to use; teachers can use it to lead a whole class, or can assign selected topics or sections to small groups of students. Because the text is student-friendly, students can use it independently, too. *Grammar & Writing for Standardized Tests* can be integrated into and used to complement any English curriculum over the course of a full year, or for shorter time periods in preparation for a standardized test. For more suggestions on pacing, see pages T10–T12.

A glance at the table of contents shows that the Student Text is divided into two main sections: one that is dedicated to essay writing (more specifically, writing to a prompt), and one that is dedicated to multiple-choice grammar and usage items. Most students will have already received instruction in some or all of the skills covered in the Student Text. Depending on grade level and students' ability, teachers should decide how to allocate and present the program contents accordingly—in sections or by topic, for instance. Instead of administering the practice tests after students have completed all of the topics, teachers may choose to administer one of them before beginning the text in order to assess students' level of readiness, and to identify skills that may need reinforcement and practice.

Getting Started

Below are some suggestions for how to begin to incorporate *Grammar & Writing for Standardized Tests* into your existing program.

- Evaluate the essay-writing process you currently teach. If you provide students with more than one class session to prewrite, write, and proofread their work, then you will have to develop strategies that will allow students to do all of this within a designated time frame such as 25–30 minutes. For instance, you may want to start by allotting one full class session to complete the entire process, and then gradually decrease the allotted time until students become comfortable with 25–30 minutes. Or, you may want to break up the entire writing process into its component steps first, and have students practice completing one stage at a time within an allotted amount of time. See, for example, the two step-by-step models on pp. 73–80 for recommendations on how much time to allocate to each step.

- When grading your students' work, use the scoring guidelines and rubrics that will be used by the scorers of the test your students will be taking.

- Make sure your students understand the rubric, or scoring guidelines, you will be using to grade their essays. Closely examine with them the criteria of each score level, so they learn to appreciate the differences between the scores. For example, ask students to try and anticipate how "*keen* critical thinking and solid reasoning" (score of 6) differs from "*strong* critical thinking" (score of 5), and so on. For a detailed description of the scores 1–6 (the scoring guidelines established for most standardized tests), see pp. 5–6 in the Student Text.

- Read with your students the scored sample essays (pp. 7–10), and have them use the language of the rubric to analyze them. Ask students to discuss in detail why each essay received the score that it did. For instance, have them compare the essays for relevant evidence, supporting details, word choice, sentence structure, and grammar and usage.

- Remind students that they are probably already familiar with the writing process that they will practice in this book. The difference is that now they must learn to complete this process within a designated time frame. Preparation is of the essence, and for that reason the writing process, as outlined below, should be deeply instilled—indeed, almost "automatic"—when students open their exams and begin their essays. It is important to remind students regularly that their essays will be judged first in terms of development—how well they support their views with a progression of facts, details, and ideas, and whether they do so in a unified, coherent manner. Their essays will be judged holistically, or based on the impression they make as a whole, rather than on their individual attributes.

The Writing Process

STEPS	TASKS
Prewriting	• Narrow the topic • Use graphic organizers to gather and group ideas and details • Order ideas for effectiveness • Draft a thesis statement
Drafting (Writing)	• Write an essay from prewriting notes • Make sure to draft a strong introduction that includes thesis statement • Use relevant examples to support point of view • Draft a strong conclusion
Revising	• Read essay for coherence and unity • Make sure essay is free of fragments or run-ons, or any other errors in grammar and usage • Replace any vague or dull words with precise ones

- Point out to students that the Student Text provides two step-by-step models that show how two student writers completed the entire writing process—from prewriting to revising—under time constraints. These models can be used as a guide to illustrate for students how to apply this process to their writing.

- Grammar instruction, too, can be integrated into the revising phase of the writing process. After students write a timed (or even un-timed) essay, teach one of the topics from the grammar and usage section of the book. Then have students review their own essays (or exchange them with peer editors) to check for correct use of the grammar just taught.

- Make sure that students understand that when they take a college admissions exam, they will have to only identify or fix errors in grammar, usage, or paragraph structure, not formally name or explain grammatical terms.

- Encourage students to periodically refer to the appendices of this book to familiarize themselves with commonly confused words, idioms, and for additional test-taking tips. Have them analyze their progress, strengths, or weaknesses by filling out the student self-evaluation on pp. 215–216.

The following pages provide three pacing charts with suggested study plans. The first plan, based on a 30-week schedule, is to be used for preparation beginning approximately eight months before taking a standardized test. The second and third plans, representing 20- and 12-week schedules, are meant to be used for more intensive preparation. Notice that pp. T13–T14 provide a list of additional prompts for practice.

Full-Year Course (30 weeks)

The chart below sets out a suggested study plan for students who begin preparation approximately eight months before they take a standardized test. Teachers should keep in mind that online, too, they can access two additional practice tests that can be printed out in standard 8½ x 11 in. format.

WEEK	ASSIGNMENT
1	Introduction (pp.1–2); Essay Overview (pp. 4–10); Topic 1 (pp. 11–12)
2	Topic 2 (pp. 13–16)
3	Topic 3 (pp. 17–20); Topic 4 (pp. 21–24)
4	Topic 5 (pp. 25–28)
5	Topic 6 (pp. 29–33)
6	Topic 7 (pp. 33–34); Topic 8 (pp. 35–36)
7	Topic 9 (pp. 37–40)
8	Topic 10 (pp. 41–42); Topic 11 (pp. 43–46)
9	Topic 12 (pp. 47–53); Topic 13 (pp. 53–54)
10	Topic 14 (pp. 55–58)
11	Topic 15 (pp. 59–62)
12	Topic 16 (pp. 63–64), Topic 17 (pp. 65–68)
13	Topic 18 (pp. 69-70); Topic 19 (pp. 71–72)
14	Step-By-Step Models (pp. 73–80)
15	Multiple-Choice Overview (pp. 86–90); Topic 20 (pp. 91–96)
16	Topic 21 (pp. 97–102)
17	Topic 22 (pp. 103–108)
18	Topic 23 (pp. 109–112); Topic 24 (pp. 113–116)
19	Topic 25 (pp. 117–122)
20	Topic 26 (pp. 123–128)
21	Topic 27 (pp. 129–132); Topic 28 (pp. 133–138)
22	Topic 29 (pp. 139–144)
23	Topic 30 (pp. 145–150)
24	Topic 31 (pp. 151–156)
25	Topic 32 (pp. 157–162)
26	Topic 33 (pp. 163–166)
27	Topic 34 (pp. 167–170)
28	Topic 35 (pp. 171–176)
29	Practice Test 1 (pp. 177–192)
30	Practice Test 2 (pp. 193–208)

Half-Year Course (20 weeks)

The chart below sets out a suggested study plan for students who begin intensive preparation five or six months before they take a standardized test. Teachers should keep in mind that online, too, they can access two additional practice tests that can be printed out in standard 8½ x 11 in. format.

Week	Assignment
1	Essay Overview (pp. 4–10); Topic 1 (pp. 11–12)
2	Topic 2 (pp. 13–16); Topic 3 (pp. 17–20)
3	Topic 4 (pp. 21–24); Topic 5 (pp. 25–28)
4	Topic 6 (pp. 29–33); Topic 7 (pp. 33–34); Topic 8 (pp. 35–36)
5	Topic 9 (pp. 37–40); Topic 10 (pp. 41–42)
6	Topic 11 (pp. 43–46); Topic 12 (pp. 47–53)
7	Topic 13 (pp. 53–54); Topic 14 (pp. 55–58)
8	Topic 15 (pp. 59–62); Topic 16 (pp. 63–64)
9	Topic 17 (pp. 65–68); Topic 18 (pp. 69–70); Topic 19 (pp. 71–72)
10	Step-By-Step Models (pp. 73–80); Multiple-Choice Overview (pp. 86–90)
11	Topic 20 (pp. 91–96); Topic 21 (pp. 97–102)
12	Topic 22 (pp. 103–108); Topic 23 (pp. 109–112)
13	Topic 24 (pp. 113–116); Topic 25 (pp. 117–122)
14	Topic 26 (pp. 123–128); Topic 27 (pp. 129–132)
15	Topic 28 (pp. 133–138); Topic 29 (pp. 139–144)
16	Topic 30 (pp. 145–150); Topic 31 (pp. 151–156)
17	Topic 32 (pp. 157–162); Topic 33 (pp. 163–166)
18	Topic 34 (pp. 167–170); Topic 35 (pp. 171–176)
19	Practice Test 1 (pp. 177–192)
20	Practice Test 2 (pp. 193–208)

"Crash" Course (12 weeks)

The chart below sets out a suggested study plan for students who begin intensive preparation three months before they take a standardized test. Teachers should keep in mind that online, too, they can access two additional practice tests that can be printed out in standard 8½ x 11 in. format.

WEEK	ASSIGNMENT
1	Essay Overview (pp. 4-10); Topic 1 (pp. 11–12); Topic 2 (pp. 13–16)
2	Topic 3 (pp. 117–20); Topic 4 (pp. 21–24); Topic 5 (pp. 25–28); Topic 6 (pp. 29–32)
3	Topic 7 (pp. 33–34) Topic 8 (pp. 35–36); Topic 9 (pp. 37–40); Topic 10 (pp. 41–42); Topic 11 (pp. 43–46)
4	Topic 12 (pp. 47–53); Topic 13 (pp. 53–54); Topic 14 (pp. 55–58); Topic 15 (pp. 59–62)
5	Topic 16 (pp. 63–64); Topic 17 (pp. 65–68); Topic 18 (pp. 69–70); Topic 19 (pp. 71–72); Step-By-Step Models (pp. 73–80)
6	Multiple-Choice Overview (pp. 86–90); Topic 20 (pp. 91–96); Topic 21 (pp. 97–102)
7	Topic 22 (pp. 103–108); Topic 23 (pp. 109–112); Topic 24 (pp. 113–116)
8	Topic 25 (pp. 117–122); Topic 26 (pp. 123–128); Topic 27 (pp. 129–132)
9	Topic 28 (pp. 133–138); Topic 29 (pp. 139–144); Topic 30 (pp. 145–150); Topic 31 (pp. 151–156)
10	Topic 32 (pp. 157–162); Topic 33 (pp. 163–166); Topic 34 (pp. 167–170); Topic 35 (pp. 171–176)
11	Practice Test 1 (pp. 177–192)
12	Practice Test 2 (pp. 193–208)

Additional Prompts for Practice

If, in addition to the prompts found throughout the Student Text, students need extra practice, below are six additional prompts.

> Thomas A. Edison once said, "Our greatest weakness lies in giving up. The most certain way to succeed is always to try just one more time."

Do you agree or disagree? Support your position with examples from history, literature, readings, or personal experience.

> It is often said that the harder you work, the luckier you become.

Do you agree or disagree? Support your position with examples from history, literature, readings, or personal experience.

> Thomas Jefferson once said, "The care of human life and happiness, not its destruction, is the first and only legitimate object of good government."

Do you agree or disagree? Support your position with examples from history, literature, readings, or personal experience.

> In our culture, people sometimes refer to "the American dream." As society changes, so too does the meaning of the phrase. Today, "the American dream" means _____.

Write an essay that completes the above statement. Use examples from history, literature, readings, or personal observations to support your point of view.

> Eleanor Roosevelt once said, "You gain strength, courage and confidence by every experience in which you really stop to look fear in the face. You are able to say to yourself, " 'I lived through this horror. I can take the next thing that comes along.' "

Do you agree or disagree? Support your position with examples from history, literature, readings, or personal experience.

Martin Luther King, Jr. once said, "The ultimate measure of a man is not where he stands in moments of comfort and convenience, but where he stands at times of challenge and controversy."

Do you agree or disagree? Support your position with examples from history, literature, readings, or personal experience.

Online Writing Evaluation

To save time, teachers can choose to implement into their curriculum one of the Web-based writing evaluation programs currently available. Using these services, teachers can submit their students' essays, and instantly receive feedback and scores based on the rubrics typically used on standardized tests. One of these evaluation services, for example, is called Criterion. It is available from ETS, the same company that administers the SAT and PSAT/NMSQT. Another one, available from CTB, is called Writing Roadmap.

Notes

Notes

Grammar & Writing
for Standardized Tests
Timed Essay & Multiple Choice

Martin E. Lee

Senior Series Consultant
Beverly Ann Chin
Professor of English
University of Montana

Senior Consultant
Mel Farberman
Director of English Language Arts, K–12
Bay Shore, NY, U.F.S.D.

Sadlier-Oxford
A Division of William H. Sadlier, Inc.

Acknowledgments

The publisher wishes to thank for their comments and suggestions the following teachers, who read portions of this text prior to publication.

Susan Simundson
District Facilitator, English Department
Tamalpais Union High School District
Larkspur, CA

Jackie Kucker
College Counselor
Benjamin Cardozo High School
Bayside, NY

Photo Credits

Corbis: 17, 53, 59, 113; Bettmann: 11, 41, 151, 157; Richard Cummins: 65; Ric Ergenbright: 133; Robbie Jack: 91; Wolfgang Kaehler: 55; Lester Lefkowitz: 63; Danny Lehman: 117; Gabe Palmer: 129; Roger Ressmeyer: 33; Reuters/Amit Dave: 123; Pierre Ducharme: 21; Jim Ruyman: 35; Connie Ricca: 25; Flip Schulke: 13; Underwood & Underwood: 29; FoodPix/PictureArts/Martin Jacobs: 103; Getty Images/Stone/James Randklev: 97; Index Stock Imagery/Steve Dunwell: 37; Picture Desk/The Kobal Collection/United Artists: 47; Superstock/Lisette Le Bon: 43; The Granger Collection, New York/Carl Van Vechten: 69; The Image Works/Eastcott-Momatiuk: 145; WPA Photograph Collection, Louisiana Division, New Orleans Public Library: 109

Address inquires to:
Permissions Department, William H. Sadlier, Inc., 9 Pine Street, New York, New York 10005-1002.

Printed in the United States of America
ISBN: 0-8215-0763-X
456789/09 08 07 06 05

TABLE OF CONTENTS

Multiple Choice: Grammar and Usage

*Extra practice available at **www.writingforstandardizedtests.com**.
See page T5. (Teacher access only.)

**Answer rationales, as well as two additional Practice Tests, available at
www.writingforstandardizedtests.com. See page T5. (Teacher access only.)

Introduction

The writing section of the SAT* consists of two parts: an essay-writing component and a multiple-choice component. Together, the two parts of the writing section test understanding of standard written English. The ACT* is another standardized college entrance exam that tests similar skills but is organized differently. On the SAT, you will be given 25 minutes to plan and write an essay in response to a prompt and 35 minutes to complete the multiple-choice items.

The Essay

The essay-writing component of the SAT asks you to plan and compose a persuasive essay on a broad topic. That topic will appear in the form of a statement or statements followed by a writing assignment. Your essay will be read and graded by two qualified, experienced teachers who do not know you or what school you attend. Neither teacher will know the score the other one gives your essay, but if the two scores differ by more than one point, a third teacher will be asked to read your essay. Each will grade your essay with a score that ranges from a low of 1 to a high of 6, with a total combined score ranging from 2–12. An essay not written on the given assignment will receive a score of 0.

One of the following three kinds of essay prompts will appear on the test you take:

- **Respond to a Statement or to a Quotation** This type of prompt presents a statement or quotation followed by an assignment. The assignment will ask you to consider the statement or quotation, think about whether you agree or disagree with it, and then plan and write an essay that persuasively presents your viewpoint. You will be instructed to support your position with facts and ideas drawn from your studies, readings, current events, or personal experiences and observations.

- **Complete a Statement** In this type of prompt, you are presented with an incomplete statement followed by a blank. Your assignment will be to plan and write an essay that completes the statement. Once again, you will be instructed to support your views with facts and ideas drawn from what you have learned or experienced.

- **Respond to Two Statements or Quotations** This kind of prompt presents two contradictory statements or quotations followed by an assignment. The assignment will ask you to consider the two statements or quotations, and then to plan and write an essay in support of one of them. Here, too, you will be instructed to support your views with facts and ideas.

You should be prepared for any of these prompts. The good news is that although the kind of prompt may differ from test to test, the gist of your writing assignment will be essentially the same for each: to take a firm stand on an issue and support your viewpoint convincingly.

*SAT is a registered trademark of the College Entrance Examination Board and ACT is a registered trademark of ACT, Inc., neither of which was involved in the production of, or endorses, this product.

The Multiple-Choice Items

The multiple-choice items in this book are similar to those in the writing section of the SAT: Identifying Sentence Errors, Improving Sentences, and Improving Paragraphs. (The comparable section of the ACT, called the English Test, has multiple-choice items testing the same kinds of grammar, usage, and punctuation skills as the SAT.)

- **Identifying Sentence Errors** These items ask you to detect an error within a sentence or indicate that there is no error. They test your knowledge of basic grammar, sentence structure, and word choice.

- **Improving Sentences** The items in this section require you to choose the best way to fix any errors by selecting the most effective form of a sentence from the answer choices. They test your ability to use standard English not only correctly, but gracefully as well.

- **Improving Paragraphs** These items ask you to make choices about improving the logic, unity, or coherence of a flawed essay. They put your knowledge about writing and grammar to the test by asking you to identify the best way to revise a poorly constructed or grammatically incorrect sentence. They might also ask you to delete or relocate a sentence, or to combine sentences. In addition, you may be asked to rephrase a sentence so that it could be a topic sentence, or to choose the best way to begin or conclude an essay.

How to Use This Textbook

Test taking is like any task—the more you practice it, the less daunting it becomes. Working through the topics and activities in this textbook diligently can diminish some of the anxiety and mystery associated with writing for standardized tests. It can help you to become more relaxed and confident in a test-taking situation.

Take a moment to look over the table of contents. You will see that your book is divided into two main sections: one that addresses the essay portion of the writing section, and one that addresses the multiple-choice portion. Flip through the pages in your text to see what the topics look like. Observe repeating features, such as those that direct you to look back or ahead to related pages. Look at exercise sets or a practice test to get a sense of what awaits you. Observe, too, the sample scored essays as well as the step-by-step models—two essays presented from start to finish to emphasize the importance of the prewriting phase of the writing process. Then flip to the appendices to see the additional information they provide.

Working through the topics in each section of your text will not only help sharpen your persuasive writing skills and grammar and usage skills, but its focused instruction, practice, and test-taking strategies and tips will also help you be successful on the writing section of the SAT and comparable parts of the ACT.

Good luck!

The Essay:
Writing to a Prompt

The Essay: Writing to a Prompt

A persuasive essay is one that you write to convince readers that your opinion is right, or to persuade someone to take action. To create a successful work of persuasion, you need to present logical arguments and support them with valid evidence. To receive a high score on the essay part of the writing section, you will need to get your points across not only forcefully and intelligently, but also skillfully, demonstrating a varied vocabulary and smooth transitions between ideas.

What Makes a Good Essay?

Think of the charismatic people you know, those who can deliver a convincing argument or speech. A good persuasive essay is like one of these people; it uses appeal along with perceptive thinking to sway an audience. The audience for the essay that you will write for the SAT will be college or high school writing teachers. To receive a high score, you need to know what they will be looking for when they read your essay.

What Your Readers Will Expect

The readers who will grade your essay know that you will have had only 25 minutes (maybe more, depending on the test) to plan, write, and look over it. Therefore, they will not expect a polished composition. They will, however, expect you to present your ideas clearly and effectively, and in a style that exhibits skilled control of language. Although they will not expect you to have expertise on the topic, they will expect you to take a firm position and to make your best case. They will judge your essay holistically, or based on the impression it makes as a whole, rather than on its individual attributes.

The readers will pay careful attention to the way you present your argument. They will read to see whether you develop and support your views with a progression of facts, details, and ideas, and whether you do so in a unified, coherent manner. They will expect you to use the conventions of standard written English, although they will find a conversational tone acceptable, even effective, as long as you avoid clichés and slang, and use idiomatic expressions correctly. The readers will notice whether or not you demonstrate a command of the language.

In short, the readers grading your essay will be looking for essentially these elements:

- relevant evidence
- a clear, logical presentation of ideas
- correct use of standard written English
- an effective, appealing style

How Long Should Your Essay Be?

When you take a standardized test, the length of your essay will be limited to the number of lines on your answer sheet. You will be provided with scrap paper, which you may want to use for the prewriting skills you will learn in this book. In confining yourself to the number of lines on your answer sheet, keep the following in mind: *quality over quantity.* Say what you wish to say, but be concise. Use only the best of your ideas.

Also, try to keep your handwriting legible and your margins narrow so that you can fit all of your ideas on the answer sheet. Be sure to write as neatly as you can—you want the readers to be able to read your essay and the corrections you make.

Scoring Essays

Scoring guidelines for most standardized tests typically spell out the distinctions between the scores 1–6. These guidelines have been established to distinguish an outstanding persuasive essay from one that is successful, for example, or to differentiate between one that is adequate and one that is lacking.

Below is a summary of the scoring guidelines.

- **Score of 6: Outstanding** Essays that merit this score are clearly and insightfully developed and written; they display keen critical thinking and solid reasoning. The writer effectively presents and supports a point of view by providing relevant examples and evidence. The writing is focused and the ideas are well organized and presented smoothly, coherently, even elegantly. The writing displays an exceptional command of language and word choice, and it skillfully incorporates a variety of sentence types and structures. Essays this good are mostly free of mistakes in grammar, usage, and mechanics.

- **Score of 5: Successful** Essays that receive this score are effectively developed and written. The writer demonstrates strong critical thinking skills and thoughtfully presents and supports a point of view. Ideas are well organized and supporting facts and details are generally appropriate and presented in a logical and coherent manner. The writing is focused, and demonstrates a solid command of language and vocabulary. It integrates a variety of sentence types and structures. These essays may include minor flaws in grammar, usage, and mechanics.

- **Score of 4: Adequate** Essays in this scoring category are competently thought through and adequately written, but contain some weaknesses. The writer competently develops, presents, and supports a point of view, using supporting facts and details that are sufficient. The writing is, for the most part, focused and coherent, and demonstrates an adequate but variable command of writing conventions and vocabulary. The writer includes some variety in sentence structures and types. The essay contains some errors in grammar, usage, and mechanics.

- **Score of 3: Lacking** Although essays in this category may demonstrate some critical thinking, they are neither competently developed nor adequately written, and may be marred by a variety of weaknesses. For example, the writing may not sufficiently or consistently support the writer's point of view because of the use of insubstantial evidence. Also, it may display lapses in focus and/or coherence. In addition, although the writing may demonstrate some facility with language, the writer's word choice is neither consistently strong nor wholly appropriate. Furthermore, the writing is flawed by faulty sentence structure as well as by an assortment of flaws in grammar, usage, and mechanics.
- **Score of 2: Seriously Flawed** Essays that receive this score are critically limited; they demonstrate many weaknesses. These essays show poor critical thinking, and are neither well organized nor clearly focused. The writer's point of view is vague or inconsistent, and is insufficiently supported by facts, details, or other evidence. The writing displays little coherence or exhibits lapses in a clear progression of ideas. Also, it contains little evidence of competent language use; the word choice is weak or even erroneous. Furthermore, the writing shows frequent sentence structure errors, and is also diminished by very serious errors in grammar, usage, and mechanics.
- **Score of 1: Thoroughly Deficient** Essays in this group are fundamentally flawed and demonstrate very little or no proficiency. If these essays do present a feasible point of view, it is either poorly developed or not developed at all. Evidence in support of the writer's view is vague or missing. The writing is disorganized, wholly incoherent, and therefore difficult to follow. Furthermore, the writer's intent is clouded by grave fundamental mistakes in word choice and sentence structure, and by an abundance of serious errors in grammar, usage, or mechanics.

How Do I Get a Top Score?

Below are some pointers to help you to get a top score:

- Open strong; close memorably.
- Let readers know what to expect by including a clear and compelling thesis statement.
- Provide a variety of evidence, including personal observations, to support your viewpoint.
- Recognize other points of view, particularly when you are asked to agree or disagree with a statement.
- Use precise, vivid language wherever you can.
- Do not use big words if unsure of their meaning.
- Make sure each paragraph is unified and that the main idea is either clearly implied or included in a topic sentence.

- Use transitional words and phrases to establish coherence.
- Make sure all paragraphs help to support your thesis statement.
- Vary the lengths, types, beginnings, and structures of your sentences.

Sample Essays

Below is a writing prompt similar to one you might encounter on a standardized test. Three examples of essays follow, each written in response to the prompt. The first essay is one that would most likely receive a score of 6. The second would most likely receive a score of 4, and the last one, a score of 2.

Read the prompt and the writing assignment. Then read each essay critically to gain a sense of how the scoring process works, and to have a gauge by which to measure your own writing.

DO NOT WRITE AN ESSAY THAT ADDRESSES ANY OTHER TOPIC. AN ESSAY ON A DIFFERENT TOPIC WILL NOT BE ACCEPTED.

Consider the following statement. Then write an essay as directed.

> **"Universities should be safe havens where ruthless examination of realities will not be distorted by the aim to please or inhibited by the risk of displeasure." Is that an important role for universities? What do you think?**

<u>Assignment</u>: Write an essay in response to the above statement. Support your viewpoint with ideas, facts, and details gained from your readings, observations, or personal experience.

Essay that would typically earn a score of 6

The most important thing about the college years is not what we think it is when we fill out our college applications. Most of us probably think about the quality of the academics first, particularly if we already have identified a field of study or future career that interests us. We expect, certainly, that our college years will be a time during which we grow and mature. But, mostly, we envision those years as a time when we will absorb and begin to become proficient in a body of knowledge that we will use and build upon in our professions. This is certainly a part of the college experience. However, the college years are also a time when we, within the accepting and open-minded environment a campus provides, learn to think for ourselves, and develop our individuality as a result.

A good example of this process can be found in the life of Charlayne Hunter-Gault, the first African American woman to be admitted to and graduate from the University of Georgia. Hunter-Gault wanted to attend the university for its outstanding journalism program, but in 1959 the school was designated for whites only, and Hunter-Gault was denied admission. Hunter-Gault and a fellow classmate enlisted the help of an attorney to fight the school's decision and, after a long legal battle, a judge ruled in favor of the two students. Although initially the university was not a "safe haven," Hunter-Gault's experience of integrating the university—thereby creating a place where the ruthless examination of realities indeed was not inhibited by the aim to please—she opened her mind to possibilities she would not have considered before. She went on to have a successful career in newspaper and television journalism.

My wise older sister, a senior in college, also has been pounding into my head this notion of exploring ideas unfettered by rigid conventions. Because of college, she has been able to develop her own views on the world around her. She says, and I agree, that when we are growing up, there are pressures to conform. These pressures, both subtle and not-so-subtle, are pervasive. In school, for example, there is pressure to receive high grades. To do so, we do what we think our teachers and parents want and expect us to do. Outside of school, there is peer pressure to act in certain ways and to dress and talk like everybody else does. Yes, in our lives conformity is the name of the game and we are rewarded for being good at it. But this is unproductive because of one true, key idea: The world is constantly changing. If change is a constant, why are we so keen on maintaining the status quo through blind conformity?

This is where college should come to the rescue. Instead of conformity, we need flexibility. Flexibility emerges from freedom of thought; it comes from freely making connections among ideas and fields of study. If the college experience encourages and prepares us to think for ourselves, if it emboldens you to open your mind, then it will be doing a great service to us and to society as a whole. So, for my money—and a lot of it will go to the college of my choice!—I want a safe haven in return. I want my money's worth of open-mindedness and honest exploration and examination of ideas.

Why this essay receives a 6:

- It supports a clear thesis with convincing, relevant ideas presented in a well organized and sensible progression.
- The paragraphs are unified and coherent; it uses a variety of sentence structures and precise vocabulary.
- It has a pleasant, conversational tone.
- It has a minimum of errors, such as the pronoun shift ("us. . . you") in paragraph 4, sentence 4.

Essay that would typically earn a score of 4

The most important thing about the college years is that during that time we learn to and are encouraged to be open-minded and to think for ourselves. We are able to develop our individuality as a result of this. This may not be what most of us think when we fill out our college applications. At that time, we think that those years will be a time when we will learn a body of knowledge that we can later apply in our professional lives. We also think that college will be a time for growing up and maturing, and learning to live with others. This is certainly true, but more importantly, we will develop our skills at reasoning freely in an uninhibited way.

I think the college years serve a vital function in our lives and that is all about the environment a campus can provide. In that environment we get to freely explore ideas. There we comfortably participate in open-minded discussions about many important topics. It is a time for freely making connections among ideas big and small. It is a time when we learn to think for ourselves. This is what my older sister tells me and I think she is right! She has experienced this herself and has been telling me that college is a place where you learn to see things in a different light.

When we are growing up, there are pressures to be and act like everybody else. These pressures are everywhere. In school, there is pressure to get high grades, which is what our teachers and parents want. There are peer pressures to act, dress, talk, and think alike, too. We all use the same expressions, wear the same clothes and we shop in the same stores where we are buying the same brands. There is always pressure to be liked or to be known as a star athlete. However, this is not helpful to developing as an individual.

In my view, conformity shortchanges us all. Being good at being and acting like everybody else is wrong because of one big idea. That idea is that conforming helps us to fit in today, but in the long run stifles us, as the world is always changing. Since change is what we can expect, we should focus more on thinking in new ways than in maintaining the status quo by thinking as everybody else.

So, we need to change the way we think and college is the place where that happens. In college we can learn to think flexibly and free. If we can be flexible in the way we think about ideas, we can make the connections needed to be ready for the unexpected. If college prepares us to think for ourselves and be open-minded, students and society benefit. Therefore, learning to reason for ourselves and not focusing on pleasing others is the best lesson to learn in college.

Why this essay receives a 4

- It adequately supports a thesis with ideas presented in a fairly well organized and sensible progression.
- It uses some variety in sentence structure and displays an adequate com-

mand of language.

- It has a pleasant, conversational tone.
- It has some errors in grammar, usage, and mechanics.

Essay that would typically earn a score of 2

The most important thing about college years is that we don't have to please anybody any more and only please ourself and that way really learn stuff. At college we don't have to do what our high school teachers say or our parents. We can be like ourselves there and be ruthless and brave there and we also connect ideas like getting older, getting wiser, learning about history, and science and philosophy. We also meet all kinds of different people too. And since they are doing what we do we can grow together.

College is when we learn what we should learn to support us and our families when college is over. We can learn to think like we want because in college nobody has to take the same classes or get up or go to sleep the same time, in short we grow up because we learn to be on our own. I've got a brother in college who tells me constently that life in his dormatory is where he learns everything worth learning because him and his buddies talk all hours about important stuff. We don't get to do that in high school except on the phone.

In college my brother tell me they hold nothing back and and teachers hold nothing back and that's better for everybody in the discussions. Everybody gives their opinions all the time. I can learn a lot from that. On the other hand; in high school I was trying all the time to do what my teachers wanted us to do and not what I thought was right you know. I was afraid to think stuff for myself. In college that will be different too. I will learn more on account of that I will be doing things for me only and will get better grades because of it and without trying to.

In summary, we need to go to college to grow up and to think like grownups. You get much smarter and ruthless in college if you go all four years I think. Because the longer you get to think about things the better it will be and the more uninhibited you get and that's good. That is my opinion and I believe it is right.

Why this essay receives a 2

- It shows poor critical thinking, is weakly organized, and its ideas are haphazard and undeveloped.
- Its thesis is vague, unfocused, and not well supported with ideas or facts.
- It demonstrates poor language skills and weak word choice.
- It contains frequent errors in sentence structure, grammar, usage, and mechanics.

Reading Carefully

Read the following:

> George Bernard Shaw once noted, "Liberty means responsibility. That is why most men dread it." Do you agree or disagree? Support your position, using examples from your personal experience, literature, history, or current events.

Playwright George Bernard Shaw (1856–1950)

Yヒou have just read an essay prompt much like one you might find on a standardized test. To help you to achieve the best results when writing your response to a prompt, you should have a well-rehearsed, efficient writing plan. This plan should include all that you will do *before* you begin to write.

Getting Under Way

The very first step in this prewriting process is to read the prompt carefully. Before you write a single word, you must make sure that you will specifically address only the topic you have been asked to address. Here's how:

- First, read the prompt carefully.
- Then, read the prompt again to clarify your task.
- Finally, identify key words and ideas in the prompt as you read it a third time.

Identifying Key Ideas

One way to identify key ideas is to underline them. Another way is to use a strategy known as **looping**. To loop, you link circled words or groups of words.

> George Bernard Shaw once noted, "Liberty means responsibility. That is why most men dread it." Do you agree or disagree? Support your position, using examples from your personal experience, literature, history, or current events.

Think about other ways to identify what is important in this prompt. Share your ideas with classmates.

Reading carefully to identify key words and ideas is an important prewriting step, and it prepares you for the next step: narrowing your focus.

TEST-TAKING TIP

You should spend no more than five or six minutes in the prewriting phase. Can you estimate time? To practice estimating time, work with a partner and take turns guessing when 1, 3, or 5 minutes have elapsed. You will need one watch or clock between you.

Exercise: Identifying Key Ideas

Now you try it. First, read the prompt. Then, read it again. Next, identify key ideas and words by looping or underlining them. Answers will vary.

1. Eleanor Roosevelt once said, "Friendship with oneself is all important, because without it one cannot be friends with anyone else in the world." Do you agree or disagree? Support your viewpoint, using examples from your personal experience, observations, or studies.

2. As countries go, the United States is a wonderful one. But like all nations, it is a work in progress. There is room for improvement. If I were a lawmaker, I would work to develop laws that would better the lives of all Americans. The direction I would turn my attention to first is _____.

3. On February 15, 1959, poet Carl Sandburg addressed a joint session of Congress to reflect on the 150th anniversary of the birth of Abraham Lincoln. In the address he said, "Not often in the story of mankind does a man arrive on earth who is both steel and velvet, . . . as hard as rock and as soft as drifting fog, who holds in his heart and mind the paradox of terrible storm and peace unspeakable and perfect." Are the qualities Sandburg describes those required of all great leaders? What do you think? Support your viewpoint, using examples from your studies or personal experience.

4. "Figuring out who you are is the whole point of human experience," journalist and author Anna Quindlen once remarked. Do you agree or disagree? Support your position, using examples from your studies or personal experience.

5. Helen Keller once said, "Character cannot be developed in ease and quiet. Only through experience of trial and suffering can the soul be strengthened, ambition inspired, and success achieved." What do you think? Support your viewpoint, using examples from your studies or personal experience.

Narrowing Your Focus

Anthropologist Margaret Mead once wrote, "Never doubt that a small group of thoughtful, committed citizens can change the world. Indeed, it's the only thing that ever has." To what extent do you agree or disagree with this observation? Support your position with examples taken from your studies, reading, or personal observations.

Civil Rights activist Martin Luther King, Jr. (1929–1968)

You have just read an essay prompt that is typical of those you will see on standardized tests. Read it again. It asks you to consider one point of view on a wide-ranging issue. It asks you to take a position on that issue and then to defend that position persuasively. But you know that you have only a limited time in which to do it. This means that you have to limit the breadth of your response so that you can address an aspect of the topic sufficiently. Essay prompts are purposely broad so that you can always write from a perspective you are familiar with.

So, how do you begin? How can you avoid wasting time with false starts? How can you focus your ideas in a few good paragraphs?

Getting Started

The first step in planning a successful persuasive essay is to **narrow your focus**. You should narrow your focus so that:

- your response is limited enough to be manageable, given the test's time and length constraints
- you can write knowledgeably about what you know
- you can provide clear, specific examples that support your opinions

If you happen to know a lot about a historical event that can support your argument, then write about it. If you have a relevant personal experience that will support or illustrate your position, then you can also use that. A work of fiction too, can provide a narrow, clear focus for your essay if you can write knowledgeably about it.

A narrow focus is important in writing an effective persuasive essay. Simply take one or two minutes to focus your thinking in order to limit the scope of your response. You will save time in the end.

With practice, you can improve your skill at narrowing broad topics. Let's look at a way to do this.

Using a Topic Web

A topic web is an organizing tool you can use to narrow the focus of your essay. Study the example below. Think about the choices this writer has made in response to Mead's position.

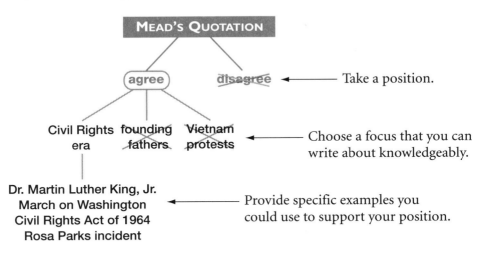

MEAD'S QUOTATION

agree   ~~disagree~~ ◄——— Take a position.

Civil Rights founding Vietnam ◄——— Choose a focus that you can
    era   ~~fathers~~ ~~protests~~   write about knowledgeably.

Dr. Martin Luther King, Jr.
March on Washington ◄——— Provide specific examples you
Civil Rights Act of 1964   could use to support your position.
Rosa Parks incident

Notice that this writer has chosen to focus on the Civil Rights era as a way to support the idea that "a small group of thoughtful, committed citizens can change the world." He or she may include the example of the March on Washington led by Martin Luther King, Jr., which helped the Civil Rights Act of 1964 get passed. This writer might also decide to use the Rosa Parks incident as another example.

You Try It

Can you think of a personal experience that you can use to support Mead's quotation? Perhaps you witnessed or were part of an event in your local community or school that initiated change. Complete the topic web below to help you narrow your focus.

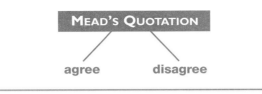

MEAD'S QUOTATION

agree   disagree

Topic webs will vary.

Using a Pro-Con Chart

Another tool you can use to narrow your writing focus is a pro-con chart. This chart can help when you are responding to a prompt that requires you to consider both sides of an issue. Using the chart helps you to see quickly which point of view you can most easily and forcefully support.

Here is how one student used a pro-con chart to examine Mead's view:

- In the Pro column, he lists examples to support the idea that individuals and small groups can make a difference.
- In the Con column, he lists other things that affect change and reasons why individuals and small groups may not make a difference.

Notice how he uses phrases, abbreviations, and other shortcuts to help speed up this part of the writing process.

Pro	Con
Civil Rights era— Martin Luther King, Jr. Lunch counter, other demonstrations Rosa Parks Brown vs. Bd. of Ed. marches speeches	change takes time, and small groups don't have the resources Majority rules; radicals, activists marginalized, fail to make impact sm. groups work against one another
Amer. Revol.— Founding fathers Paul Revere and other riders patriots Minutemen Constitutional Convention Sons of Liberty Gandhi in India	economics, power, land big factors, too great for indiv. and small groups to affect change Religious differences, prejudices run too deep for individual efforts to overcome

This student recognized that he could quickly generate many convincing ideas to choose from in the Pro column. He then decided to write his essay in support of Mead's view, and to narrow his focus to rely mainly on examples from the Revolutionary War period and the Civil Rights era.

Remember, although the prewriting stage is an important step, you will spend most of your time writing your essay. Since you have only a limited amount of time to plan, write, and look over your essay, make sure that you spend no more than two minutes narrowing your focus.

Exercise: Narrowing Your Focus

Read each prompt below and narrow the focus of your response to it. Cite examples that you would use to support your argument. You may wish to use a topic web or a pro-con chart to guide you. Answers will vary.

1. Mahatma Gandhi once said, "It is unwise to be too sure of one's own wisdom. It is healthy to be reminded that the strongest might weaken and the wisest might err." Do you agree or disagree? Support your position, using examples from your studies, personal experience, or observations.

   _____

   _____

   _____

2. Complete the statement: "The personal achievement I am most proud of is

   _____

   _____

   _____."

3. Albert Einstein once said, "Everything that is really great and inspiring is created by the individual who can labor in freedom." Do you agree or disagree with this statement? Support your position, using examples from your studies, personal experience, or observations.

   _____

   _____

   _____

4. Complete the statement: "If I could change one thing about the world, it would be _____

   _____

   _____."

5. Your neighborhood has been given a gift of $5 million to fund either infrastructure upgrades or community arts programs. How would you spend the money to improve life for you and your neighbors?

   _____

   _____

   _____

Gathering and Grouping Ideas

In 1859, ardent abolitionist John Brown and his small group of followers attempted to raid the armory at Harper's Ferry to secure arms for a slave revolt. His bold effort has been both highly praised and severely condemned. Whatever one's viewpoint, one can certainly argue that Brown's violent act ignited the Civil War.

Abolitionist John Brown (1800–1859)

Brown acted. He led *by example*. What do you think: Is example the best way or even the only way to influence others? Present your viewpoint, supporting it with evidence from your reading, studies, or observations.

Getting Under Way

To write an effective persuasive essay, you must support your viewpoint with strong ideas and examples. One way to begin is to list them in a quick but organized way. List statistics, historical facts, and ideas based on common sense to make your case. Keep in mind that ideas or illustrations gathered from personal experience can be as persuasive as those gathered from reading or study. Don't shrink from using your own observations to support your position!

You don't have a lot of time to spend on this step— perhaps 2 or 3 minutes.

The teachers who will read and grade your essay know how limited your time is. They will read mainly to see how persuasively and clearly you have made your case. Knowing this, you need to be discriminating. You may not need all of your ideas. Choose your best ones—those that are the most compelling. Cross out those you won't need to use. Remember, you will write four or five paragraphs *at most*. Aim to write a strong essay, not necessarily a long one.

> **TEST-TAKING TIP**
>
> Since the time you should spend on this phase of the prewriting process is brief, *do not write full sentences*. Use phrases, key words, or abbreviations to list supporting ideas and details.

Using a T-Chart to Gather and Group Ideas

One way to gather ideas is to use a T-chart. Look at the next page to see how one student used this tool to list, group, and choose ideas to make her case. Notice the categories into which she divided her supporting ideas and the timesaving abbreviations and shortcuts she used.

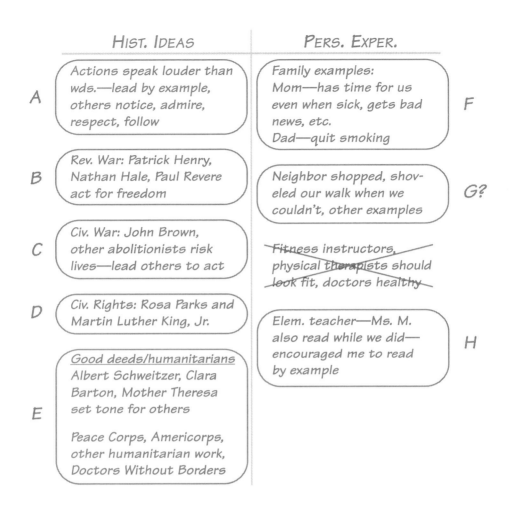

HIST. IDEAS	PERS. EXPER.

A Actions speak louder than wds.—lead by example, others notice, admire, respect, follow

F Family examples: Mom—has time for us even when sick, gets bad news, etc. Dad—quit smoking

B Rev. War: Patrick Henry, Nathan Hale, Paul Revere act for freedom

G? Neighbor shopped, shoveled our walk when we couldn't, other examples

C Civ. War: John Brown, other abolitionists risk lives—lead others to act

~~Fitness instructors, physical therapists should look fit, doctors healthy~~

D Civ. Rights: Rosa Parks and Martin Luther King, Jr.

H Elem. teacher—Ms. M. also read while we did— encouraged me to read by example

E *Good deeds/humanitarians* Albert Schweitzer, Clara Barton, Mother Theresa set tone for others

Peace Corps, Americorps, other humanitarian work, Doctors Without Borders

You can see that this student separated those ideas learned through reading and study from those learned through personal experience. To link related ideas, her strategy is simple:

- Ring the ideas she will use in the essay.
- Cross out all the ideas she will not use.
- Label all the rings that go together with the *same* capital letter.

What do you think of the way this student gathered and grouped ideas? Explain what you might do differently. Discuss your conclusions with a classmate.

Practicing the key strategies of gathering and grouping ideas will help you to get better and faster at this phase of the essay-writing process. And doing so also prepares you for the next step in the prewriting process: choosing the best order to present your ideas.

Exercise: Using a T-Chart

Read each prompt below. Take time to carefully narrow the focus of your response. Then fill the T-chart with brief notes that support your viewpoint, and ring and label the ideas that go together. Answers will vary.

1. Many have said that pain and suffering build character. What do you think? Use examples from your experience, observations, readings, or studies to write an essay about this issue.

2. Should the legal driving age in your state be lowered or should it stay as it is? What do you think? Use supporting examples from your experience and observations or from any information you have gathered from readings or studies to write an essay expressing your viewpoint on this issue.

3. Statesman Adlai E. Stevenson once said, "All progress has resulted from people who took unpopular positions." Do you agree? Use examples from your experience, observations, readings, or studies to write an essay on this idea.

4. Some have said that punishment keeps people in line. Others argue that rewarding good behavior is a more successful approach. What do you think? Use examples from your experience, observations, readings, or studies to write an essay expressing your viewpoint.

Choosing a Thesis Statement and Ordering for Support

Consider the following prompt:

> College sports is a big business. In most instances, football and basketball programs generate a great deal of revenue and publicity for their schools. Some of the athletes go on to professional careers.
>
> Should these football and basketball players be treated as student athletes while at the university, or as paid professionals?

College football game

Suppose that after considering the pros and cons of this issue, a student chooses to write an essay in favor of the viewpoint that athletes in those sports should be treated as professionals. Here are some notes he might have quickly jotted down in support of that position:

- *Demanding schedule of practices/games: little time left for classes, studying; need to take light course load, academics take backseat anyway*

- *Earn lots of $ for school: TV revenues, ticket prices, marketing of jerseys, other paraphernalia—players should share in profits*

- *Some athletes leave school early to turn pro anyway*

Once you have gathered and grouped the notes you intend to use and develop in your essay, you need to choose an order for them that best supports the argument you wish to make. So, the first thing to do is to write a thesis statement— the main idea of your argument. Usually, a thesis statement is placed at the beginning of the introductory paragraph, but you can place it in the middle or the end of the paragraph. If necessary, use two sentences to formulate your thesis statement—that's how important it is.

Writing a Thesis Statement

A thesis statement not only lets a reader know your viewpoint; it also helps *you* to focus on that viewpoint as you write. Your thesis statement, which should emerge from your prewriting, should present your position as if it were a fact. So, write it clearly and firmly. Make every effort to make plain for readers what your essay will deliver.

Below is a thesis statement written by a student who supports the viewpoint that certain college athletes should be treated as professionals:

> Since many athletes who contemplate a professional career play for a college only to showcase their talents, they should be treated and paid as the pros they will shortly become and not be required to take a heavy courseload.

It's a pretty forceful statement, isn't it?

Here are two more examples of thesis statements. Each is in response to a prompt adapted from Topic 3, and each takes a firm stand:

> **Prompt:** Should the legal driving age in your state be lowered or kept as it is?
>
> **Thesis Statement:** Keep the driving age where it is or even raise it! Many teens are self-absorbed and careless; they think they are immortal, and they are too young to drive safely and according to the rules.
>
> **Prompt:** All progress has resulted from people who took unpopular positions.
>
> **Thesis Statement:** Most people only begrudgingly accept new ideas, even good ones. Therefore, progress will always face an uphill battle.

TEST-TAKING TIP

In organizing your essay, you might also want to consider using the five-paragraph format. Start by writing an introductory paragraph and then include three paragraphs for the body. Organize the three paragraphs in a logical order (for example, in decreasing or increasing order of importance). Finish with a strong concluding paragraph.

Ordering for Support

Once you know what your thesis statement will be, it is time for the final, brief, prewriting step: choosing a clear, easy-to-follow, but effective order for presenting supporting ideas. Here is one way to order your ideas:

- Hook readers with your introduction, which should include the thesis statement.
- Between your two best ideas, arrange your other arguments in a logical order.
- Use your strongest argument last for a powerful finish.

You can order your ideas in different ways. Be creative. Think about ways to make an impression on readers. Don't just simply write your ideas down arbitrarily, no matter how good they are. Order them so that your essay has a beginning, middle, and end.

You Try It

Read again the sample notes about student athletes shown on the previous page. Add new ideas, and then choose an order for them that makes sense. Discuss your plan with a classmate.

Exercise 1: Choosing the Better Thesis Statement

Each pair of thesis statements below addresses the same prompt from essentially the same point of view. Circle the one that is more effective. If you think they are equally effective, circle both. Then explain your choice.

1. Should our government spend more or less money on school programs in the arts?

   If we want a nation of dull, narrow-minded, and uninspired citizens, then undoubtedly we must cut spending on school arts programs.

   I think that increasing government funding for school arts programs is a fabulous idea.

2. Should physical fitness classes be required of all students?

   All students need to start healthy habits that will last a lifetime.

   There are several very important medical and social reasons why all students should take physical education classes.

3. Is the use of force ever an appropriate way to resolve a conflict?

   There are bound to be occasions, particularly when intolerable abuses play a part, when, after all other means have failed, force should be applied as a solution of last resort.

   Sadly, using force is the best way to solve a great many of the world's problems.

4. Should we rely more or less on our first impressions?

   If first impressions had guided people throughout history, who would ever have taken that first bite of a lobster?

   Do we always correctly judge someone's character at a first meeting, enjoy a record on first hearing it, or understand someone's viewpoint immediately? We don't, do we?

5. Should the minimum working age be lowered?

   In the past, American children worked too many hours at dangerous factory jobs; today, with so many safety rules in place, it is time to reevaluate the guidelines that govern minimum working age.

   Anyone knows that kids can work every bit as hard and every bit as long as grown-ups can.

Exercise 2: Writing Thesis Statements

Read each prompt below. Take a position. Then, write a thesis statement that lets readers know your viewpoint. Answers will vary.

1. If we have a limited amount of money to spend on transportation, should we spend it on more and better public transportation options, or on better roads and highways for our cars and trucks?

   _____

   _____

2. Do emotions and intellect contribute to success in sports, or are physical attributes and skills all that matter?

   _____

   _____

Exercise 3: Ordering Supporting Ideas

Below are four thesis statements. Read each. Then list three ideas in support of the statement. *Think:* **Each idea should be a key idea for a different paragraph.**
Answers will vary.

1. Voting in national elections should be mandatory, not optional.

   _____

   _____

2. Some period of service to our country, military or otherwise, should be required of all young Americans.

   _____

   _____

3. The most important factor in any educational system is the quality of the teachers in the classrooms.

   _____

   _____

4. If we ignore what has happened in the past, we are bound to make many of the same mistakes in the future.

   _____

   _____

Opening Strong, Finishing Memorably

Consider the following prompt:

> In 1803, Thomas Jefferson purchased the Louisiana Territory from Napoleon. In doing so, he nearly doubled the size of the United States for about 4 cents an acre. Some have said that this purchase was one of the three events essential to the creation of the modern United States. The writing of the Declaration of Independence and the writing of the Constitution were the other two.

Do you agree that Jefferson's land purchase from France belongs in this exalted company? Support your viewpoint.

Writing a Strong Opening

Just as a boldly colored flower will attract any bee in the vicinity, a strong opening to an essay will capture a reader's attention. In contrast, a dull or confusing opening can put off a reader by creating a negative first impression.

Lewis and Clark were among the first to explore the territory acquired by the Louisiana Purchase.

Not only do the initial sentences you write provide a reader with an opportunity to develop an interest in your viewpoint, but they also are your first and best chance to do so. So take advantage of this opportunity. Hook your readers!

Read the following opening paragraph that supports the importance of the Louisiana Purchase in the creation of the modern United States.

> What would America be like today if Jefferson had never purchased the Louisiana Territory from the French? The purchase of that rich land from Napoleon was unequivocally essential to the creation of the United States as we know it. Jefferson's wise purchase was not only among the very best real estate deals ever, but it also fundamentally changed both the shape and history of our country.

A paragraph like this will make readers sit up and take notice. It engages them. It makes them eager to read on. Here's why:

- It has a provocative first sentence.
- It uses bold, precise, and stirring language.
- It is thoughtful but not pretentious.
- It is not overly long.
- It includes a compelling thesis statement—"Jefferson's wise purchase . . ."—that lets readers know what to expect.

A powerful opening paragraph should have all five of these components. Notice that the sample opening paragraph on the previous page began with a question. Asking a sensible, thoughtful question or two at the beginning can be an effective strategy to grab readers' full attention. Here are some other strategies:

- Begin with a short anecdote related to your topic.
- Make an unpredictable connection between your topic and something else.
- Don't reveal your thesis statement until the end of the paragraph.
- Avoid opening with sentences that start with *It is* or *There are.*

You Try It

The writer's opening paragraph for the Louisiana Purchase essay will be followed by paragraphs that detail how Jefferson's purchase was essential to the creation of the modern United States. The body of this essay will also provide supporting details that highlight the growth of the United States as an economic power as a result of the purchase of the Louisiana Territory. It will show how America's increased size and wealth helped democracy and freedom to flourish.

Here is another prompt:

> Today's astronauts are fearless explorers of space. But compared to early seafaring and landfaring explorers and adventurers, and the obstacles and uncertainties they faced, these modern pioneers have it easy.
>
> What do you think?

Take a position. List some ideas you would include in an essay on this topic. Then write a strong opening for it. Use one or more of the strategies presented in this lesson.

> **TEST-TAKING TIP**
>
> Starting with a strong opening is important, but if your thesis statement isn't perfect at first, don't fret. Just complete your essay, and then go back and adjust your thesis statement later.

Writing a Memorable Conclusion

A polished essay needs a memorable ending nearly as much as it needs a strong beginning. If your ending is trite, tired, or ill-fitting, you can leave readers unconvinced of the arguments you have carefully constructed throughout the body of your piece. Your concluding sentence (or sentences) should fit naturally within the last paragraph of your essay. Your ending should be catchy without being too cute. Here are some ways to end your essay memorably:

- Review your main idea, this time using different words.
- Be witty. You may even want to pose another question.

Here is an example of how one might end the early explorers-versus-astronauts essay:

> Lewis and Clark exhibited remarkable daring and resourcefulness throughout their journey into the unknown. If they had been modern astronauts rather than explorers of the past, this undaunted team would have made their farewells to Houston, left their orbits, foraged for supplies on the moon, and then gone straight on to Mars.

You Try It

Write your own powerful ending for either of the prompts presented in this lesson.

Exercise 1: Writing Strong Openings

TEST-TAKING TIP

A clever ending is not absolutely necessary, but you have to write a conclusion that stems from the ideas within the essay. Don't simply repeat yourself, and don't just stop writing.

The following opening sentences should be stronger. Think about what makes each one weak, and then write an improved version. Answers will vary.

1. There are many, many reasons why Lewis and Clark would make awesome astronauts today.

_____

_____

2. In my opinion, Jefferson paid way too much for the Louisiana Territory.

_____

_____

3. Actually, even though I am not old enough to vote, the purchase of New York City for a pittance gets my vote as the best real estate deal ever, hands down.

_____

_____

4. I think that early seafarers were nuts to head out into unknown waters.

_____

_____

5. Did early adventurers always "depend on the kindness of strangers" on their journeys of discovery, or was that good fortune rarely the case?

_____

_____

Exercise 2: Writing Strong Openings from Thesis Statements

Read each thesis statement below. Then think of a sentence or two to accompany it to make a strong opening paragraph. Write your paragraph in the space provided. Answers will vary.

1. Had all colonials been asked to vote on the Declaration of Independence, they would have rejected it.

   _____

   _____

2. Although scientists don't always achieve the results they hope for, research is essential to our growth and learning, and should always be supported.

   _____

   _____

3. Funding space exploration is a waste of time and money.

   _____

   _____

4. The purchase of the Louisiana Territory and the subsequent westward expansion helped all groups of Americans but one—the Native Americans.

   _____

   _____

5. If our government is willing to spend billions of dollars on one scientific pursuit, that single quest most certainly should be space exploration.

   _____

   _____

Exercise 3: Writing Effective Closings

The five opening paragraphs that you wrote in Exercise 2 begin essays that need effective closing statements. Reread each of your paragraphs. Think briefly about what supporting ideas or details you would include in each essay. Then, on a separate sheet of paper, write a powerful ending for each one. Be sure to include a memorable final sentence. Answers will vary.

Choosing the Right Words

Sometimes events occur that change things forever.
Read the following sentence from an essay identifying the Wright brothers'
groundbreaking first flight more than a century ago as one such event:

> **People looked up as the odd-looking thing flew by them.**

Now read this one:

> **The shivering but astonished bystanders
> stared up at the gray sky as the ungainly
> wooden flying contraption rose, dipped,
> and then sailed gracefully by.**

The second version is better because dull,
overused, or vague words have been
replaced with precise words. The revised sentence presents a clearer and more vivid picture
of the scene at Kitty Hawk, North Carolina.

The Wright brothers in the Wright
Model A airplane

When you write to persuade, as you will have to do on your standardized test
essay, the words you choose will influence a reader's response to your viewpoint.
One caution: Do not try to impress readers by using flowery, multisyllabic words
when precise, straightforward words will get your point across.

Using Precise Language

When you write, keep the following in mind: with *precise*
words you can express *precise* thoughts. Follow these
guidelines:

- Use precise, specific nouns rather than general ones.

  Vague: Many people were fascinated with the idea of
  flight.

  Better: Scientists, physicists, and inventors were
  fascinated with the idea of flight.

- Use vivid, precise verbs.

  Vague: Many said that astrophysicist Samuel Langley,
  not two bicycle mechanics, would be the first to fly.

  Better: Many predicted that astrophysicist Samuel Langley, not two
  bicycle mechanics, would be the first to fly.

- Use accurate, specific modifiers to make your points. Try to avoid using words
  such as *nice, great, pretty, fine, kind of, cute,* and *sort of* in your descriptions.

  Vague: The brothers searched for a great place to test their gliders.

  Better: The brothers searched for a remote place to test their gliders.

**TEST-
TAKING TIP**

Word choice, also
known as diction,
affects the precision and impact
of your writing.
Choose words
that exactly fit the
message you are
conveying.

When you choose your words, be aware of a word's connotation, or the feeling a reader associates with it. For example, consider each of the following sets of synonyms. Think about which word in the pair usually has a positive connotation and which generally has a negative connotation:

clever and *crafty*   *slim* and *skinny*   *fragrance* and *odor*   *prudent* and *inhibited*

Using Sensory Language

Effective writing appeals to one or more of a reader's five senses. Sensory details describe what you see, hear, smell, feel, or touch. Using them in your essay will help you to create a vivid picture of what you are describing or arguing.

Compare these two sentences. Which paints a more vivid picture of the scene?

> He stood on the hill, looked out across the sand, and smelled the sea air in the breeze.

or

> He stood among the tufts of waving grass on the hill, looked out across the shifting dunes, and inhaled the crisp, salty air that wafted up to greet him.

Use sensory details to help you convey your meaning precisely and to create a powerful image for the reader.

Using Figurative Language

Have you ever called someone "a handful," "a loose cannon," or a "string bean"? If so, you have used figurative language. Figurative language is composed of words and phrases that suggest more than their literal meanings, and often makes comparisons or connections to explain or enhance a concept. The most common kinds of figurative language are similes and metaphors. A simile suggests a similarity between seemingly dissimilar things by comparing them, using the words *as* or *like*. A metaphor too, suggests a similarity by comparing dissimilar things, but does not use the words *as* or *like*.

Other kinds of figurative language include hyperbole, or exaggeration, and personification, or language that attributes human qualities to things that are not human.

Study these examples:

> **Simile:** The glider soared <u>like</u> the gulls that it shared the skies with.

> **Metaphor:** A cluster of rolling hills, <u>a rumpled sleeve in the distance</u>, was the destination.

> **Hyperbole:** Once the lanterns and canned goods arrived, <u>the humble shack was converted into a grand hotel</u>.

> **Personification:** The <u>grasses waved in approval</u> and the <u>winds voiced their song of praise</u>.

Exercise 1: Using Precise Nouns

Improve each sentence by replacing the vague nouns with specific ones. You may have to make other changes for grammatical correctness.
Answers will vary; sample answers provided.

1. <u>People</u> were present to capture the <u>event</u> on film. Camera crews, game

2. The inventor brushed the wing with a <u>liquid</u> to protect it from humidity. sealant

3. The brothers built a wooden <u>structure</u> in which to store equipment. shack

4. The shelves in the shop were covered with all sorts of <u>tools</u>. mallets, drills, saws, and wrenches

5. The <u>thing</u> hit the ground with the <u>sound</u> of splintering wood. plane, crack

Exercise 2: Using Vivid Verbs

Improve each sentence by replacing the vague verbs with vivid ones. You may have to make other changes for grammatical correctness.

1. The concerned onlookers immediately <u>went</u> to where the glider crashed. raced

2. She <u>looked</u> out of her window at a sight no one had seen before: a flying machine soaring high above the river. stared

3. The awkward machine stayed aloft for a few seconds and then <u>fell</u> into the soft mud. crashed

4. It was a bumpy road from the beginning for the determined aviators, who <u>had</u> a series of heartbreaking failures during that six-month period. experienced

5. The news of the success <u>hit</u> the media, and by the next day, the inventors were the toast of the town. stunned

Exercise 3: Using Expressive Adjectives

Improve each sentence by replacing the vague, overused, or empty adjectives with expressive ones. You may have to make other changes for grammatical correctness.

1. The flying machine had an <u>interesting</u> appearance. awkward

2. Considering the time of year, it was a <u>fine</u> day for a flight. perfect

3. A group of <u>good</u> engineers gathered for the demonstration. skillful

4. "What a <u>nice</u> job those two did, and with so little outside help!" superb

5. The early flight enthusiasts such as Santos-Dumont, Langley, and Graham Bell were <u>well-known</u> men. celebrated

Exercise 4: Using Sensory Details

Imagine that you have witnessed a unique event, one that has created a significant change in the world, such as the first flight, phone call, or moon landing. Fill in the chart below with sensory details you could use for a persuasive essay focusing on whether one event can change things forever. First choose your topic. Then, under each heading, list sensory details that would capture vividly the impact of that event. Answers will vary.

Topic: _____

SIGHTS	SOUNDS	SMELLS	TASTES	SENSATIONS

Exercise 5: Improving a Paragraph

Read the paragraph below. Then rewrite it so that it comes to life. Add vivid verbs, precise nouns, and expressive adjectives. Add sensory details to help a reader to picture what you are describing. Include figurative language to enliven your revision. Answers will vary.

We walked up to the top of the dune to watch the world change right before our eyes. There were three of us, Kevin, Hannah, and myself. From there, so high up, we could see the pretty ocean in one direction and the inland waterways in the other. It was a fine day, really nice. We sat there and waited for a bit. Then, off to the left, we saw the thing take off. Holy mackerel! Wow! There was a person in it. It flew toward us, sort of, for I don't how long, and then dropped to the ground. None of us had ever seen anything quite like that before. No one had! History was being made right smack before our eyes. This event changed the way we lived, in more ways than one. Many inventions or events can do that.

_____

_____

_____

_____

_____

_____

Supporting Your Ideas

Good writers start out with a strong idea, or thesis statement, and then work to support and illustrate it. **Elaboration** is the writing technique of supporting an idea by using facts, examples, descriptions, details, comparisons, quotations, and personal experience.

Read the following:

> The admission price of rock concerts is too high and should be lowered.

Rock group in concert

What do you think? Support your position with information based on what you have learned or experienced.

Making Your Case

Consider using the following elaboration strategies whether you agree or disagree with the thesis statement or idea presented for your consideration. Included with each strategy is an example that could be used to agree or disagree with the opening statement.

TEST-TAKING TIP

Aim for *quality* over *quantity*. Coming up with a few rich ideas is a better strategy than coming up with many weaker ones.

- **Provide Facts and Statistics:** Provide background for your argument by including *objective* information. Strengthen your position with names, dates, and numbers. For example, you could provide current rock concert ticket prices.
- **Include Details:** Clarify and reinforce your position with specifics. For instance, you might include information on other expenses besides ticket prices that concert fans incur when they attend concerts, such as the cost of refreshments, and souvenirs such as T-shirts.
- **Make Comparisons:** Compare this topic with information you may have on other, related topics. For example, you could compare concert admission prices with admission prices to movies or ball games.
- **Use Personal Experience:** Give examples from your personal perspective. For instance, maybe you had to forgo attending a concert because of the exorbitant ticket prices.

Using an Idea Web

You can use an idea web to help you develop supporting ideas for a thesis statement. Examine the one on the next page written in support of the view that concert ticket prices are *not* too high.

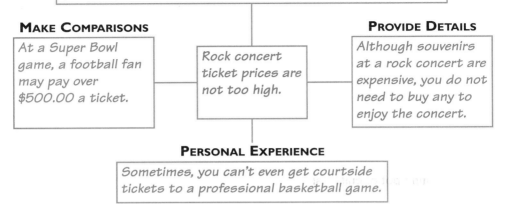

PROVIDE FACTS AND STATISTICS

Rock concert ticket prices range from $145.00 to $500.00 to sit by the stage, but courtside tickets to an NBA playoff game sometimes cost over $1,000.00

MAKE COMPARISONS

At a Super Bowl game, a football fan may pay over $500.00 a ticket.

Rock concert ticket prices are not too high.

PROVIDE DETAILS

Although souvenirs at a rock concert are expensive, you do not need to buy any to enjoy the concert.

PERSONAL EXPERIENCE

Sometimes, you can't even get courtside tickets to a professional basketball game.

Exercise: Completing an Idea Web

Read the following:

> The school day is too short and so is the school year; American students are falling behind those in other countries simply because they are not in school enough.

What is your view of this issue? Think about it and write a thesis statement. Then complete the idea web below to show ideas you might use to develop your case.

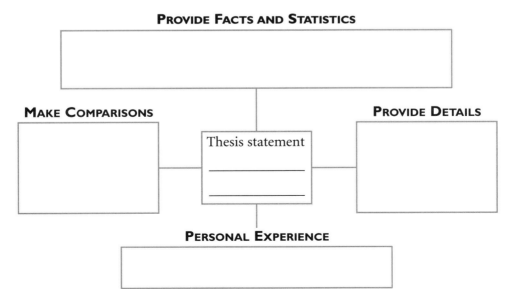

PROVIDE FACTS AND STATISTICS

MAKE COMPARISONS

PROVIDE DETAILS

Thesis statement
_____
_____

PERSONAL EXPERIENCE

Unity in Paragraphs

If you have ever played on a team or worked on a committee, you know that success is more likely to be achieved when everyone involved works toward the same goal. The same holds true for a piece of writing.

Read the following, written in support of the position that America is truly a melting pot of cultures. The writer has focused on tap dance as an example of an American art form that really owes much to other cultures.

Tap dance, although thought to be a classic American art form by many, owes its origins to Africa and Ireland. Its subsequent evolution here provides a clear example that America is, in fact, a melting pot of cultures. Tap dance was brought to America on slave ships—on deck the captives moved to the unfamiliar sounds of the fiddle, banjo, and hornpipe by adapting an African step called *giouba*. Some ships were two-masted sailing vessels. Later, African-American dancers became adept at copying Irish jigs, reels, and other dances of the period. Over time, these artists created elaborate variations using African steps such as the *slide*. The form of dancing they cre- ated—with improvisation, syncopation, and an emphasis on rhythm rather than on melody—would later become the basis of what today we call tap dancing.

Tap legend Gregory Hines (1946–2003) accepts an award.

What do you think of this paragraph? You will probably agree that it is pretty good except for one glaring weakness—a sentence that does not belong. Which do you think it is?

The sentence describing the ships is *not relevant* to the main idea of the passage: the beginnings of the art of tap dance in America.

Writing Unified Paragraphs

When you write a paragraph, all of your sentences must illustrate and support one main idea. When they do, your paragraph has unity. To give the paragraph about tap dance unity, you should delete the irrelevant sentence.

Here are three ideas about unity to keep in mind as you write essays:

- If you group ideas carefully in the prewriting phase, it will be easier for you to write unified paragraphs.
- If new ideas come to you as you are writing (and they will!), make sure that you place them in the paragraphs in which they belong.
- One way to unify an *essay* is to introduce your thesis statement in the first paragraph, then connect the topic sentence of each of the following para- graphs to that thesis statement.

Exercise 1: Eliminate Irrelevant Sentences

Read the planned main idea of the paragraph. Then identify the sentence that should be eliminated to maintain paragraph unity. Cross it out. Be prepared to explain your choice.

1. **Tap dance has again become a very popular form of entertainment.**
   - Tap dance classes at studios, recreation halls, and senior citizen centers are regularly packed.
   - More than 40 cities have annual tap dance festivals.
   - ~~Savion Glover is an established tap dance star.~~

2. **Juba (William Henry Lane) established himself as the greatest tap dancer in the world.**
   - In the 1840s, Juba enjoyed a reputation as the "King of all Dancers."
   - ~~Juba often danced with white performers.~~
   - Juba emerged from many dance contests as the clear winner.

3. **Drums were outlawed, but the beat went on.**
   - ~~*Giouba* was an African step.~~
   - After a slave revolt in 1739, slaves were not allowed to keep drums or other loud instruments.
   - Slaves kept the beat alive through improvisation.

Exercise 2: Create a Unified Paragraph

Read the following paragraph. Rewrite it so that it is unified. Delete or revise sentences as needed.

Should you ever need proof that America is a melting pot of cultures, simply think about the foods we eat. If you look around at the restaurants that line our streets, you are likely to see a Hunan restaurant next to an Indian one, and a Mexican *taqueria* across the street. Down the block, an Italian restaurant serves pasta while its neighbor, a Japanese eatery, serves sushi. You can also get all the rice and noodle dishes you could want at the Vietnamese, Thai, or Cambodian restaurants just a few blocks away. And nearby, the Asia Society is having an exhibition of seventeenth-century screen paintings and serving sushi. I plan either to visit that exhibit or to see the Russian folklore on display at the historical society. There are so many multicultural events happening at once here! In fact, you don't even have to leave school grounds to get a taste of this culinary cultural mix. Just take a look at what the cafeteria is serving today: burritos with rice and beans. Pass the salsa. Hold the ketchup.

To create a unified paragraph, delete sentences 5–7, or edit sentence 5 to focus only on the food served, and delete sentences 6 and 7.

Coherence and Transitions

It is one thing to make sure that all the ideas in a paragraph belong together. It is quite another thing to make sure that these ideas are clearly presented and easy to follow.

Read the following, taken from an essay written in support of saving school arts programs.

Violin section of an orchestra

> We live in a time when school districts are facing cutbacks in funding for arts programs. Sadly, music education is one of the first programs to suffer the consequences of decreased funding. Once a staple of a well-rounded education, music appreciation may be dropped from school curricula. This is unfortunate, not only because all students are given the opportunity to learn to play and enjoy an instrument in music classes, but also because music enriches their lives in so many powerful ways. First, it broadens their understanding of the creative process. Second, it provides an outlet for emotional expression and an avenue for nonverbal, nonvisual communication. In doing so, it hones learning styles and types of intelligences that other subjects may not. Furthermore, music education helps to build multicultural awareness.

You may notice that the paragraph has unity—all sentences support the writer's viewpoint that losing school music education programs would deprive students of a valuable learning experience. Notice too, that the sentences flow smoothly and logically from one to the next. The writer's ideas, then, are easy to follow because they were not simply placed in a slapdash order on the page.

We can also say that this paragraph about music education has **coherence**. A piece of writing has coherence when its ideas are arranged in an orderly way so that the connection between those ideas is clear.

Carefully organizing your ideas is essential to writing coherently. When you write an essay, you will be able to achieve coherence more easily if you choose and apply an *organizational plan* to your paragraphs. You want your readers to follow your thoughts easily and to understand the points you are making.

TEST-TAKING TIP

The *Improving Paragraphs* part of the multiple-choice section of a standardized test may ask you to improve the coherence of a paragraph. Aim to select the answer choice that best fits the context of the paragraph; to do this you need to have a strong sense of the main idea of the essay.

Choosing an Organizational Plan

You can choose from among several organizational writing plans. The chart below lists and describes some plans that will work well when you are writing to present your point of view convincingly.

ORGANIZATIONAL PLAN	DESCRIPTION
Chronological Order	Presents events in order of occurrence; useful for writing a narrative passage, for describing the steps in a process, or for writing about a historical event
Spatial Order	Organizes details in a clear spatial order, that is, from east to west, near to far, or top to bottom; useful for describing a person, place, or object
Order of Importance	Provides details in order of decreasing importance; useful when writing to persuade, describe, or evaluate
Comparison and Contrast	Shows similarities and differences between two or more things; useful when writing to compare or evaluate subjects or features
Pro and Con	Presents positive and negative aspects of actions, processes, and products
Cause and Effect	Presents causes and their effects; useful for analyzing reasons and results

Using Transitional Words

To write a coherent passage, you need to show clearly how ideas relate to one another. Words that show these clear connections, or transitions, are called transitional words. The chart below presents a selection of transitional words.

ORGANIZATIONAL PLAN	TRANSITIONAL WORDS
Chronological Order	before, during, after, since, once, meanwhile, first, next, suddenly, at the same time, as soon as, whenever, as, now, later
Spatial Order	above, below, behind, beside, here, there, across, next to, opposite, near, where, outside, within
Order of Importance	first, second, last, more important, least, better, most of all, best, furthermore, significantly, moreover, least of all, in addition
Comparison and Contrast; Pro and Con	however, in contrast, on the other hand, similarly, conversely, nevertheless, yet, although
Cause and Effect	because, therefore, so, as a result, since, thus, consequently, for that reason, accordingly

Identifying an Organizational Plan

In the following paragraph, the writer has chosen to use *order of importance* as the organizational plan. Notice how the transitional words support that plan and help to make the ideas easy to follow.

> It is not easy to imagine life without the piano. First of all, it is a versatile musical instrument. Second, it is a handsome piece of furniture. In addition, it is and has long been a status symbol. Furthermore, the piano is and has been a muse for popular and classical composers.

Applying Other Strategies to Achieve Coherence

In addition to choosing a writing plan and inserting transitional words, there are other strategies you can use to improve the coherence of your writing.

- **Use Repetition.** Add to the coherence of your writing by repeating words and phrases, grammatical structures, or both. Through repetition of key words, phrases, and grammatical structures (see Topic 31, Parallel Construction), you can emphasize key points and also help readers to link similar ideas you have expressed in separate sentences. Read the following:

> Since it first appeared on the scene, the piano has had an impact as large as its size. It has played a large role in the development of music education and music appreciation. Since the early twentieth century, the piano has played a large role in the American home and in bringing families together to appreciate music. It has been a symbol of that appreciation.

Notice the repetition of *since, played a large role,* and *appreciation.*

- **Use Synonyms.** You can help to create coherence by substituting synonyms. Read on:

> A stylish art deco Steinway was on display at the 1939 World's Fair in Flushing Meadows, New York. People flocked to the United States Pavilion where the piano was on view. They marveled at the elegant instrument.

Notice the use of the synonyms *elegant, instrument,* and *on view.*

- **Use Pronouns.** You also can create coherence by using pronouns. Read on:

> The exhibit featured two dozen historic pianos, including an 1850 Chickering, as well as one by Cristofori, and several others of notable provenance, all magnificent instruments.

Notice the use of the pronouns *one* and *others.*

When you plan and write paragraphs, always aim for coherence, or flow. You should use clear, precise language and:

- organize your thoughts and present them in a logical order for the reader.
- guide the reader by using transitions, repetition, synonyms, and pronouns.

Exercise 3: Revising to Form a Coherent Paragraph

Read the paragraph below. It supports the viewpoint that losing arts programs in schools would not be a great loss. Rewrite it to make it better. Insert transitional words and combine or separate sentences as needed.
Answers will vary. Accept a paragraph that displays coherence.

    I am always hearing people bemoan the lack of funding for arts programs in our schools. Why are they so upset? The reasons for dumping frivolous programs in order to focus on those that are far more meaningful are many and convincing. Replacing interesting but superfluous courses like photography and music appreciation with additional reading and math courses would help our students raise their standardized test scores and hone the skills they need for success in college and in the workplace. Adding more social studies courses would help create better-informed citizens. And what is the argument against replacing arts classes with more science courses? What is more important: to have more art historians and violinists, or more physicists, biologists, doctors, and researchers? We should spend money on textbooks, not paintbrushes. Our students need to be better educated in core subjects. They can discover art on their own time.

Exercise 4: Revising for Coherence and Unity

Read the following passage, which gives one person's explanation of why it is necessary to change today's high school curriculum. Then rewrite it. Improve coherence and unity by applying all the strategies you have learned so far. Feel free to divide it into two unified paragraphs. Answers will vary. Accept a paragraph that displays coherence.

    If I were responsible for planning high school curricula, I would make several key changes. These changes are necessary as a result of the world getting smaller and smaller and our need to understand it well getting bigger and bigger. It is not acceptable to be ignorant of what goes on in other parts of the globe. Our citizens need to be armed with the information and skills they need to navigate smoothly within this new and changing world. For their own sense of well-being, they need to be able to grasp key global issues, not just solve simultaneous equations. When they study languages, our students need to learn Asian and Middle Eastern languages too, not just French or Italian. France is a beautiful country though. They need to know key features of governments in addition to key tenets of trigonometry. If I were creating a curriculum, I would reduce the number of math requirements beyond algebra and have kids take additional world cultures and world history courses. Chances are that that this will create citizens better prepared to meet the needs of the constantly changing global climate. We will need to grasp what is going on in the world when we read the paper or watch the news so that we can act wisely. If we are called upon to serve overseas, we ought to know more when we embark than the name of the ship we will leave on.

Varying the Structure of Your Paragraphs

Read the following paragraph:

> People were openly hostile to them. They shot at them. Woodrow Wilson called them "a picture of arrogance and wealth, with all its independence and carelessness." In the early 1900s, automobiles were hated and feared by many. They were seen as unsafe and, what was worse, designed for the privileged only.

The 1908 Model T Ford

Sometimes, new ideas, no matter how ingenious or advantageous, are at first unappreciated, even unpopular. The appearance of Henry Ford's Model T is an example of this phenomenon. Initially, many people were reluctant to see its value. But we now know that Ford's reliable and affordable car altered the way we live in America in ways that few other inventions or events have.

In the opening paragraph, the topic sentence is located within the body of the paragraph. A topic sentence states a paragraph's main idea. The sentences before and after it provide supporting ideas and examples. Below is the opening paragraph with the topic sentence placed where you may be more accustomed to seeing it—right in the beginning:

> In the early 1900s, automobiles were hated and feared by many. People were openly hostile to them. They shot at them. Woodrow Wilson called them "a picture of arrogance and wealth, with all its independence and carelessness." They were seen as unsafe and, what was worse, designed for the privileged only.

When you write, it is important to vary the structure of your paragraphs. You can do this by varying where you place your topic sentence.

Placing Your Topic Sentence

Each paragraph you write should either imply the main idea or contain a topic sentence that states it plainly. You can place the topic sentence at the beginning of the paragraph, within the body, or at the end. Here again is the opening paragraph, shown this time with the topic sentence as its concluding sentence:

> People were openly hostile to them. They shot at them. Woodrow Wilson called them "a picture of arrogance and wealth, with all its independence and carelessness." They were seen as unsafe and, what was worse, designed for the privileged only. In the early 1900s, automobiles were hated and feared by many.

Which of the three versions of this paragraph do you like best? Why?

Exercise 1: Writing and Placing a Topic Sentence

None of the following paragraphs has a topic sentence. Read each paragraph. Then write a topic sentence for it and tell where in the paragraph you would place it. Answers will vary; sample topic sentences provided.

1. In 1898, the first car was sold in the United States. By the turn of the century, there were 8,000 automobiles registered in the country. Eight years later, 200,000 cars were registered. By 1910, that figure was nearly half a million.

   Between 1898 and 1910, the number of cars sold in the United States increased by

   almost half a million.

2. Just before World War I, when most cars were prohibitively expensive, the purchase price of a new Model T was a relatively low $360. Add to that its annual upkeep and running expenses of less than $100 ($1,500 was a typical estimate for most other cars), and you can see why the car was quite a bargain. In fact, one aficionado calculated that it would cost him about $10 to walk a thousand miles, but less than $8 tooling along that distance in his Model T!

   Although many people could not afford a new car in the early 1900s, the Model T

   was reasonably priced and affordable to most middle-class Americans.

Exercise 2: Writing Unified, Coherent Paragraphs

Read each topic sentence and the list of supporting details and ideas below it. Then, on a separate sheet of paper, write a unified, coherent paragraph incorporating those details and ideas. Place the topic sentence where it will be most effective. Answers will vary.

People embraced Henry Ford's practical Model T.

extremely low priced

very durable

motorists enjoyed new freedom

women welcomed the Model T as much as men did

became like a new member of the family

quote from Georgia farmer: "Your car lifted us out of the mud. It brought joy into our lives."

Cars like the Model T afforded people a new sense of freedom.

simple to operate, anyone could do it

easy to shift gears and control

increased people's range of movement and activity

Edith Wharton quote: "The motor-car has returned the romance of travel . . ."

no longer reliant on railroad schedules, routes, and destinations

started idea of new kind of adventure—the car trip

What Is and Isn't a Sentence

Read the following paragraph:

> There is more that is wrong with television than is right with it. When all is said and done, is a waste of time. When you consider that working and sleeping are the only things we spend more time doing than watching TV. Television may be a very successful advertising medium, it also is a successful sleeping agent, it discourages concentration and effort. What good is TV if it can do no more than divert us from real thinking and acting? Do we really need the instant gratification TV provides? If it comes at the expense of time we certainly could spend more productively.

A family watching television

The reason the paragraph is difficult to digest is that it is filled with groups of words that are *not* sentences. Instead, it is mostly made up of sentence fragments and run-on sentences. By definition, a **sentence** is a group of words that expresses a complete thought and is syntactically independent. In English, every sentence has two main parts: a complete subject and a complete predicate.

A **complete subject** is a noun, a group of words acting as a noun, or a pronoun, plus any modifiers that describe what or who the sentence is about. A **complete predicate** is a verb or verb phrase plus any modifiers and complements, or words that complete the meanings of verbs.

When you write, be sure to write complete sentences. Avoid fragments and run-ons, such as those that ruin the opening paragraph.

Fixing Fragments

A group of words that is punctuated as a sentence but fails to express a complete thought is called a **sentence fragment**. Sentence fragments lack subjects, verbs, or both.

To fix a fragment:

- Add a subject or verb to complete the thought.

  > When all is said and done, is a waste of time.
  > When all is said and done, **television** is a waste of time.

- Attach the subject or verb to the sentence fragment before or after it, if it makes sense to do so.

  > If it comes at the expense of time we certainly could spend more productively.
  > **Do we really need the instant gratification TV provides** if it comes at the expense of time we certainly could spend more productively?

- You also can fix fragments by dropping or replacing words.

> Television producers whose allegiance is to the advertisers that pay for the programs.
> Television producers' allegiance is to the advertisers that pay for the programs.

Fixing Run-ons

A run-on sentence is two or more sentences that are masquerading as a single sentence because of incorrect punctuation. Sometimes no punctuation separates the two sentences; sometimes a comma does. Don't let any of this fool you. If you spot one of these run-on sentences in your essay, fix it.

To fix a run-on sentence:

- Separate the sentences using capitalization and end punctuation.

> **Run-on:** Television may be a very successful advertising medium, it also is a successful sleeping agent.

> **Fixed:** Television may be a very successful advertising medium. It also is a successful sleeping agent.

- Use a conjunction preceded by a comma to separate the sentences.

> **Run-on:** Television may be a very successful advertising medium, it also is a successful sleeping agent.

> **Fixed:** Television may be a very successful advertising medium, but it also is a successful sleeping agent.

- Insert a semicolon, or a semicolon with a transitional word or phrase followed by a comma.

> **Run-on:** Television provides instant gratification, it discourages concentration and effort.

> **Fixed:** Television provides instant gratification; unfortunately, it discourages concentration and effort.

- Turn one of the sentences into a subordinate clause.

> **Run-on:** Television provides instant gratification, it discourages concentration and effort.

> **Fixed:** Although television provides instant gratification, it also discourages concentration and effort.

TEST-TAKING TIP

The run-on sentences on this page have one thing in common: each has only commas separating its independent clauses. This error is called a *comma splice*. Be on the lookout for comma splices— they appear more frequently than run-ons without any commas.

Exercise 1: Fixing Sentence Fragments

Rewrite each item to correct the fragments. Use the strategies presented so far. If a group of words *is* a sentence, do not make any corrections.
Answers may vary; sample answers provided.

1. Difficult to escape the influence of television. It is difficult to escape the influence of television.

2. The only things Americans do more than watch TV. The only things Americans do more than watch TV are sleep and work.

3. By the age of twenty. Most people will have been exposed to more than 20,000 hours of television watching. By the age of twenty, most people will have been exposed to more than 20,000 hours of television watching.

4. For each decade we live, we can add 10,000 hours of TV watching to our accomplishments. Correct as is.

5. Programming designed for instant gratification. Programming is designed for instant gratification.

6. What you otherwise could do with those 10,000 hours. What you otherwise could do with those 10,000 hours would undoubtedly be more productive.

7. A typical undergraduate student spends about 5,000 hours completing a bachelor's program. Correct as is.

8. Requires little effort. Television viewing requires little effort.

Exercise 2: Fixing Run-on Sentences

Rewrite each item to correct the run-ons. Use the strategies presented so far. If a group of words *is* a sentence, do not make any corrections. Answers may vary; sample answers provided.

1. Television helps us to pass the time, it diverts us from serious thinking. Television helps us to pass the time. It diverts us from serious thinking.

2. Most television programs, even the newest ones, are not better than those made thirty years ago. Correct as is.

3. Television offers neat solutions many are too simple for the real complexities of life. Television offers neat solutions; however, many are too simple for the real complexities of life.

4. Television screens are getting larger and larger every year, sets themselves are getting thinner and thinner. Television screens are getting larger and larger every year, but sets themselves are getting thinner and thinner.

5. Some families make an effort to watch only public television or educational programming, while others go for the popular game shows, sitcoms, and reality programs. Correct as is.

6. Televisions are getting to be huge, living rooms across the country are turning into screening rooms. Televisions are getting to be huge, <u>and</u> living rooms across the country are turning into screening rooms.

7. I calculated the number of hours I spent watching TV one week, I was astonished to find that I sat in front of the tube for twenty-five hours! <u>When</u> I calculated the number of hours I spent watching TV one week, I was astonished to find that I sat in front of the tube for twenty-five hours!

Exercise 3: Rewriting to Eliminate Fragments and Run-ons

The passage below presents one student's viewpoint on the future impact of television. First, read it through. Then, on a separate sheet of paper, rewrite it to eliminate all fragments and run-ons. Use a variety of strategies. Then compare your version with those of your classmates. Answers will vary.

We are becoming a nation of home theaters. The movie theaters near our homes have been replaced by theaters in our homes. In our living rooms and family rooms. In our basements, too. These new home theaters have every amenity. Great sound systems, amazingly sharp pictures, comfortable seating, professional lighting, not to mention the most important thing of all—flat-screen televisions the size of highway billboards.

Individual movie theaters already on the way out. Multiplex movie theaters will follow. After all, why spend ten dollars or more to see a movie that you are not even guaranteed to enjoy when you can curl up in front of a 96-inch screen in the luxury of your home theater, choose from among hundreds of movies, concerts, sporting events, and documentaries? Undisturbed by cell phones or people talking loudly when you are trying to listen, or tall people blocking your view when you are trying to see the screen. In addition, you can speed through the dull or gory parts.

As home theaters and all that is part of home theaters become commonplace. Video stores will follow movie theaters and multiplexes into history's dustbin. Like the dinosaurs. Now subscribers can purchase packages bundled by cable companies to offer a wide range of viewing choices. No more unplayable tapes, corrupt DVDs, no more long lines waiting to pay and no more late night trips to return videos before they are overdue. Changing times in the video world, indeed.

As TVs get bigger and look and sound better. We will watch even more TV than we do now, programs won't improve along with the equipment. Depend on it. Count on spending even more time-wasting hours in front of the screen. Our imaginations will be the first things to go. And thoughtfulness will follow. Our ability to concentrate, too. We will one day become a nation of couch potatoes with fabulous TVs. We are already well on our way there. And we can get there without having to leave the comfort of our homes.

Varying Sentence Structure and Type

Imagine that you are a passenger on a bus riding alone through a flat desert on a road as straight as a carpenter's rule. You look around and see that there is nothing to grab your attention. Only the railroad tracks to your right fill the emptiness.

Writing is similarly dull when each sentence is as alike as one railroad tie is to the next. Read the following paragraph that is part of an essay in reaction to a statement made by movie star John Wayne: "Courage is being scared to death and saddling up anyway."

John Wayne in a movie role

> **Courage means standing up for what you believe in. Courage means not turning the other cheek. Courage means doing what is right. It does not mean doing what is popular. Courage means doing what is best. It does not mean doing what is easiest. It means saddling up for your principles. It means not hiding from the truth.**

Paragraphs with sentences only like these, which all basically have the same structure, are sure to put off readers. On the other hand, paragraphs that have a variety of sentence patterns will enliven writing.

To keep your readers interested in your essay, you should vary your sentence structures, types, and lengths. Good writing depends on variety.

Varying Sentence Types

Every sentence may be classified into one of four types. Vary the types of sentences you use to best fit your purpose.

A declarative sentence makes a statement. It ends with a period.

> **John Wayne played a brave man in *Stagecoach*.**

An imperative sentence gives a command or makes a request, and usually ends with a period.

> **"Keep an eye out for bandits," Wayne warned the fearful passengers.**

An exclamatory sentence expresses strong feelings and always ends with an exclamation point.

> **Skirting danger at every turn, the rattling stage pulled into Dodge early, and its passengers and payroll were saved!**

An interrogative sentence asks a question. It ends with a question mark.

> **Who, other than John Wayne, would you want to lead your wagon train?**

Varying Sentence Structures and Lengths

There are four basic sentence structures. Use a variety of structures when you write.

A simple sentence has *one* main clause, which has a subject and a predicate.

> **The brave soldiers held the high ground.**

A compound sentence contains *two or more* main clauses. The clauses are linked by a coordinating conjunction, and are usually preceded by a comma or a semicolon.

> **The soldiers huddled in the trenches, but their general paced above them in plain sight.**

A complex sentence has one main clause and *one or more* subordinate clauses.

> **After watching the others leap from the plane, the young parachutist summoned all his courage and followed suit.**

Think: This sentence begins with a subordinate clause.

A compound-complex sentence has *two or more* main clauses and *one or more* subordinate clauses.

> **The young woman tentatively walked onto the high diving board, and although she had butterflies in her stomach, she bravely waited for the signal from her coach below.**

You also will improve the quality of your writing by mixing long sentences with short ones. Lengthen choppy sentences by combining sentences or by adding descriptive details and facts. Shorten long compound and complex sentences by dividing them into simple sentences. Keep in mind that a string of similarly long compound or complex sentences can be tedious to read.

Here is a way to break up the compound-complex sentence about the nervous diver:

> **The young woman tentatively walked onto the high diving board although she had butterflies in her stomach. She bravely waited for the signal from her coach below.**

Varying Sentence Beginnings

Study these ways to add diversity to your sentences by varying the way they begin.

Start with an **adverb**.

> **Gallantly, Wayne urged his troops to charge the enemy's line.**

Start with a **prepositional phrase**.

> **With great gallantry,** Wayne urged his troops to charge the enemy's line.

Start with a **participial phrase**.

> **Displaying great gallantry,** Wayne urged his troops to charge the enemy's line.

Start with a **subordinate clause**.

> **As gallantly as he could,** Wayne urged his troops to charge the enemy's line.

Start with the **predicate**.

> **Into the enemy's line charged** Wayne and his gallant troops.

Vary the kinds of sentences you write to make your viewpoint clearer. Vary them also *to show emphasis*; for instance, place a short sentence between longer ones so that it will stand out. Read the following:

> There was a mad scramble on the rig when the crew noticed an enormous iceberg moving toward them at one knot. The weather conditions were frightening and added to the chaos. Winds shook the rig's platform and huge waves crashed against it. **Fear was on everyone's face.** The only thing left to do was to pull the rig's several massive anchors up and try to haul the heavy structure out of danger.

You Try It

Here again is the opening paragraph:

> Courage means standing up for what you believe in. Courage means not turning the other cheek. Courage means doing what is right. It does not mean doing what is popular. Courage means doing what is best. It does not mean doing what is easiest. It means saddling up for your principles. It means not hiding from the truth.

Rewrite it, focusing on using a variety of sentence types and structures. Try to vary the ways that the sentences begin. Also, try to write both long and short sentences. Add information or ideas, as needed, to add to the clarity and variety.

_____

_____

_____

_____

_____

_____

Exercise 1: Varying Sentence Types

Your topic is what courage means to you. On that topic, write an example of each of the four sentence types. Look back as needed to remind yourself of the different sentence types. Answers will vary.

1. declarative sentence: _____

_____

2. imperative sentence: _____

_____

3. exclamatory sentence: _____

_____

4. interrogative sentence: _____

_____

Exercise 2: Varying Sentence Structures

In the exercise below, write sentences agreeing or disagreeing with the idea that we learn most from situations that require courage. Write sentences using each of the four basic kinds of sentence structures. Look back as needed to remind yourself of the different sentence structures. Answers will vary.

5. simple sentence: _____

_____

6. compound sentence: _____

_____

7. complex sentence: _____

_____

8. compound-complex sentence: _____

_____

Exercise 3: Varying Sentence Lengths

Use your sentences from Exercise 2. On a separate sheet of paper, revise each to change its length. Use the strategies presented in this lesson. Answers will vary.

Exercise 4: Rewriting to Vary Sentence Beginnings

Read each sentence. Then revise it by changing the way it starts. For each sentence, write two new versions. Add, change, or delete words as needed. Answers will vary.

1. Sadly, many people do not seem to be concerned enough with protecting the environment.

   _____

   _____

2. The issue of global warming will be with us for generations to come.

   _____

   _____

3. Observers in small planes search vigilantly for potentially treacherous icebergs.

   _____

   _____

4. When the survivors spoke of the event, they all had different reactions.

   _____

   _____

5. With great care, the soldiers picked up the land mine and moved it to where special squads could disarm it.

   _____

   _____

6. Admitting to a fear is the first step toward overcoming it.

   _____

   _____

7. As weather conditions worsened in the Atlantic, the threat of collisions increased.

   _____

   _____

8. In difficult situations, we typically find ourselves choosing between the lesser of two evils.

   _____

   _____

Exercise 5: Rewriting a Dull Passage

"Don't trust anyone over thirty." That was common advice during the turbulent 1960s. Read the passage below, which shows part of one student's response to that statement. Then rewrite it to enliven it by varying the types, structures, and lengths of your sentences. Use a mixture of strategies. Divide, combine, rearrange, revise, and even add or delete sentences. If you wish, break up the passage to create more than one paragraph. Use transitional words to add coherence. Then, compare your version with those of your classmates.

Of course we should trust people over thirty years old. The students in the 1960s who said that we shouldn't were wrong. I think we should trust people over forty, too. I trust anyone over fifty and over sixty. I trust my grandparents. I trust my friends' grandparents. I think we should trust anyone who was once our age and has had experiences like those we are now having and has learned from them. We should trust that as people age and experience more things, they learn more about life. We can learn from their mistakes. Our country does not consist of two societies—one with people over thirty and one with people under thirty. It is not two societies. It is one society made up of people of all ages. It is a better society when people trust one another. I don't trust anyone under thirty who doesn't trust people older than they are.

Answers will vary.

Avoiding Clichés and Slang

Read the following passage written for a test sometime in the not-so-distant future. It is part of a response to a prompt asking students to address the suggestion that the build-up to or preparation for an event may be as powerful, exciting, or enriching an experience as the event itself:

> When we got the news, we were all pleased as punch. "Groovy," said my grandfather. "Cool," my mother added. "Awesome," my brother chipped in. You see, our reservations for a family space flight had just come in. We were a "go." When I saw the price tag, I was, like, "Whoa!" It nearly knocked my socks off. But that was the only downside. I was happy as a clam. We were all happy as clams. The liftoff date was set in stone. All our i's were dotted and t's crossed. Nothing could rain on our parade.

NASA space station

You will probably agree that this passage suffers from a lack of formal English. It might be acceptable in a letter to a friend, but not in a persuasive essay.

This is not to say that persuasive writing must always be stiff and formal. Feel free to use informal, everyday words and phrases—they can give your sentences a personal touch and can make dialogue sound natural. They can add spirit to your writing. But you should use them judiciously.

Clichés and Slang

Clichés are expressions or idioms that have become trite from overuse—stay away from them in your writing. *Works like a horse, raining cats and dogs, slept like a log,* and *pretty as a picture* are some examples. Find a better way to write what you mean. Slang, which is composed of newly made-up terms, or new meanings attached to existing terms, can add genuineness and immediacy to your writing. But slang is always changing, so watch out: When you include slang words and expressions in your writing, you limit your audience. And when your audience is a pair of teachers reading to see how precisely, eloquently, and effectively you make your case, you are better off staying away from slang.

> **TEST-TAKING TIP**
>
> Idioms, such as *That's how the cookie crumbles,* are common expressions that we use in conversation. A conversational style is fine to use in your writing, but don't overdo it.

You Try It

Reread the opening paragraph about the family space flight. Then rewrite it, replacing the clichés and slang. Answers will vary.

_____

_____

_____

_____

_____

Exercise: Eliminating Clichés and Slang

Read each sentence below. Then replace the underlined clichés and slang with language that is more appropriate and more expressive, too. Make changes in the wording as needed. Answers will vary; sample answers provided.

1. When our father began poring over family space-trip packages <u>like a hawk</u>, we knew he had <u>something up his sleeve</u>. attentively poring over space-trip packages; in mind

2. We knew we would have to <u>cough up an arm and a leg</u>—nearly $20 million— for the trip. pay a hefty price

3. We all wanted to go. That was a <u>no-brainer</u>. a certainty

4. <u>Dudes</u> across the country, who all think the idea of a family space vacation is <u>way cool</u>, are vying for tickets. People; intriguing

5. Our family won't need to <u>downsize</u>, since the spaceship's living quarters have room for five. leave anybody home

6. When my little brother heard that the ship's <u>cribs</u> have 84-inch TVs, he was <u>on cloud nine</u>. apartments; ecstatic

7. Preparing for the trip was <u>no sweat</u>. It included flying in a jet fighter at 2.5 times the speed of sound, riding in a centrifuge capsule, diving into a 40-ft antigravity tank in a spacesuit, and becoming familiar with a spacecraft's controls. It was <u>a piece of cake</u>. not difficult; an easy assignment

8. We didn't all have to look <u>buff by doing billions of reps and working out</u>; we just had to get a checkup. get into top physical shape by exercising vigorously and consistently

9. We were <u>all over our responsibilities</u> in all the preparations for liftoff. We took our responsibilities for the journey seriously.

10. "I hope your ship's commander won't be <u>wet behind the ears</u>," my friend Frank teased. "Maybe he trained as <u>like</u> a surfer or snowboarder before someone put him in front of a ship bound for outer space." new to this job; eliminate *like*

Avoiding Wordy and Empty Sentences

Imagine that two visitors from another galaxy were asked to identify *the most unusual or unexpected thing* they saw on their visit to Earth, and then to write a paragraph explaining why it deserves that honor. Compare the following paragraphs.

Komodo dragon

> To me—and I'm no expert on Earth's long and turbulent history—it looked like it could have been an episode out of the earthling movie *Jurassic Park*. What I mean is the setting was a beach on the central Indonesian island, the island of Komodo. Less than 100 feet from where I stood, a huge lizard suddenly appeared and ferociously attacked a deer. On account of the attack, the deer's hind legs were broken. Then the enormous reptile—it was really big, let me tell you—moved in for the kill. What I want to say is that I thought I was witnessing a scene from Earth's Age of Dinosaurs. It was certainly the most unusual thing I saw on this trip, and I saw many, many odd things on this little planet.

> The most unusual thing I saw on this trip could have been an episode out of the earthling movie *Jurassic Park*, or a scene from Earth's Age of Dinosaurs. The setting was a beach on the central Indonesian island of Komodo. Less than 100 feet from where I stood, a lizard the size of an alligator ferociously attacked a deer, driving it into the surf and breaking its hind legs. Then it moved in for the kill. Prior to this trip, I would have thought that an event like this could only have taken place before there were humans living on Earth!

You will probably agree that the first passage includes sentences that decrease the effectiveness of the writer's description. The second version is tighter and has no redundancies. It is much better.

Fixing Wordy Sentences

When you write, aim for brevity. Avoid wordy sentences. Choose your words carefully and economically. When your writing includes words that don't add anything new, you will slow down your readers. You will obscure the points you are making, and lower your score, too.

To fix a wordy sentence:

- cut out any unnecessary words and drop or trim any wordy expressions, or
- replace it with a shorter, more succinct sentence.

Look at the examples below:

WORDY SENTENCE	REVISED SENTENCE
What I want to say is that Komodo dragons are formidable predators.	Komodo dragons are formidable predators.

Fixing Empty Sentences

Empty sentences are those that simply repeat ideas or those that make a statement without providing any new information. You should avoid empty sentences when you write. When you include empty sentences in your essay, they too will obscure the points you are making, and lower your score.

To fix an empty sentence, cut it out, or add the supporting details, facts, and ideas that will help the sentence add meaning or clarity to your thought.

Look at the examples below:

EMPTY SENTENCE	REVISED SENTENCE
Komodo dragons are the largest lizards in the world. There are no lizards as large as the Komodo dragon.	Komodo dragons are the largest lizards in the world.

You Try It

Read the following passage. Rewrite it to eliminate wordiness and empty sentences. Use the strategies presented in this lesson.

I know that it wasn't until the beginning of the twentieth century that scientists became aware of Komodo dragons. In the year 1928, the island of Komodo was officially proclaimed a wilderness area. Today, the dragon is classified as an endangered species, partly because of the fact that it has a very limited habitat—the most limited of any large carnivore in the world. No meat eaters of its size have a habitat that small. Thank goodness that the days when tourists descended upon the island to enjoy the entertainment of watching the lizards maul goats offered to them are long gone. In regard to those days, they are history. Indonesia has protected the dragon's habitat by designating much of it a national park. The reason why is because the Komodo dragon itself is now regarded as a national treasure. It is revered by Indonesians who are 100% right to do what they can to save it. Paragraphs will vary.

Exercise 1: Fixing Wordy and Empty Sentences

Read each sentence below about Komodo dragons. Then, revise each one to cut out the excess. Make changes in the wording as needed. Revisions will vary; sample answers provided.

1. It is a true fact that at present there are an estimated 3,000 to 5,000 Komodos in the world.

   At present, there are an estimated 3,000 to 5,000 Komodos in the world.

2. What I want to add to that is that now there are more than 200 of the dragons living in captivity.

   Now there are more than 200 of the dragons living in captivity.

3. Komodo dragons are bred in three zoos in Indonesia, while other zoos, which are located around the world, are showing interest in developing breeding programs of their own.

   Komodo dragons are bred in three zoos in Indonesia, while other zoos around the world are showing interest in developing breeding programs of their own.

4. Not surprisingly, the Komodo dragon in many cases has been the subject of mythmaking.

   Not surprisingly, the Komodo dragon has been the subject of mythmaking.

5. In spite of the fact that very few instances of people being attacked by the dragons have been reported, many fear that the giants are man-eaters.

   Although very few instances of people being attacked by the dragons have been reported, many fear that the giants are man-eaters.

6. Humans are not the main item on a Komodo dragon's menu. We are not what the dragons hunger for the most.

   Delete second sentence.

7. What Komodo dragons prefer is a meal of snake, bird, small mammal, deer, pig, water buffalo, or another dragon.

   Komodo dragons prefer a meal of snake, bird, small mammal, deer, pig, water buffalo, or another dragon.

8. They are also known to be scavengers, because of the fact that they can be seen lumbering along beaches looking around for dead fish and other carrion.

   They are also known to be scavengers who can be seen lumbering along beaches looking for dead fish and other carrion.

9. To kill large prey, the dragons lie camouflaged in the brush along game trails and attack by ambush. Unsuspecting pigs and deer don't see the dragons until it is too late because they are hiding.

Eliminate *because they are hiding*, or delete the second sentence.

10. "I've seen other instances of the dragons' predatory behavior. What I want to say is that I once saw a cluster of them digging through a nest of bird eggs."

"I've seen other instances of the dragons' predatory behavior. I once saw a cluster of them digging through a nest of bird eggs."

Exercise 2: Fixing a Passage

Read the following passage about the nature preserve on Komodo. It contains both wordy and empty sentences. Rewrite it to eliminate unnecessary words and expressions. Keep in mind as you revise to never use more words than you need—don't use two words or expressions when one is enough.

Komodo, one of the homes of these giant lizards, is an island in central Indonesia that the country preserves, as is, to sustain the animals' continued existence. In regard to the most common habitat on the island, it is the savanna. Its tall grasses offer both food and cover for deer, the dragon's primary prey, the animal it hunts more than any other. What is clear is that the deer can hide in these grasses. Scattered about the drier parts of the savanna are tall lontar palms that have giant fan-shaped leaves. In the damp parts of the grassland, stunted jujube trees grow along with tamarind trees. In the island's gullies and along the streams that run down the steep, nearly vertical hills are tropical monsoon forests. Because of the fact that the forests are dominated by kapok trees, tamarinds, ferns, and tropical plants, they have a decided aura of primitiveness. These forests seem to me to be from another, earlier time, when giant lizards thrived.

Paragraphs will vary; sample paragraph provided.

Komodo, one of the homes of these giant lizards, is an island in central Indonesia

that the country preserves to sustain the animals' existence. The most common

habitat on the island is the savanna. Its tall grasses offer both food and cover for

deer, the dragon's primary prey. Scattered about the drier parts of the savanna are

tall lontar palms that have giant fan-shaped leaves. In the damp parts of the grass-

land, stunted jujube trees grow along with tamarind trees. In the island's gullies and

along the streams that run down the steep hills are tropical monsoon forests. These

forests are dominated by kapok trees, tamarinds, ferns, and tropical plants, and have

a decided aura of primitiveness.

Read the following passage.

> Was Krakatoa the most destructive volcanic eruption ever? Was it Tambora, 68 years earlier? Many know about the 1883 eruption on Krakatoa. Few know of the eruption of Mount Tambora. Tambora's burning ash streamed from the volcano. It hissed into the sea. It cooled quickly. It formed pumice. The pumice clogged harbors. It disrupted trade for months.

The volcano of Krakatoa

Notice that the passage includes a series of short, choppy sentences. Although short sentences can be powerful, too many strung together create a repetitive, abrupt rhythm. They are boring to read. They also can be hard to follow, because each idea is given equal emphasis and the connection between ideas is unclear.

To capture and keep your readers' attention, avoid using choppy sentences. You should make every effort to vary the lengths of your sentences. You can create this variety by combining sentences that express closely related ideas. There are several ways to do this.

Using Coordinating Conjunctions

A way to combine short sentences of *equal importance* is to join them with a coordinating conjunction. The most common coordinating conjunctions are *and*, *but*, and *or*.

In the examples below, coordinating conjunctions have been used to combine choppy sentences into smoother, more readable ones.

CHOPPY SENTENCES	COMBINED SENTENCES
Was Krakatoa the most destructive volcanic eruption ever? Was it Tambora, 68 years earlier?	Was Krakatoa the most destructive volcanic eruption ever, or was it Tambora, 68 years earlier?
Many know about the 1883 eruption on Krakatoa. Few know of the eruption of Mount Tambora.	Many know about the 1883 eruption on Krakatoa, but few know of the eruption of Mount Tambora.
The pumice clogged harbors. It disrupted trade for months.	The pumice clogged harbors and disrupted trade for months.

Using Subordinating Conjunctions

Sometimes, the ideas expressed in two short sentences are *not* of equal importance. You can join short sentences like these with a subordinating conjunction. (Sometimes, you can use a subordinating conjunction to begin a sentence.) Here are some common subordinating conjunctions:

before	after	when	while	where	wherever
whenever	because	since	so	so that	
as	unless	if	although	until	

In the examples below, subordinating conjunctions have been used to combine choppy sentences into smoother, more readable ones.

CHOPPY SENTENCES	COMBINED SENTENCES
1816 was known as the "year without a summer." Ash and debris from Mount Tambora shrouded the atmosphere.	1816 was known as the "year without a summer" because ash and debris from Mount Tambora shrouded the atmosphere.
Mount Tambora erupted. Sources of fresh water became contaminated. Crops and forests died.	After Mount Tambora erupted, sources of fresh water became contaminated, and crops and forests died.
Debris from the Tambora eruption chilled parts of the planet. It contributed to crop failures. It contributed to famine. It contributed to epidemics.	Since debris from the Tambora eruption chilled parts of the planet, it contributed to crop failures, famine, and epidemics.

Using Relative Pronouns

You can also use the relative pronouns *who, whom, which,* and *that* to combine sentences. Below are two examples.

CHOPPY SENTENCES	COMBINED SENTENCES
The eruption of Mount Tambora was ten times more powerful than that of Krakatoa. Krakatoa is 900 miles away from Tambora.	The eruption of Mount Tambora was ten times more powerful than that of Krakatoa, which is 900 miles away from Tambora.
Thomas Jefferson retired to Monticello in 1809. He did this after completing his second term. He had such a poor corn crop in 1816. He applied for a $1,000 loan.	Thomas Jefferson, who retired to Monticello in 1809 after completing his second term, had such a poor corn crop in 1816 that he applied for a $1,000 loan.

Exercise I: Combine Sentences

TOPIC **15**

Combine the following sets of sentences. Use coordinating or subordinating conjunctions or relative pronouns, and add or remove words as needed.
Answers may vary; sample answers provided.

1. Miguel is interested in volcanoes. He is interested in earthquakes.

   Miguel is interested in volcanoes and earthquakes.

2. Rice crops were ruined. Corn crops were ruined. Floods destroyed surviving crops.

   Rice and corn crops were ruined, and floods destroyed any surviving crops.

3. Mr. Matsui is a scientist. He studies natural catastrophes.

   Mr. Matsui is a scientist who studies natural catastrophes.

4. Some boats got out safely. Rafts of pumice trapped many boats in the harbor.

   Although some boats got out safely, rafts of pumice trapped many others in the

   harbor.

5. The historian read through boxes of records. She found what she was looking for.

   The historian read through boxes of records until she found what she was

   looking for.

6. The villagers stopped in their tracks. They looked up at the erupting volcano. It was time to leave the area.

   When the villagers stopped in their tracks and looked up at the erupting volcano,

   they knew it was time to leave the area.

7. Ash poured down the slope. People looked up in fear.

   As ash poured down the slope, people looked up in fear.

8. The island used to have a large population. It doesn't have as many inhabitants now.

   The island used to have a large population, but it doesn't have as many

   inhabitants now.

Topic 15: Avoiding Choppy Sentences   **61**

9. The Northern Hemisphere was severely affected by the eruption. The Southern Hemisphere suffered little damage.

   The Northern Hemisphere was severely affected by the eruption, but the Southern

   Hemisphere suffered little damage.

10. A group of geologists took a trip to Indonesia. They wanted to learn more about the eruption. They wanted to see what the land looks like today.

    A group of geologists took a trip to Indonesia because they wanted to learn more

    about the eruption and see what the land looks like today.

Exercise 2: Revise a Paragraph

The paragraph that follows is not only dull, but it is also hard to read because it contains a series of choppy sentences. Make it better. Improve it by combining sentences or sentence parts, and changing or deleting words as you need to. Be sure to insert commas where they are needed. Paragraphs will vary.

    We climbed for several hours. The climb was slow and demanding. I was thirsty. I was tired. I stopped frequently to drink. I also stopped often to rest. We finally reached the summit. We were on the northern part of the rim. I looked into the caldera. I looked across to the other side. The view was amazing. It took my breath away. I was filled with awe. I was filled with emotion.

_____

_____

_____

_____

_____

_____

_____

_____

_____

Exercise 3: Write a Paragraph

On a separate sheet of paper, write a paragraph of your own. Include only short sentences. Then give it to a classmate to fix by combining some of the sentences. Then discuss the changes. Paragraphs will vary.

Using the Active Voice

Voice is the form of a transitive verb that shows whether the subject of a sentence performs or receives an action. (Transitive verbs express an action that is directed toward a person or thing in a sentence; they require an object to complete their meaning.)

Read and compare the following sentences.

> **Only one fatality was suffered by visitors to amusement parks that year.**
>
> **That year visitors to amusement parks suffered only one fatality.**

Roller coaster in an amusement park

In the first sentence, the verb *suffer* is in the **passive voice.** The passive voice is made up of verbal phrases that always include a form of *be* followed by the main verb's past participle. When a verb is in the passive voice, the subject *receives* the action it names. In the opening sentence, the subject, *fatality*, receives the action.

In the second sentence, the verb *suffer* is in the active voice because the subject *performs* the action named by that verb. In that sentence, the subject, *visitors*, performs the action. Keep in mind the following:

- Use the active voice *whenever possible* when you write your essay. Using the active voice will make your sentences more forceful, direct, and economical.
- Use the passive voice when you wish to stress the *action* rather than the *performer*, or when that performer is unknown.

You can write any transitive verb in the active voice. Study these examples.

PASSIVE VOICE	ACTIVE VOICE
Amusement parks are visited by 320 million people each year.	320 million people visit amusement parks each year.
6,500 injuries were reported by the Consumer Product Safety Commission.	The Consumer Product Safety Commission reported 6,500 injuries.
Injuries are not broken down by ride by the CPSC.	The CPSC does not break down injuries by ride.

Only transitive verbs can indicate voice; *being verbs* cannot. Being verbs can be lifeless, so replace them with transitive verbs in the active voice whenever you can.

> **Clark and Claire were riders in the first roller coaster car.**
>
> **Clark and Claire rode in the first roller coaster car.**

Exercise: Using the Active Voice

Read each sentence. Then rewrite it in the active voice. Replace *being verbs* with *transitive verbs*. Make changes in the wording as needed. Make no changes if you think the sentence works well as written.

Revisions will vary; sample answers provided.

1. In 2002, 13 million people were visitors at Tokyo Disneyland.

   In 2002, 13 million people visited Tokyo Disneyland.

2. In that same year, Japan's Universal Studios resort was visited by more than eight million people.

   In that same year, more than eight million people visited Japan's Universal Studios resort.

3. 120 miles an hour is the speed reached by Japan's Steel Dragon roller coaster.

   Japan's Steel Dragon roller coaster reaches the speed of 120 miles an hour.

4. 400 feet is the height people are dropped from when they ride Ohio's Top Thrill Dragster.

   People drop 400 feet when they ride Ohio's Top Thrill Dragster.

5. The Tower of Terror in Australia soars to a height of 328 feet.

   Correct as is.

6. A small girl was injured when she fell during a teacup ride in San Diego.

   A small girl injured herself when she fell during a teacup ride in San Diego.

7. During the last 40 years, 58 injuries were suffered by amusement park visitors.

   During the last 40 years, amusement park visitors suffered 58 injuries.

8. Do you think amusement park safety should be governed by federal regulations?

   Do you think the federal government should provide regulations to ensure amusement park safety?

9. Roller coasters are considered too dangerous by some critics.

   Some critics consider roller coasters too dangerous.

10. On the other hand, roller coaster design has drawn the attention of engineers seeking to create the ultimate ride.

    Correct as is.

Using Commas, Semicolons, and Colons

How willing are people to allow new information to replace long-accepted beliefs? Read the following sentence from a paragraph written in response to that question.

> A reporter a photographer and I met with an archaeologist a professor at the University of Arizona a historian studying the region and a local resident who was to be our guide.

It is a confusing sentence, isn't it? How many people were at this meeting: 3? 4? 5? 6? You would know the answer if this sentence were punctuated properly.

Native American cliff dwellings

Using Commas

Commas signal pauses. They guide readers to take a break as they read and, in doing so, they help to prevent misunderstandings.

WHEN TO USE COMMAS	EXAMPLE
• to separate three or more items in a series	We visited sites in Colorado, Utah, Arizona, and New Mexico.
• to separate independent clauses of a compound sentence when they are joined by coordinating conjunctions	The Anasazi moved into the Four Corners area in the thirteenth century, but then something went terribly wrong. (Note: Place the comma *before* the coordinating conjunctions *and*, *but*, *for*, *or*, *nor*, or *so*.)
• to set off a subordinate clause	While we were hiking, John spotted two stone structures.
• to set off nonessential appositives	The Anasazi, a civilization that arose as early as 1500 B.C., built a network of settlements.
• to set off introductory prepositional phrases	Within the last decade, archaeologists have begun to gain new understandings about why the Anasazi left their homes.
• to set off words that interrupt flow	We were intrigued, as many were before us, by how the village dwellers scaled the cliffs.
• to separate two or more adjectives of equal rank that precede a noun	It was a steep, perilous climb back up to the plateau.

Also, use commas to set off the direct quotations you use. Remember always to place a comma *before* the quotation mark when your sentence extends beyond it.

"The climb is not as easy as it looks," our guide told us.

Do not use commas in the following situations:

- between parts of a compound predicate

  A long walk brought us to a ledge and provided us with a 180° view of the surrounding desert.

- after a final adverb clause (unless it is *nonessential* and interrupts the flow)

  The Anasazi tried to make their new homes attractive after they moved into them.

- to set off *essential* appositives—those necessary to the sentence's meaning

  My friend Thomas met us at the visitor center.

Using Semicolons and Colons

A semicolon signals a longer pause than a comma, but a shorter pause than a period. It can replace a period, but not a comma. Use a semicolon:

- in place of a period to separate two simple sentences.

  As many as 30,000 people lived in the Four Corners area one thousand years ago; many resided in Chaco Canyon.

- before an adverb that links two clauses. Notice the comma after the adverb.

  The Anasazi were fearful of something; therefore, they left their villages and moved south and east.

- to separate items in a series when those items already contain commas.

  A reporter, a photographer, and I met with an archaeologist, a professor at the University of Arizona; a historian studying the region; and a local resident, who was to be our guide.

  The meaning of this sentence is clear. Three people met three others.

A colon serves as a signal to pay close attention to what follows. Use one before an extended quotation, an explanation, an example, or a series. Here are two uses you may have for colons in your essay writing:

- to introduce a list

  At the site we saw the following: stone walls, petroglyphs, ladders, corncobs, and loopholes for sentries.

- to introduce material that clarifies or illustrates a point

  Just gathering water was a hazardous chore: The Anasazi had to climb up and down a treacherous cliff.

Learn the uses of commas, semicolons, and colons that are new to you. You want to use every tool at your disposal to clarify your ideas so that readers can follow them.

Exercise 1: Using Commas

Read each sentence. Then place commas where they are needed.
If none are needed, leave the sentence as it is.

1. We flew into Phoenix, drove to Flagstaff, and from there drove east to visit the ruins at Wupatki.

2. Settlements were established high up in the cliffs for protection and defense.

3. These settlements, well preserved by the dry climate and stone overhangs, led the explorers who came upon them to refer to the builders as Cliff Dwellers.

4. Some archaeologists, who are not rock climbers, underestimated the skill and courage it took to live high up in canyon walls.

5. Our guide and interpreter, Leroy, took us up the trail to the ledge of the ruin.

6. In contrast to those living in cliff houses, some Anasazi settled in walled towns.

7. Gasping and sweating, we scrambled up to a ledge 500 feet above the canyon floor.

8. "Something drove the Anasazi to retreat to cliffs and fortified villages," Leroy told us.

9. In fact, what happened to the Anasazi has been the biggest puzzle facing archaeologists who study their ancient, complex culture.

10. For many years, experts focused on environmental explanations for their sudden departure.

11. Using tree ring data, researchers determined that a long drought seized the Southwest at the end of the thirteenth century.

12. Anasazi may have chopped down trees for roof beams, nearly deforesting the region.

13. Environmental issues don't explain everything.

14. Now archaeologists think the Anasazi lived in a climate of constant terror, and among the things they feared were execution and even cannibalism.

15. Until recently, due to a perception that ancient cultures were peaceful, archaeologists have been reluctant to recognize that the Anasazi might have been violent.

Exercise 2: Using Commas, Semicolons, and Colons

Read each sentence. Then place commas, semicolons, or colons where they are needed.

1. As typically defined, the Southwest includes all of Arizona and New Mexico; the southern parts of Utah, Nevada, and Colorado; and the northern Mexican states of Sonora and Chihuahua.

2. For every modern city in the Southwest, such as Tucson, Phoenix, or Albuquerque, there are small villages inhabited, in some cases for hundreds of years, by Native Americans.

3. And, for each of these villages, there are thousands of ruins of native settlements.

4. Complex irrigation canals, dug without the benefit of metal tools, are associated with several of the towns.

5. In the second half of the thirteenth century, war came to the Southwest; neighboring settlements attacked one another in grisly, violent encounters.

6. From the eleventh and twelfth centuries, there is scant archaeological evidence of true warfare; however, there is evidence of executions.

7. Archaeologists now generally agree: Environmental catastrophes which, in turn, led to violence, caused the Anasazi to flee the Four Corners region.

8. The Anasazi, although they lived in a time of fear and paranoia, produced much great beauty: villages such as Mesa Verde's Cliff Palace, petroglyph panels, and beautiful pottery.

9. Now, back in the present, Thomas, my friend; our guide Leroy, an interpreter; Jenna, a photographer; and I started off for the mesa early in the day.

10. Native Southwesterners today are comprised of descendants of those settlers who inhabited the region before the Europeans appeared, and of those who arrived during the late prehistoric period.

11. Modern Pueblo peoples of Arizona and New Mexico are unquestionably descendants of the ancient prehistoric settlers; many still dwell in villages constructed during prehistoric times.

12. In 1599, the Spanish settler Don Juan de Oñate described Native American settlements as follows: Houses adjoin houses with square plazas. They have no streets, and in the pueblos, which contain many plazas, one goes from one plaza to the other through alleys.

Making Changes

If you are like most writers, your essay will not be perfect right away. So, as soon as you have finished writing, it is time to start looking for ways to make improvements. You want to be sure to leave a few minutes to review your work to see whether you can present your argument more clearly or more logically. You also want to be sure that you have followed the conventions of standard English.

Zora Neale Hurston (1891–1960)

Use the following checklist as a guide for revising your essay.

Fixing Paragraphs

- Is each paragraph unified and does each have a topic sentence?
- Does each paragraph contain sufficient supporting ideas and details? Are all the details related to the topic sentence?
- Do all the paragraphs support your thesis statement?
- Have you used transitional words and phrases to make your paragraphs coherent?
- Are the paragraphs organized and arranged in the most effective way for making your case?
- Did you grab readers with a strong opening? Is your closing argument strong enough?

Fixing Sentences

- Are there any run-ons or fragments?
- Have you correctly used commas, semicolons, and colons?
- Have you varied the types, the lengths, the beginnings, and the structures of your sentences?
- Are any sentences too wordy? Is there a need to combine sentences to avoid choppiness?

Fixing Word Choice

- Are there dull or vague words you could replace with more precise, vivid, or expressive ones?
- Are your verbs in the active voice as much as possible?
- Is your essay free of clichés and slang?

> **TEST-TAKING TIP**
>
> Leave two or three minutes to reread and improve your essay. Look back to the first *Overview* (pages 4–10) for further review of the key elements of a persuasive essay.

Using Editor's Marks

You will make changes in your essay—you can count on it. It is important to show these changes clearly. You want readers to consider only your best version.

You can use the common editorial marks below to help you to show your changes quickly and clearly. They are convenient to know, but if you don't use them on the day of your test, that is fine—just make sure that the marks you make are easy to understand.

EDITORIAL MARK	HOW IT IS USED
⁋ new paragraph	⁋Place the symbol before the word that will begin the new paragraph.
= capitalize	the oldest city in the Americas may be Caral, in Peru.
∧ insert	The city flourished *about* 5,000 years ago.
delete	Is it the most ancient city in all the world?
⊙ insert period	Caral was a 180-acre complex of residences, plazas, and pyramids.
∧ insert comma	Caral, Peru, was discovered in 1905.
∨ insert end punctuation	The cache of goods unearthed was amazing !
⁀ transpose	The native Peruvians were first in Caral, 3,500 years before the Spaniards arrived.

You Try It

Use editor's marks to revise the following paragraph.

I have often heard the Americas described as the "New World." We should drop that designation immediately, since there was nothing new about the region when the Europeans arrived first. Pre-columbian North and South America featured well-established and great civilizations, cultures, and urban centers. For example, in caral, a city few are unfamiliar with, archaeologists' recent discoveries have opened eyes. They found that Caral was not only a very ancient and complex settlement, but a huge one, too. One of its pyramids, for instance, covers an area the size of four football fields. What were the cities in the Old World like when Caral was at its height fifty centuries ago?

Fixing Flawed Essays

The following essays contain errors. Correct the errors and make each essay better. Use editor's marks to help show your changes.
Corrections may vary; sample corrections provided.

Essay 1

Many of my classmates might disagree but I think it is
a good idea to have all students wear school uniforms. I
know that having to wear the same thing *that* as everyone else
wears
sounds boring and old-fashioned, and that many students
would find the idea stifling. Some might even say that
having to wear what everyone else does goes against our
democratic heritage and that it limits our freedom of
choice. however, I am ~~totally~~ in favor of the idea, as the
advantages of uniforms far outweigh their disadvantages

**TEST-
TAKING TIP**

If you choose to
add a sentence,
long clause, or
phrase, place the
correct editorial
mark where your
addition belongs in
the essay, then write
your new group of
words either to the
left or to the right
of the passage.

For one thing making everybody wear a ~~drab~~ uniform
relieves us all of the pressure to look good and to fit in. And it certainly would be
beleaguered
a great boon to those unfortunates among us who are poor dressers. These souls
would get relief from the steady diet of cold shoulders or even ridicule that
they've been long exposed to for having bad taste. For another thing uniforms in
a uniform
school would eliminate social class barriers if all students wear ~~the same thing,~~
no one would be able to tell who is rich and who is not just by looking at the
labels on their ~~sweaters,~~ blouses, and jeans. And in addition, popular clothing
relatively
costs bundles of money whereas uniforms are cheap.

Some of my classmates would argue that dressing as they like helps them to
define who they are. Many might say that it provides them with an outlet for self-
and individuality
expression. But as I see it, requiring students to wear school uniforms is a positive measure. Whereas clothing is so often a way of separating people, uniforms
can bring people together. So to the question of school uniforms, my answer is:
Bring them on

Essay 2

Ozone is a pale blue poisonous gas with a ~~strong~~ *pungent* odor that is made up of three oxygen atoms instead of two, as in the oxygen that is part of the air that we breathe. Ozone is concentrated in a layer between 12 and 20 miles above the Earth's surface. There, it acts as a shield that absorbs most of the ultraviolet radiation from the sun before it reaches us. The less ozone there is, the more ultraviolet light will get through. The disappearance of the ozone layer is a reason for *great* concern and the single most serious environmental problem we face on the planet.

The ozone layer protects all *living* organisms and is vital to their survival. *W*ithin the last thirty years ~~or so~~, scientists have discovered that the amount of ozone in the atmosphere has been decreasing. They have become aware too of a seasonal "ozone hole" above Antarctica that is larger than the continental United States and is growing in size. Whether the growth of this hole is naturally occurring or ~~a cause~~ *whether it is caused by* of chlorine atoms released by CFCs or other pollutants, the loss of ozone is a developing dilemma that the world needs to work *on* together to fix.

The shrinking concentration of ozone is bad news for several reasons. For one thing, if we don't stop the expansion of the hole, we will experience many more incidences of skin cancers, tum*o*rs, and cataracts caused by the increase in radiation. In addition, we may find our coastal cities flooded by the melting of the Antarctic shelf. And since ozone absorbs heat, *w*e may find changes in temperatures, and in wind and rain patterns, too. Furthermore, the *increased* radiation would kill single-celled ~~animals~~ *plankton* in our oceans ~~and cause~~ *causing* an imbalance in the food chain and a decrease in worldwide levels of oxygen, the gas *that* we breathe is essential to life on the planet.

We citizens of the world need to focus on this *very* important issue. We need to research what can be done to stem the rapid expansion of the ozone hole. As hard on industry and as unappealing to some politicians as this task may be, the consequences of doing nothing are frightening. ~~So~~ we need to act decisively to replenish the precious ozone layer.

Model A: From Prompt to Finished Essay

Read the following prompt, and then observe the steps one student took to write an essay based on it.

> By participating in community service, high school students can learn first-hand how local government functions as well as experience its many benefits—both for communities and volunteers. Therefore, volunteer community service should be part of the high school curriculum, as biology or algebra is. Do you agree? In an essay, support your opinion using knowledge from your studies, observations, and personal experience.

Step 1: Read Carefully

The first step this writer takes is to reread the prompt to clarify her task. In doing so, she uses the strategy of identifying key ideas by underlining them.

> By participating in community service, high school students can learn first-hand how local government functions as well as experience its many benefits—both for communities and volunteers. Therefore, volunteer community service should be part of the high school curriculum, as biology or algebra is. Do you agree? In an essay, support your opinion using knowledge from your studies, observations, and personal experience.

Step 2: Narrow Your Focus

To help narrow the focus of her response, this student chooses to make a pro-con chart. By quickly listing reasons for and against the concept of required community service, she can more easily identify the position for which she can make her strongest case. She saves time by using abbreviations and by not writing complete sentences. She stops as soon as she decides what side she will take (in this case, in support of the idea).

Pro	Con
rich personal learning exper.	too busy; schoolwork already takes too much time
serves greater good; feels good	have family respons.; need time for p.t. job, baby sittg., etc.
learn citiz. skills, how democ. works	can do comm. serv. as adult
meet people, make contacts, devel. interpers. skills	less time for extra curric. activ. like sports
good social stud. learning exper.	
gd. for coll. applic.	

Total time for reading closely and narrowing focus: no more than 2–3 minutes

Step 3: Gather and Group Ideas

The next step in the prewriting process is to gather supporting ideas, facts, and details you will use in the essay, and to group those that belong together in the same paragraph. To do this, this writer makes a T-chart. She uses it to list any more ideas she can think of, and to add details to those she already has. Again, she uses abbreviations to speedily list ideas. Although a new chart is shown here, to save time, a student writer could continue to use the first chart. She simply could change the headings and move some ideas from the left side to the right by circling them and using arrows.

Good for student	*Greater good*
rich personal learning exper.	the more participants in democ., the better
meet people, make contacts	learn citiz. skills
devel. interpers. skills, listening skills, patience, etc.	become better-informed citizen, wiser voter
good social stud. learning exper. —how people in organiz. work togeth. to solve probs.	gov. saves $ by using volunts.
gd. for coll. applic. gd. for fut. job opps.	

She decides to write a thesis statement that supports the idea that active participation in community service is a good idea, both for students and society. She will put this in her opening paragraph.

In examining her supporting ideas, she sees how she might group them into three paragraphs: one to explain ways in which community service is good for all, one to explain ways it would be good for a student's learning and personal growth, and one to show how community service could advance a student's college and career opportunities. She will also include a closing paragraph, in which she will tie together her ideas by restating her thesis with different words.

Step 4: Order Ideas for Effectiveness

In ordering ideas, this student writer chooses to do the following:

- Hook readers with the introduction and thesis statement.
- Between her two best ideas, she will arrange her other arguments in a logical order.

She now is ready to write her persuasive essay in support of making community service mandatory for high school students. She thinks about how to open strong and close powerfully.

Total time to gather, group, and order ideas: no more than 4–5 minutes

Step 5: Write the Essay

The writer has a sufficient amount of time left to write and then polish her essay. She writes quickly, but as legibly as she can. She makes her hand-writing small enough to make sure to have room to fit her essay in the space provided.

People whose idea of service to the U.S. is participating in the military are only half right. This country needs volunteers right here at home, to help government better meet the needs of its citizens and, as President Kennedy reminded us, to help citizens better meet the needs of their government. Requiring high school kids to participate in community service not only provides them with a rich personal learning experience, but it also benefits society.

Living in a democracy is not a gift, but a responsibility. One responsibility all citizens share is to understand how government functions. High school students, although most of them are not yet old enough to vote, can participate in government in important ways on a local level. Students' involvement in civic activities through volunteer work can help prepare them to be better-informed citizens and wiser voters. What's better for a democracy like ours than that? And one more thing: Volunteers save our cities money.

Student volunteers not only help the communities they serve, but they also help themselves. Their involvement in community service enriches their education as they learn about the workings of civic organizations, and learn first-hand how people work together to make and carry out decisions. Students can learn how to listen to other views. They can learn how to compromise. They can learn how to handle failure. They can learn patience. In short, they can acquire better "people" skills.

Another benefit of community service is that colleges and future employers will look favorably upon their service. Also, there are networking opportunities that await them when they work with others toward common goals. But most importantly, they will experience a sense of pride and accomplishment simply for participating responsibly in such a worthy endeavor.

Requiring high school students to participate in service to their communities is something that they owe to themselves and to their friends and neighbors. It is a win-win idea whose time has come. Just imagine the advantages to all when that first graduating class of better-informed, more actively involved citizens leaves campus.

Step 6: Polish the Essay

With her remaining two or three minutes, the writer reads over her essay and looks for ways to improve it. She uses editorial marks to show her changes.

People whose idea of service to the U.S. is participating in the military are only half right. This country needs volunteers right here at home, to help government better meet the needs of its citizens and, as President Kennedy ~~so aptly~~ reminded us, to help citizens better meet the needs of their government. Requiring high school kids to participate in community service not only provides them with a rich personal learning experience, but it also benefits society.

Living in a democracy is not a gift, but a responsibility. One responsibility all citizens share is to understand how government functions. High school students, although most of them are not yet old enough to vote, can participate in government in important ways on a local level. Students' involvement in civic activities through volunteer work can help prepare them to be better-informed citizens and wiser voters. What's better for a democracy like ours than that? ~~And one more thing:~~ *In addition, using* Volunteers save**s** our cities money.

Student volunteers not only help the communities they serve, but they also help themselves. Their involvement in community service enriches their education as they learn about the workings of civic organizations, and learn first-hand how people work together to make and carry out decisions. *With an open mind,* Students can learn how to listen to other views, *and* ~~They can learn~~ how to compromise. They can learn how to handle failure. They can learn patience. In short, they can acquire better "people" skills.

Another benefit of community service is that colleges and future employers will look favorably upon their service. Also, there are networking opportunities that await them when they work with others toward common goals. But most importantly, they will experience a sense of pride and accomplishment simply for participating responsibly in such a worthy endeavor.

Requiring high school students to participate in service to their communities is something that they owe to themselves and to their friends and neighbors. It is a win-win idea whose time has come. Just imagine the advantages to all when that first graduating class of better-informed, more actively involved citizens leaves campus.

Model B: From Prompt to Finished Essay

Read the following prompt, and then observe the steps one student took to write an essay based on it.

> Living in a democratic society such as the United States is a responsibility that all citizens share. If I could choose one environmental issue facing our nation or the world that requires our immediate attention, it would be _____.

Step 1: Read Carefully

The first step this writer takes is to reread the prompt to clarify his task. In doing so, he uses the strategy of identifying key ideas by looping them.

> (Living in a democratic society) such as the United States (is a) (responsibility that all citizens share.) If I could (choose one) (environmental issue facing our nation or the world) that (requires) (our immediate attention), it would be _____.

Step 2: Narrow Your Focus

To help him narrow the focus of his response, he quickly makes a topic web to list key environmental issues to consider. Although he sees that all of the issues are important enough to address, he selects the disappearance of rain forests because it is a serious issue that he knows a lot about through his studies.

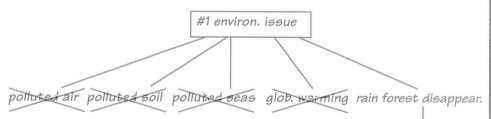

```
                    #1 environ. issue

polluted air  polluted soil  polluted seas  glob. warming  rain forest disappear.

                                                              importance of r.f.
                                                              causes of disappear.
                                                              define probs.
                                                              deforestat. rate
```

Total time for reading closely and narrowing focus: no more than 2–3 minutes

Step 3: Gather and Group Ideas

Next, the writer needs to gather and group ideas, facts, and details to use to support his viewpoint on the importance of saving rain forests. For this purpose, he uses an idea web. Notice again how he uses abbreviations.

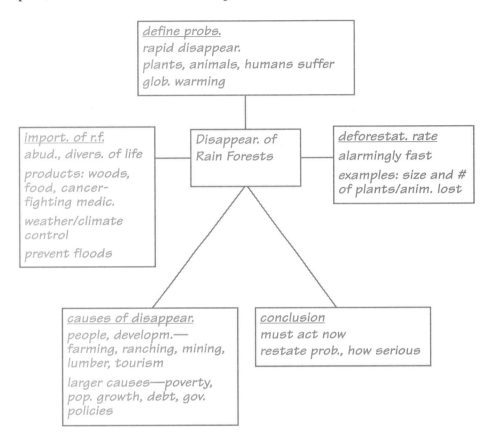

Step 4: Order Ideas for Effectiveness

In ordering ideas, this student chooses to do the following:

- Hook readers with the introduction and thesis statement.
- Between his two best ideas, he will arrange his other arguments in a logical order.

He now is ready to write persuasively in support of the idea that the disappearance of rain forests is the most troubling environmental issue facing us today. He numbers the groups of ideas to indicate the order in which they will appear. He thinks about how to open and close the essay.

Total time to gather, group, and order ideas: no more than 4–5 minutes

Step 5: Write the Essay

The writer has a sufficient amount of time left to write and then polish his essay. He writes quickly, but as legibly as he can. He makes his hand-writing small enough to make sure to have room to fit his essay in the space provided.

Rain forests are the world's most bountiful gardens. Under the rain-forest canopy exists an abundance and diversity of life greater than exists in the rest of the world combined. But rain forests are extremely fragile environments that are vulnerable to human disturbance. Because of their importance to people and wildlife the world over, the loss of these tropical forests is the most serious and troubling environmental issue we face today.

Rain forests provide the world with an extraordinary wealth of riches. For one thing, they are a plentiful source of hardwoods, foods, and key medications—at least 2,000 plants in rain forests have been identified as possessing cancer-fighting properties. In addition, healthy rain forests do more than provide indispensable resources. They also reduce erosion, and by doing so, help to act as a natural buffer against wind damage and coastal flooding. However, when the forests are cleared, carbon dioxide is unleashed into the atmosphere and contributes to disastrous global warming.

Tropical deforestation is warming the Earth and depriving it of critical products. It is happening at a very fast rate. Alarmingly, studies tell us that more than 30 million acres of rain forest are lost each year, a rate that is equivalent to about a football field a second. In the process, the deforestation wipes out between 10,000 and 20,000 species of plants and animals a year, or about two species per hour. And if this tragic loss isn't enough to grab our attention think about the other inhabitants of rain forests: people. The rapid destruction of the forests threatens the cultural and physical survival of the indigenous groups, who are helpless to stop it.

The causes of tropical deforestation are many, but have one thing in common: All of them are the result of human involvement. Farming, ranching, mining, logging, tourism, and development contribute explicitly. But the underlying causes such as poverty, debt, rising populations, and short-sighted governmental policies are complicated and hard to fix. The future is dire and we need to act responsibly now, for the disappearance of rain forests would surely spell doom for us and for all the plants and animals that are part of the complex web of interdependencies in our ecosystem.

Step 6: Polish the Essay

With his remaining two or three minutes, the writer reads over his essay and looks for ways to improve it. He uses editorial marks to show his changes.

Rain forests are the world's most bountiful gardens. Under the rainforest canopy exists an abundance and diversity of life greater than exists in the rest of the world combined. But rain forests are extremely fragile environments that are vulnerable to human disturbance. Because of their importance to people and wildlife the world over, the loss of these tropical forests is the most serious and troubling environmental issue we face today.

Rain forests provide the world with an extraordinary wealth of riches. For one thing, they are a plentiful source of hardwoods, foods, and ~~key~~ *vital* medications—at least 2,000 plants in rain forests have been identified as possessing cancer-fighting properties. In addition, healthy rain forests do more than provide indispensable resources. They also reduce erosion, and by doing so, help to act as a natural buffer against wind damage and coastal flooding. However, when the forests are cleared, carbon dioxide is unleashed into the atmosphere and contributes to disastrous global warming. *Not only is* Tropical deforestation ~~is~~ warming the Earth and depriving it of critical products. It is *also* happening at a ~~very fast~~ *staggering* rate. Alarmingly, studies tell us that more than 30 million acres of rain forest are lost each year, a rate that is equivalent to about a football field a second. In the process, the deforestation wipes out between 10,000 and 20,000 species of plants and animals a year, or about two species per hour. And if this tragic loss isn't enough to grab our attention, think about the other inhabitants of rain forests: people. The rapid destruction of the forests threatens the cultural and physical survival of the indigenous ~~groups~~ *tribes*, who are helpless to stop it.

The causes of tropical deforestation are many, but have one thing in common: All of them are the result of human involvement. Farming, ranching, mining, logging, tourism, and development contribute explicitly. But the underlying causes such as poverty, debt, rising populations, and short-sighted governmental policies are complicated and hard to ~~fix~~ *alleviate*. The future is dire and we need to act responsibly now, for the disappearance of rain forests would surely spell doom for us and for all the plants and animals that are part of the complex web of interdependencies in our ecosystem.

Your Turn

Now it is time to put what you have learned about writing essays to the test.

Knowing What Your Readers Do and Do Not Expect

The people who will be reading your essay *do not* expect fully polished compositions. They know that you have only 25 minutes (or more, depending on the test) to plan, write, and look over your essay. They do, however, expect you to express your ideas clearly and effectively. They do not expect you to have expertise on a topic; they do expect you to take a stand and to make your strongest case.

Readers will pay careful attention to your presentation. They will read to see whether you develop and support your argument with facts, details, and ideas, and whether you do so in a unified, coherent manner.

You are expected to use standard English, although you may apply a conversational tone, as long as you avoid clichés and slang. Readers will pay attention to whether or not you demonstrate a command of the language.

In addition, readers will expect you to take the time to review your essay, and to make changes that will improve it.

TEST-TAKING TIP

Look back at *What Makes a Good Essay* on pages 4 and 5 for additional reminders about what to expect in the essay portion of standardized tests. Remember: The prompt will be broad enough so that you will be able to write from a familiar perspective.

Paying Attention to Length

When you write your essay, you will need to confine it to the lines provided on the answer sheet. No additional paper will be available to you. Knowing this, you should keep the following in mind: *How well you write is more important than how much you write.* Don't shortchange yourself. Say what you need to say, but be concise. Include only your best ideas. Strive for quality, not quantity.

You can aim to write 3–5 paragraphs. If you write only three, make sure that they are loaded with information!

You should make a point of keeping your handwriting small enough to fit your essay on the lines provided for you. Write and revise as neatly as you can, too. You want readers to be able to read your essay and any revisions that you make.

Look at the checklists below. Use them as a guide for writing and revising your essays.

Writing Better Essays

- ☐ Have I started my essay with a strong opening?
- ☐ Have I included a compelling thesis statement that lets readers know what to expect?
- ☐ Have I used precise, bold language and replaced dull or vague words with better ones?
- ☐ Have I made sure that my essay is free of clichés and slang?
- ☐ Have I posed a thoughtful argument?
- ☐ Have I written neatly?
- ☐ Have I closed powerfully?

TEST-TAKING TIP

Look back at Topics 5–17, as needed, to review the components of essay writing in more detail.

Writing Better Paragraphs

- ☐ Is each paragraph unified?
- ☐ Does each paragraph have a topic sentence, or a main idea that is clearly implied?
- ☐ Have I included enough supporting ideas and details that are all relevant to the topic?
- ☐ Do all the paragraphs support the thesis?
- ☐ Have I used transitional words and phrases to make the paragraphs coherent?
- ☐ Have I varied the organizational structure of the paragraphs?
- ☐ Have I organized and arranged the paragraphs so that they will effectively make a case?

Writing Better Sentences

- ☐ Have I made sure that there are no fragments and run-ons?
- ☐ Have I correctly used commas, semicolons, and colons?
- ☐ Have I varied the types, the lengths, the beginnings, and the structures of the sentences?
- ☐ Have I avoided writing wordy, empty, or choppy sentences?
- ☐ Can I combine or break apart sentences to make them better?
- ☐ Have I avoided empty sentences?
- ☐ Have I used verbs in the active voice as much as possible?

Now it is time to practice writing a timed essay. You should give yourself the same amount of time that you will be given when you take a standardized test. You should also give yourself the same amount of writing space. Read the following before you turn to the next page and begin.

Reading Carefully and Following Directions

As you know, the essay portion of a standardized test will ask you to respond to a prompt by writing an essay. On the same page as the prompt, you will see an explanation of your task. You also will see specific writing guidelines and helpful pointers.

It is important to familiarize yourself with the kind of information this page provides so that you will not have to waste time reading it on the day of your test.

Review the following key ideas:

- First, read the prompt *very* carefully.
- Then, read the prompt again.
- Finally, identify key words and ideas in the prompt as you read it a third time.

TEST-TAKING TIP

Look ahead to Practice Test 1 on page 177 to see an example of a writing test opening page.

Using Your Prewriting Time Wisely

Before you begin to write, there are many useful things you can do, even within a limited time, to prepare to write the best essay you can. Carefully review these prewriting pointers:

- The prompt is a broad statement. Narrow the focus of your response to it to something that you can write about thoughtfully and knowledgeably.
- Gather ideas and key words for your essay. Use graphic organizers, phrases, and abbreviations to save time.
- Keep only your best ideas. Keep in mind that ideas gathered from personal experience can be as powerful as those gathered from reading or study.
- Group ideas that go together. Use circling and numbering to show in which paragraphs grouped ideas belong.
- Order grouped ideas in a way that will most effectively support your thesis.
- Write a thesis statement that lets your readers know what to expect.
- Do all of these things quickly but efficiently.

It is time to write. Put your best foot forward!

Writing an *Agree or Disagree* Essay

You have 25 minutes to write an essay on the following topic.

DO NOT WRITE AN ESSAY THAT ADDRESSES ANY OTHER TOPIC. AN ESSAY ON A DIFFERENT TOPIC WILL NOT BE ACCEPTED.

Consider the following statement. Then write an essay as directed.

"If you can't write well, then you cannot think well, and if you cannot think well, then others will do your thinking for you."

Assignment: Do you agree or disagree? Support your position, using examples from your personal experience, literaure, history, or current events.

WRITE YOUR ESSAY ON A SEPARATE PIECE OF PAPER.

Writing a *Complete the Statement* Essay

You have 25 minutes to write an essay on the following topic.

DO NOT WRITE AN ESSAY THAT ADDRESSES ANY OTHER TOPIC. AN ESSAY ON A DIFFERENT TOPIC WILL NOT BE ACCEPTED.

Consider the following statement. Then write an essay as directed.

If Abraham Lincoln came back to life for a week and saw America as it is today, what would please him the most about it is _____ .

Assignment: Write an essay that completes the sentence above. Explain the reasons behind your choice.

WRITE YOUR ESSAY ON A SEPARATE PIECE OF PAPER.

Go to **www.writingforstandardizedtests.com** to access additional practice sheets for Topics 20–32 and answer rationales for all of the multiple-choice items in Topics 20–35.

Multiple Choice:
Grammar and Usage

[17] I'm sure that George Washington struggled to keep his chin up during the rough winter at Valley Forge before rallying his troops to victory. [18] Abraham Lincoln must have had many sleepless nights watching the great sacrifice Americans were making to keep the country together. [19] I'm certain, too, that Dr. Martin Luther King, Jr., along with those who marched and demonstrated with him, kept his head high even though he had doubts about where all his hard work would lead. [20] Well, it led to civil rights for millions of Americans!

[21] All of these great leaders understood that despite the difficulties they faced, they needed to keep on going because what they knew to be right was worth the struggle. [22] They, and many others like them, saw the future as a distant, flickering light, not as a train bearing down on them. [23] Their view then should ours today, because although it may not always seem so, hopefulness results in success. [24] After all, since "the future is ours to make," let's make it the best can be!

1. Which sentence best states the main idea of paragraph 1?

   (A) sentence 1
   (B) sentence 2
   (C) sentence 3
   (D) sentence 4
   (E) sentence 5

   Ⓐ Ⓑ Ⓒ Ⓓ Ⓔ

2. Sentences 6 and 7 function together to

   (A) describe today's troubles.
   (B) defend adversity.
   that the future is bright.
   has learned somethin

Multiple-Choice Formats: Identifying Sentence Errors, Improving Sentences, Improving Paragraphs

In addition to an essay component, standardized writing tests include a multiple-choice section that tests your understanding of standard written English. In this section, you will encounter three different types of multiple-choice questions:

- Identifying Sentence Errors
- Improving Sentences
- Improving Paragraphs

You will have to either spot or fix errors, not to formally name or explain them. Let's now take a closer look at these types of multiple-choice questions.

Identifying Sentence Errors

With this type of multiple-choice item, you will have to find an error within a sentence, or indicate that there is no error. These items test your knowledge of basic grammar, sentence structure, and word choice.

Each test item is a sentence that has four words or phrases underlined and labeled A through D. Your task is to identify the underlined portion of the sentence that contains the error and to fill in the corresponding oval on your answer sheet.

In the *Identifying Sentence Errors* section, no sentence will have more than one error. You can assume that the parts not underlined do not contain mistakes. You will be instructed to fill in the oval for choice E when the sentence is error-free.

Read the following sample *Identifying Sentence Errors* item:

Each of the <u>members</u> of the all-star team <u>had</u> <u>their</u> <u>own</u> TV in the locker
          A   B   C   D

room. <u>No error</u>
      E

Choice C is correct because *Each*, the antecedent of the pronoun *their*, is singular, and therefore requires a singular pronoun. The error is in the pronoun-antecedent agreement.

To help you to successfully respond to an *Identifying Sentence Errors* item:

- Read the sentence very carefully. "Listen" for an error by imagining how the sentence would sound if read aloud.
- Reread the sentence, focusing on the underlined portions.

- Be alert to errors that commonly appear on standardized tests.

Some kinds of sentence errors are more likely than others to appear in this portion of the test. See the list below.

Topics commonly tested in *Identifying Sentence Errors* items:

- Subject-verb agreement
- Idioms
- Pronoun-antecedent agreement
- Comparisons
- Adjectives and adverbs
- Verb forms or tense
- Word choice (i.e., *accept* vs. *except*)
- Pronoun choice
- Double negatives
- Parallel construction

Topics 20–32 address these and other grammar and usage issues. They provide practice answering *Identifying Sentence Errors* test items. Working through these topics will help you to be on the lookout for, or to "hear," these common errors. Keep in mind that within any given topic, one or more of the practice multiple-choice items may include subject matter introduced in a previous topic.

Improving Sentences

In contrast to the *Identifying Sentence Errors* section, where you are asked only to spot mistakes, the items in the *Improving Sentences* section of the test require you to fix any errors by choosing the most effective form of the given sentence. *Improving Sentences* items continue to test your ability to use standard written English not only correctly, but gracefully, too.

Like the *Identifying Sentence Errors* items, these items test grammar, sentence structure, and word choice. In contrast to the *Identifying Sentence Errors* items though, these usually do not focus on individual words or phrases, but rather on the structure of the entire sentence.

Each *Improving Sentences* test item is a sentence with part or all of it underlined. Following the sentence are five answer choices. The first one, (A), repeats the sentence exactly as it is originally given. The next four choices, (B) through (E), rephrase *only the underlined portion*. Each is a possible replacement for it. Your job is to pick the answer choice that *best* improves the sentence.

Once you determine which answer choice results in a sentence that is grammatically correct, is neither awkward nor ambiguous, and best expresses the intended meaning of the original sentence, you should then fill in the corresponding oval on your answer sheet. You should choose (A) only if you think that the original sentence needs no revision.

Read the following sample *Improving Sentences* item:

> Athabasca Glacier, which flows down from the Columbia Ice Field, <u>giving us a look back to a time</u> when the world was dominated by ice.

(A) giving us a look back to a time

(B) giving us a look back

(C) gives us a look back to a time

(D) looking back to a time

(E) looks back at a time

The original sentence is a fragment. Choice (C) is correct because it is the only one that contains the necessary predicate and does not alter the intended meaning of the sentence. Choice (E) is incorrect because even though it would create a complete, correct sentence, it changes the meaning of the original sentence by implying that the glacier has the ability to see itself.

To help you to successfully respond to an *Improving Sentences* item:

- Read the sentence very carefully. "Listen" for any errors.
- Save time by not reading choice (A), as it is exactly the same as the underlined portion.
- Read choices (B) through (D). Eliminate right away those that do not improve the sentence.
- Pick the choice that "sounds" best to you.
- Never choose an alternative that significantly changes the meaning of the original sentence, even if it is grammatically correct and stylish.

In some cases, you may be presented with two or more answer choices that are grammatically correct. When this occurs, follow this rule of thumb: Always choose the answer that most gracefully and effectively completes the sentence without changing its meaning.

An *Improving Sentences* item may contain more than one kind of error. Remember, a large part of or the whole sentence will be underlined. Be sure the answer choice you pick addresses and corrects all of the errors. Keep in mind though, that the original sentence may be correct as given. If this is the case, you should choose (A).

Some kinds of sentence errors are more likely than others to appear in this section. See the list below.

Topics commonly tested in *Improving Sentences* items:

- Run-on sentences
- Modifiers
- Subordination/coordination
- Subject-verb agreement
- Comparisons

- Sentence fragments
- Parallelism
- Redundancy or wordiness
- Verb forms and tenses
- Pronouns

Topics 20–32 address these and other grammar, usage, and style issues. They provide practice answering *Improving Sentences* test items. Keep in mind that within any given topic, one or more of the practice multiple-choice items may include subject matter introduced in a previous topic.

Improving Paragraphs

In the *Improving Paragraphs* section, the multiple-choice items test your ability to improve the logic, unity, or coherence of an essay. Because the essays in this section are intended to be early drafts, they contain parts that need to be rewritten. These items will put your knowledge of grammar to the test, too. More specifically, you may be asked to identify the best way to:

- revise a poorly constructed or grammatically incorrect sentence.
- delete or relocate a sentence.
- combine sentences.
- rephrase a sentence so that it could be a topic sentence.
- begin or conclude an essay.

Many of the items in this section address the same issues that the items in the previous two sections do. However, they differ in one key way: They require you to keep the "big picture" in mind when you respond to them. When you make your selection from among the answer choices, you need to consider the *context*. To choose the best way to fix the flaws in the given essay, reread the sentences that come just before and just after the sentence(s) in question, and keep in mind the overall purpose of the essay.

All the sentences in the essay are numbered and each essay is followed by six items. Each item offers five answer choices, (A) to (E). Occasionally, choice (A) is "As it is now."

You should first read the essay before you respond to the items that follow it. Some items refer to particular sentences or parts of sentences, and require that you improve the structure or word choice, while others refer to the entire essay, or parts of it, and ask you to address the way it is organized and developed. When selecting answers, you should use the conventions of standard written English.

Choosing How to Approach the *Improving Paragraphs* Section

It is up to you how you work through these multiple-choice items—pick a method that seems to work best. Here is one way:

- Read the essay quickly, but carefully, so that you can get a good sense of what it is about.
- Refer to the text, as needed, to answer each question.

- Read each question carefully to make sure you understand what it asks you to do.
- Some questions refer to a specific sentence or pairs of sentences. When you reread the sentence(s) the question addresses, also read the portions of the essay immediately before and after it to understand the context.
- If a question is about the essay as a whole, skim it all again, as needed, to refamiliarize yourself with the content.
- When responding to items in this section, try to decide how to fix the flaw *before* you look at the answer choices.

Read the following sample excerpt and test item.

(1) Archaeologists have recently discovered a lost colony in Maine. (2) In 1606, about 20 years after Sir Walter Raleigh's North Carolina colony disappeared, James I granted a charter to a joint stock company. (3) Its mission was to establish two colonies on the Atlantic Coast. (4) One colony was Jamestown, settled on the southern Atlantic Coast. (5) The other, Popham, was on the northern Atlantic Coast. (6) Jamestown proved to be a success. (7) Popham, located northeast of Portland, Maine, lasted less than a year.

Which of the following is the best way to combine sentences 6 and 7?

(A) Jamestown proved to be a success unlike Popham, located northeast of Portland, Maine, lasted less than a year.

(B) Jamestown proved to be a success and Popham, located northeast of Portland, Maine, lasted less than a year and was a failure.

(C) Popham lasted less than a year and was located northeast of Portland, Maine, unlike Jamestown, which was a success.

(D) Jamestown proved to be a success, but, Popham, located northeast of Portland, Maine, lasted less than a year.

(E) Jamestown proved to be a success but Popham, located northeast of Portland, Maine, lasting less than a year.

Choice (D) is the best solution. It is correctly, concisely, and clearly written, and does not change the meaning of the two sentences.

You now have seen an overview of the kinds of multiple-choice questions that will appear on a standardized writing test. Topics 20–35 provide teaching and practice for this section of the exam. As you work through those topics, feel free to look back to these pages for test-taking pointers.

Subject-Verb Agreement

Read the following:

> All across the mining and cattle towns of the Wild West, theaters that held performances of Shakespearean plays was nearly as common as saloons and gambling halls.

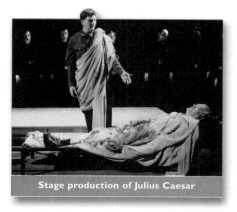

Stage production of Julius Caesar

It is true. Shakespearean plays won the hearts and minds of the American West. But Shakespeare would not have looked kindly upon this problematic opening sentence. It is incorrect because the singular verb, *was*, does not agree with the plural subject, *theaters*.

Making Subjects and Verbs Agree

When you write, make sure that your verbs agree with your subjects in number. There are two basic rules of subject and verb agreement:

- A singular subject must have a singular verb.
- A plural subject must have a plural verb.

Although you are unlikely to make the error you see in the opening sentence, you may run into other cases in which choosing the correct form of a verb is not as simple. Study the key rules and examples below.

RULES	EXAMPLES
Compound Subjects Compound subjects joined by *and* are generally plural. They require a plural verb, whereas compound subjects acting as a singular unit require singular verbs.	Cowboys and miners sit side-by-side at the performances. *but* Fish and chips is served in the hotel restaurant.
Two or more singular subjects joined by *or* or *nor* require a singular verb.	Either *Hamlet* or *Macbeth* is being performed tonight.
Two or more plural subjects joined by *or* or *nor* require a plural verb.	Tents or hotel hallways take the place of theaters from time to time.
If singular subjects are joined by *or* or *nor* to plural subjects, the subject *closest* to the verb determines agreement.	Neither drought nor storms keep audiences from the performances.

Confusing Subjects

Sometimes a subject is hard to find; it can *follow* the verb or be *separated* from the verb. Verbs must agree with subjects even when words come between them.

There is a new name for Ralston, New Mexico.
Think: "name" is the subject.

The reviews of the play are positive.

In addition, some subjects (such as those that express length or distance) are usually singular even though they sound plural.

Ten miles is not far to travel to see a play.

Collective Nouns

Collective nouns require a singular verb when the group named acts as a single unit.

The cast appreciates the gold dust tossed onto the stage.

Collective nouns need a plural verb when the group named act as individuals.

The audience arrive at the theater at different times.

Some collective nouns ending in *-s,* such as *politics*, *acoustics*, and *statistics,* can be singular or plural. Use a singular verb to indicate that the group is acting as a unit.

Statistics is not a required course for theatre majors.

Use a plural verb to indicate that the individual parts or the group is acting separately.

These statistics show that people prefer musicals to dramas.

Indefinite Pronouns

Indefinite pronouns such as *each*, *anyone*, and *everybody* are always singular.

Everybody in the mines finds relief from his or her hard work in Shakespearean plays.

Others, such as *both*, *many*, *few*, and *several* are always plural.

Several mining towns name streets after Shakespearean characters.

The pronouns *all*, *any*, *some*, *enough*, *most*, and *none* are singular when they refer to singular words, and plural when they refer to plural words.

Most of the *town* shows up each night.

Most of the *towns* welcome the performers.

Amounts

Amounts (such as percentages or fractions) are singular when the amount acts as a unit, and plural when the amount acts as many parts.

Two thirds of the seats are in the mezzanine.
Think: The fraction refers to the plural noun "seats."

Exercise 1: Choose the Verb

Circle the verb in parentheses that agrees with the subject of the sentence.

1. An opera house, like those in Tombstone, Leadville, and other towns, still (stands, stand) today. stands

2. Pool tables or even tree stumps (makes, make) serviceable stages. make

3. Several factors (plays, play) a role in determining where to stage a play. play

4. Anyone on stage (is, are) a target for fruit-throwing patrons. is

5. (Do, Does) the arrival of the troupe cause excitement in the town? Does

6. Neither Denver nor Boulder (gets, get) as cold as Aspen. gets

7. The director is someone who (knows, know) how to get the most from actors. knows

8. Five years (is, are) a long time to be on the road. is

9. Both of the buildings (was, were) built in the same year. were

10. Twenty dollars (is, are) how much it costs to ride the stage to Carson City. is

> **TEST-TAKING TIP**
>
> Mistakes in subject-verb agreement can occur when you lose sight of the subject. To find the subject, don't look within prepositional phrases or subordinate clauses.

Exercise 2: Identify the Sentence Error

One of the underlined words or phrases may contain a grammatical error. If there is one, choose the underlined part that must be changed to make the sentence correct, and fill in the corresponding oval. If the sentence has no error, fill in answer choice Ⓔ.

EXAMPLE

All of the <u>members</u> of the cast <u>has</u> to <u>put</u> on <u>their</u> own costumes. <u>No error</u>
       A   B   C   D   E

Ⓐ Ⓑ Ⓒ Ⓓ Ⓔ

Ⓑ is the correct choice because the indefinite pronoun *All* is referring to the plural noun *members,* so the sentence requires the plural verb *have.*

---

1. <u>Actors</u> often <u>had</u> to <u>dodge</u> flying fruit while <u>onstage</u>. <u>No error</u>
   A   B   C   D   E

Ⓐ Ⓑ Ⓒ Ⓓ Ⓔ

2. Neither the <u>rain</u> <u>nor</u> the strong winds <u>dampens</u> the participants' <u>spirits</u>. <u>No error</u>
         A   B   C   D   E

Ⓐ Ⓑ **Ⓒ** Ⓓ Ⓔ

3. Everybody in the <u>theater</u> <u>laugh</u> each time the <u>actor</u> <u>says</u> that line. <u>No error</u>
                        A   B   C   D   E

Ⓐ **Ⓑ** Ⓒ Ⓓ Ⓔ

4. <u>A</u> strip of <u>mountains</u> <u>cross</u> the <u>state</u> from north to south. <u>No error</u>
     A   B   C   D   E

Ⓐ Ⓑ **Ⓒ** Ⓓ Ⓔ

5. Forty <u>miles</u>, the <u>distance</u> from Deadmarsh to Lone Mountain, <u>were</u> a long
         A   B   C

distance to <u>travel</u> then. <u>No error</u>
                  D   E

Ⓐ Ⓑ **Ⓒ** Ⓓ Ⓔ

Exercise 3: Improve the Sentence

**In each of the following items, all or part of the sentence is underlined.
Beneath each sentence are five ways of phrasing the underlined part. Choice
(A) is the same as the original; the other four are different. Select the answer
choice that best expresses the meaning of the original sentence. Your goal is to
produce the most effective sentence, one that is clear and not wordy. Choose
(A) if the original sentence is better than any of the other answer choices.**

EXAMPLE

The town council have decided to build a school house in town.

(A) The town council have decided to build a school house in town.

(B) The town council has decided to build a school house in town.

(C) The town council have not decided to build a school house in town.

(D) The town councils has decided to build a school house in town.

(E) The town's council have decided to build a school house in town.

Ⓐ **Ⓑ** Ⓒ Ⓓ Ⓔ

Ⓑ is the correct choice because the subject, *The town council*, is singular
and requires the singular verb, *has.*

---

1. <u>Elfrida, like other mining towns such as McNeal, Cochise, and Pearce, have had a short, wild life.</u>

   (A) Elfrida, like other mining towns such as McNeal, Cochise, and Pearce, have had a short, wild life.

   (B) Elfrida, like other mining towns such as McNeal, Cochise, and Pearce, are having a short, wild life.

   (C) Elfrida, like other mining towns such as McNeal, Cochise, and Pearce, have a short, wild life.

   (D) Elfrida, like other mining towns such as McNeal, Cochise, and Pearce, has had a short, wild life.

   (E) Elfrida, like other mining towns such as McNeal, Cochise, and Pearce, having had a short, wild life.

Ⓐ Ⓑ Ⓒ Ⓓ Ⓔ

2. According to newspaper reports, <u>either Elfrida's citizens or its mayor were to blame for the misunderstanding.</u>

   (A) According to newspaper reports, either Elfrida's citizens or its mayor were to blame for the misunderstanding.

   (B) According to newspaper reports, either Elfrida's citizens or its mayor was to blame for the misunderstanding.

   (C) Either Elfrida's citizens or its mayor were blamed for the misunderstanding, according to newspaper reports.

   (D) According to newspaper reports, either Elfrida's citizens were to blame or its mayor was to blame for the misunderstanding.

   (E) Either Elfrida's citizens or its mayor, according to newspaper reports, were to blame for the misunderstanding.

Ⓐ Ⓑ Ⓒ Ⓓ Ⓔ

3. Mayor Smith, along with the members of the town's safety committee, <u>urge citizens to leave their firearms home.</u>

   (A) urge citizens to leave their firearms home.

   (B) urge citizens to have left their firearms home.

   (C) have urged citizens to leave their firearms home.

   (D) urges citizens to leave their firearms home.

   (E) urge citizens to leave his or her firearms home.

4. <u>Macaroni and cheese are such an easy meal to make; the hotel restaurant serves it nearly every night, to the delight of its road-weary diners, to whom comfort food is most welcome.</u>

(A) Macaroni and cheese are such an easy meal to make; the hotel restaurant serves it nearly every night, to the delight of its road-weary diners, to whom comfort food is most welcome.

(B) Macaroni and cheese is such an easy meal to make, the hotel restaurant serves it nearly every night, to the delight of its road-weary diners, to whom comfort food is most welcome.

(C) Macaroni and cheese is such an easy meal to make; the hotel restaurant serves it nearly every night, to the delight of its road-weary diners, to whom comfort food is most welcome.

(D) Macaroni and cheese are such an easy meal to make; so the hotel restaurant serves it nearly every night, to the delight of its road-weary diners, to whom comfort food is most welcome.

(E) Macaronis and cheeses are such an easy meal to make; the hotel restaurant serves it nearly every night, to the delight of its road-weary diners, to whom comfort food is most welcome.

5. <u>Stagecoach robberies is one reason why more lawmen are needed in the territory.</u>

(A) Stagecoach robberies is one reason why more lawmen are needed in the territory.

(B) Stagecoach robberies is one reason why more lawmen is needed in the territory.

(C) Stagecoach robberies are one reason why more lawmen will be needed in the territory.

(D) Why more lawmen are needed in the territory is stagecoach robberies.

(E) Stagecoach robberies are one reason why more lawmen are needed in the territory.

Verb Tenses and Forms

A **verb tense** expresses the time an action is performed.

Read and compare the following two sentences. Which is correct?

> The Athabasca Glacier, which runs down from the Columbia Ice Field, gives us a look back to a time when the world is dominated by ice.

> The Athabasca Glacier, which runs down from the Columbia Ice Field, gives us a look back to a time when the world was dominated by ice.

Athabasca Glacier

The second version is correct because of the correct shift in verb tense. The glacier runs down from the ice field now, in the present, whereas ice covered much of the planet in the past.

Identifying Six Different Verb Tenses

In English, every verb has three simple tenses and three perfect tenses. Study the table below for more information about verb tenses.

TENSE	WHAT IT SPECIFIES	EXAMPLE
Present	existing or happening now; action that happens repeatedly	I always start my hike onto the glacier in the mornings.
Past	completed in the past	I started my hike onto the glacier this morning.
Future	action that will happen; formed with the helping verbs *will* or *shall*	I will start my hike onto the glacier after a good night's sleep.
Present Perfect	action completed recently or in the indefinite past; always includes the helping verbs *have* or *has*	I have started a hike onto the glacier many times during this trip.
Past Perfect	action that happened before another action in the past; always includes the helping verb *had*	I had started my hike onto the glacier by the time the sun came up.
Future Perfect	action that will happen before a future action or time; always includes the helping verbs *will have* or *shall have*	I will have started my hike onto the glacier by the time the sun comes up.

When events occur at the same time, use verbs in the same tense.

Incorrect: I climbed onto the tour bus, but have no idea of what was ahead.

Correct: I climbed onto the tour bus, but had no idea of what was ahead.

When events do not occur at the same time (as in the opening example), shift verb tenses as needed.

Incorrect: I collected my gear before today's excursion; my friend collects hers later.

Correct: I collected my gear before today's excursion; my friend will collect hers later.

Express *true* statements in the present tense regardless of what tense you use for other verbs in the sentence.

Incorrect: I have read that glaciers were in constant motion.

Correct: I have read that glaciers are in constant motion.

Recognizing Verb Forms

Every verb has four principal parts, or basic forms, that are used to create different verb tenses. The principal parts are the present (base form), the past, the present participle, and the past participle. Study the examples below.

PRINCIPAL PART	EXAMPLE
Present (base form)	I shiver when I think of how dangerous a glacier is.
Present Participle	I am shivering as I stand on this glacier.
Past	I shivered the whole time we were there.
Past Participle *Think:* Although in this case the past participle form of the verb is the same as the past form, many times the two forms are different.	I have shivered on every visit to that freezing site.

On a standardized test, you are very likely to encounter sentences with verb form errors. The kinds of mistakes you will find will most likely involve one of the following issues:

- an incorrectly formed irregular verb (irregular verbs form past tenses, past participles, or both in a different way than by adding *d* or *ed* to the present tense form of the verb)

Incorrect: She winned the bike race to the top of the peak.

Correct: She won the bike race to the top of the peak.

- confusion between the past and past participle form of a verb

> **Incorrect:** Many visitors to the park have drove along the Ice Fields Parkway.
>
> **Correct:** Many visitors to the park have driven along the Ice Fields Parkway.

- an improper shift in verb tense

> **Incorrect:** When a hiker fell into the millwell, a team of rangers rescues him from the icy hole.
>
> **Correct:** When a hiker fell into the millwell, a team of rangers rescued him from the icy hole.

<table>
<tr><td>

TEST-TAKING TIP

There are many frequently used irregular verbs. *Break* (*broke; have, has,* or *had broken*) and *begin* (*began; have, has,* or *had begun*) are examples.

</td></tr>
</table>

- use of the preposition *of* rather than the helping verb *have*

> **Incorrect:** I would of walked further, but the signs warning about bears stopped me.
>
> **Correct:** I would have walked further, but the signs warning about bears stopped me.

Exercise 1: Fix the Verb

Replace the underlined verb with the correct form or tense of that verb. Write "no error" if the sentence is correct as is.

1. We already <u>started</u> on our hike when it began to rain. __had started__

2. Our guide told us that the Athabasca Glacier <u>was</u> about six square kilometers in size. __is__

3. I <u>have spoke</u> to the ranger, who told me that the trail was muddy. __have spoken__

4. When I finally got home, dinner <u>has been</u> on the table for an hour. __had been__

5. If the ski patrol <u>had</u> not <u>come</u>, we would have been stranded. __no error__

6. Neither New York's Central Park nor Vancouver's Stanley Park <u>was</u> nearly as large as the Athabasca Glacier is. __is__

7. I have put on my backpack and <u>will began</u> the trek to the lake. __will begin__

8. The helicopter pilot reported that he <u>had spotted</u> the lost hikers. __no error__

9. We <u>catched</u> several salmon during the afternoon. __caught__

10. My hiking companion was pleased when she saw that I <u>had brung</u> chocolate along. __had brought__

Exercise 2: Identify the Sentence Error

One of the underlined words or phrases may contain a grammatical error. If there is one, choose the underlined part that must be changed to make the sentence correct, and fill in the corresponding oval. If the sentence has no error, fill in answer choice Ⓔ.

EXAMPLE

By the time we <u>arrived</u> at the campsite, I had <u>tore</u> my <u>sleeve</u> on <u>our</u> way down
             A   B   C   D

the trail. <u>No error</u>
          E

Ⓐ Ⓑ Ⓒ Ⓓ Ⓔ

Ⓑ is correct because *tear* is an irregular verb. The past participle of *tear* is *torn*.

1. I <u>would have been</u> more careful, had I <u>knew</u> that I could <u>have been stung</u> by a
      A   B   C

bee <u>so</u> late in the season. <u>No error</u>
   D   E

Ⓐ **Ⓑ** Ⓒ Ⓓ Ⓔ

2. You've <u>saw</u> the <u>site</u> of the plane crash and also the <u>plaque</u> that <u>marks</u> the spot.
       A   B   C   D

<u>No error</u>
 E

Ⓐ Ⓑ Ⓒ Ⓓ Ⓔ

3. I filmed the <u>goats</u> <u>that</u> <u>are</u> walking along a ridge about 100 yards away, not
            A   B   C

<u>mindful</u> of us at all. <u>No error</u>
   D   E

Ⓐ Ⓑ **Ⓒ** Ⓓ Ⓔ

4. The park ranger <u>bade</u> us to <u>avoid</u> the lake trail on <u>which</u> bears
                A   B   C

had been <u>spotted</u> that morning. <u>No error</u>
        D   E

Ⓐ Ⓑ Ⓒ Ⓓ **Ⓔ**

5. <u>Because</u> the night <u>was</u> so cold, the car windows <u>are</u> covered
      A   B   C

with ice when we <u>awoke</u> the next morning. <u>No error</u>
                      D   E

Ⓐ Ⓑ Ⓒ Ⓓ Ⓔ

TOPIC **21**

Exercise 3: Improve the Sentence

In each of the following items, all or part of the sentence is underlined. Beneath each sentence are five ways of phrasing the underlined part. Choice (A) is the same as the original; the other four are different. Select the answer choice that best expresses the meaning of the original sentence. Your goal is to produce the most effective sentence, one that is clear and not wordy. Choose (A) if the original sentence is better than any of the other answer choices.

EXAMPLE

<u>From where we sitted,</u> the entire avalanche came into view.

(A) From where we sitted,
(B) From where we were sitted,
(C) From where we sit,
(D) From where we sat,
(E) From where we will be sitting,

Ⓐ Ⓑ Ⓒ **Ⓓ** Ⓔ

For consistency of tense, *sat*, the past tense of *sit* (an irregular verb), should be used. Choice **Ⓓ** is correct because it describes two events happening at the same time.

---

1. <u>We would of returned sooner,</u> but our car got a flat tire.

(A) We would of returned sooner,
(B) We would have returned sooner,
(C) We returned sooner,
(D) We would have return sooner,
(E) We would have returned sooner;

Ⓐ **Ⓑ** Ⓒ Ⓓ Ⓔ

2. We emerged from our tent <u>once the sun had rose</u>.

(A) once the sun had rose

(B) after the sun had rose

(C) once the sun had rised

(D) once the sun rose

(E) once the sun had risen

Ⓐ Ⓑ Ⓒ Ⓓ Ⓔ

3. I learned that <u>a crevasse was a crack or fissure</u> in glacial ice.

(A) a crevasse was a crack or fissure

(B) a crevasse was cracks or fissures

(C) a crevasse is a crack or fissure

(D) a crevasse will be a crack or fissure

(E) a crevasse has been a crack or fissure

Ⓐ Ⓑ Ⓒ Ⓓ Ⓔ

4. Geologists have predicted that <u>the Athabasca Glacier will continue to retreat</u>.

(A) the Athabasca Glacier will continue to retreat

(B) the Athabasca Glacier continued to retreat

(C) the Athabasca Glacier has continued to retreat

(D) the Athabasca Glacier will have continued to retreat

(E) the Athabasca Glacier will retreat

Ⓐ Ⓑ Ⓒ Ⓓ Ⓔ

5. Many animal residents of the mountains <u>migrate away or hibernate to have survived the frigid Canadian winters</u>.

(A) migrate away or hibernate to have survived the frigid Canadian winters

(B) migrate away or hibernate to survive the frigid Canadian winters

(C) have migrated away or hibernate to have survived the frigid Canadian winters

(D) will migrate away or hibernate to have survived the frigid Canadian winters

(E) had migrated away or hibernated to survive the frigid Canadian winters

Ⓐ Ⓑ Ⓒ Ⓓ Ⓔ

Adjectives vs. Adverbs

Read the following two sentences.

> I eagerly pitched my fork into the plate of grits.

> I eager pitched my fork into the plate of grits.

A s you probably noticed, the second sentence sounds awkward. That is because it contains an adjective where an adverb belongs. If you learn the rules that govern the use of modifiers, you will have an easier time noticing when they are used incorrectly on a standardized test.

A breakfast meal with grits

Understanding Adjectives

An adjective is a modifier that provides information about the noun or pronoun it describes. Adjectives answer questions such as *What kind? How many? How much?* or *Which one?*

Adjectives can appear either before or after the word they modify.

> The *grits*, creamy and white, served as a bed for the poached *salmon*.

Proper adjectives are derived from proper nouns.

> Most Kentucky *restaurants* serve grits.

A predicate adjective often follows a linking verb to modify the subject or clause of a sentence.

> The yellow grits cake *was* delicious.

The indefinite articles *a* and *an* are adjectives that refer to any one member of a group. The definite article, *the*, is an adjective that names a particular noun.

> After a *vacation*, I always want a home-cooked meal.

> I put honey on the *grits* I ordered at the restaurant this morning.

Understanding Adverbs

Like adjectives, adverbs are modifiers. Adverbs modify verbs, adjectives, and other adverbs. They tell *when, where, how, to what extent, in what manner,* or *how much.*

> We happily *visited* my aunt and uncle after lunch.

> The bowl of grits was extremely *hot*.

> Jackie stirred the grits too *slowly*.

Adverbs can also modify prepositions and prepositional phrases.

> Andrew left at ten; we left just *after*.

> My plate was filled almost *to the top*.

Adverbs also can modify subordinate clauses and complete sentences.

I'll make grits again only if everyone wants me to.

Surely, you want me to make pork chops with white grits again.

Many negatives, like *not*, *barely*, and *never*, are adverbs. These can interrupt parts of a verb phrase.

He *should* not *have* refused the side dish of grits, the signature food of the South.

Choosing Between Adjectives and Adverbs

When you have to determine whether an adjective or an adverb is needed, use the rules you have learned so far to help to guide you. Some words can be both adjectives and adverbs, so be careful. Keep the following in mind:

- Though many adverbs end in *ly*, don't count on this ending of a word to identify it as an adverb. Many adjectives too, such as *friendly*, *slovenly*, and *curly*, end with the suffix *ly*.

  He *moves* gracefully for an elderly *man*.

Think: Although *elderly* ends with *ly*, it is an adjective that is modifying the noun *man* in this sentence.

- *Good* and *bad* are always adjectives. *Well* and *badly* are adverbs, although *well* may be used as an adjective to describe a person's health.
- You can use *bad* as a predicate adjective following a linking verb. When health is not involved, be sure to use *good*, not *well*, as a predicate adjective.

  Overcooked grits taste bad. Grits with cornbread taste good.

Exercise I: Choose the Correct Modifier

Underline the modifier within each set of parentheses that correctly completes the sentence.

1. A forkful of well-cooked grits goes down (smooth, <u>smoothly</u>).

2. When the new grits cookbook came out, I (quick, <u>quickly</u>) went to the store to buy it.

3. I ate my first plate of grits (near, <u>nearly</u>) twenty years ago.

4. The first time I cooked grits, I cooked them (bad, <u>badly</u>).

5. Chocolate chips in grits taste (<u>bad</u>, badly).

6. If you continue to eat so (slow, <u>slowly</u>), we will be late.

7. Some think that grits taste (<u>good</u>, well) with red-eye gravy.

8. It can be argued (strong, <u>strongly</u>) that grits were America's first food.

9. Pocahontas would (certain, <u>certainly</u>) have been no stranger to grits.

10. One can purchase (<u>instant</u>, instantly) grits at any supermarket.

Exercise 2: Identify the Sentence Error

One of the underlined words or phrases may contain a grammatical error. If there is one, choose the underlined part that must be changed to make the sentence correct, and fill in the corresponding oval. If the sentence has no error, fill in answer choice Ⓔ.

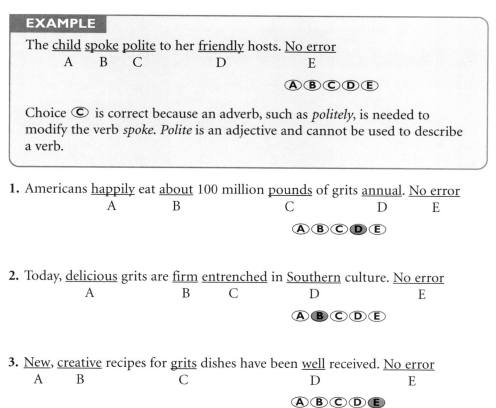

EXAMPLE

The <u>child</u> <u>spoke</u> <u>polite</u> to her <u>friendly</u> hosts. <u>No error</u>
  A   B   C   D   E

Ⓐ Ⓑ Ⓒ Ⓓ Ⓔ

Choice Ⓒ is correct because an adverb, such as *politely*, is needed to modify the verb *spoke*. *Polite* is an adjective and cannot be used to describe a verb.

1. Americans <u>happily</u> eat <u>about</u> 100 million <u>pounds</u> of grits <u>annual</u>. <u>No error</u>
            A   B   C   D   E

Ⓐ Ⓑ Ⓒ Ⓓ Ⓔ

2. Today, <u>delicious</u> grits are <u>firm</u> <u>entrenched</u> in <u>Southern</u> culture. <u>No error</u>
          A   B   C   D   E

Ⓐ Ⓑ Ⓒ Ⓓ Ⓔ

3. <u>New</u>, <u>creative</u> recipes for <u>grits</u> dishes have been <u>well</u> received. <u>No error</u>
  A   B   C   D   E

Ⓐ Ⓑ Ⓒ Ⓓ Ⓔ

4. <u>Over</u> the years, grits dishes <u>gradually</u> <u>have</u> gained <u>widely</u> acceptance. <u>No error</u>
   A   B   C   D   E

Ⓐ Ⓑ Ⓒ **Ⓓ** Ⓔ

5. The <u>instant</u> kind of <u>commercial</u> prepared grits makes up <u>about</u> a third of their
          A   B   C

annual sales. <u>No error</u>
   D   E

Ⓐ **Ⓑ** Ⓒ Ⓓ Ⓔ

6. A <u>growing</u> number of <u>talented</u> chefs are taking <u>their</u> grits <u>serious</u>. <u>No error</u>
         A   B   C   D   E

Ⓐ Ⓑ Ⓒ **Ⓓ** Ⓔ

7. <u>Near</u> fifty <u>acclaimed</u> restaurants serve <u>grits</u> dishes in <u>our</u> city. <u>No error</u>
        A   B   C   D   E

Ⓐ Ⓑ Ⓒ Ⓓ Ⓔ

8. I felt <u>anxiously</u> when breakfast <u>finally</u> arrived, because I had <u>no</u> idea what that
             A   B   C

<u>white</u> stuff on my plate was. <u>No error</u>
   D   E

Ⓐ Ⓑ Ⓒ Ⓓ Ⓔ

9. My parents and I spoke <u>often</u> and very <u>frankly</u> about <u>my</u> <u>future</u> career as
                              A   B   C   D

a chef. <u>No error</u>
          E

Ⓐ Ⓑ Ⓒ Ⓓ **Ⓔ**

10. When the letter arrived from the <u>cooking</u> institute, I opened it, <u>optimistically</u>
                                        A   B

that it was the <u>acceptance</u> letter I had been <u>nervously</u> awaiting. <u>No error</u>
                   C   D   E

Ⓐ **Ⓑ** Ⓒ Ⓓ Ⓔ

Exercise 3: Improve the Sentence

In each of the following items, all or part of the sentence is underlined. Beneath each sentence are five ways of phrasing the underlined part. Choice (A) is the same as the original; the other four are different. Select the answer choice that best expresses the meaning of the original sentence. Your goal is to produce the most effective sentence, one that is clear and not wordy. Choose (A) if the original sentence is better than any of the other answer choices.

> **EXAMPLE**
>
> The waiter <u>walked slow and steady</u>, burdened by the heavy tray of plates in his arms.
>
> (A) walked slow and steady
> (B) walked slowly and steady
> (C) walked slowly and steadily
> (D) walked slow and steadily
> (E) walked slow and careful
>
> (A)(B)(C)(D)(E)
>
> Choice (C) is correct because adverbs are needed to modify the verb *walked*. *Slowly* and *steadily* are adverbs, whereas *slow* and *steady* are adjectives.

1. The six nervous contestants <u>tried to look as calmly as they could</u> as the winner was about to be announced.

    (A) tried to look as calmly as they could
    (B) tried to look as calm as they could
    (C) tried to look as calmly as they could look
    (D) tried to look calmly as they could
    (E) tried to look as calm

    (A)(B)(C)(D)(E)

2. When the awkward waiter slipped near our table and fell flat on his back, <u>everyone thought he was hurt bad</u>.

    (A) everyone thought he was hurt bad
    (B) everyone thought he wasn't hurt bad
    (C) everyone thought he was hurt badly
    (D) everyone thought he was hurted bad
    (E) everyone thought he was hurt

    (A)(B)(C)(D)(E)

3. When you use a blender or shaker, <u>be sure the top is closed secure to avoid</u> <u>spills</u>.

(A) be sure the top is closed secure to avoid spills

(B) be sure the top is closed secure to avoid spilling

(C) be sure the top is closed tight to avoid spills

(D) be sure the top is closed securely to avoid spills

(E) be sure the top is closed to avoid spills securely

ⒶⒷⒸ**Ⓓ**Ⓔ

4. <u>I think that the following foods taste terribly</u>: spinach, cauliflower, lima beans, liver, peanut butter, and artichokes.

(A) I think that the following foods taste terribly

(B) I think that the following foods taste awfully

(C) I think that the following foods are tasting terrible

(D) The following foods taste terribly

(E) I think that the following foods taste terrible

ⒶⒷⒸⒹ**Ⓔ**

5. <u>Many people find the traditional dish of shrimp and grits (now served at some</u> <u>of the South's finest restaurants) exceptionally delicious.</u>

(A) Many people find the traditional dish of shrimp and grits (now served at some of the South's finest restaurants) exceptionally delicious.

(B) Many people find the traditional dish of shrimp and grits now served at some of the South's finest restaurants exceptionally delicious.

(C) Many people find the traditional dish of shrimp and grits (now served at some of the South's finest restaurants) exceptional delicious.

(D) Many people find the traditional dish of shrimp and grits exceptional and delicious.

(E) Many people find the traditionally dish of shrimp and grits (now served at some of the South's finest restaurants) exceptionally delicious.

ⒶⒷⒸⒹⒺ

Double Negatives

Read the following sentence.

> During the Depression, many Americans didn't have no jobs.

This sentence contains two negative words, and as a result of this, it does not mean what the writer intended. This error in standard usage is called a double negative. Do not use two negatives—one is enough. Read the corrected versions of the opening sentence below.

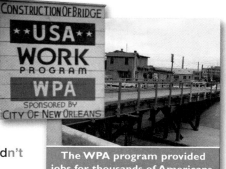

> During the Depression, many Americans didn't have jobs.
>
> *or*
>
> During the Depression, many Americans had no jobs.

The WPA program provided jobs for thousands of Americans.

Identifying Negative Words

Below are some common negative words.

no	none	never	not (-n't)	neither	barely	hardly
nobody	no one	nowhere	nothing	without	scarcely	

The words *but* and *only* too, are considered negative when they are used to mean "no more than." If this is the case, do not use them with another negative word.

Fixing Double Negatives

To fix a double negative, you need to change and/or delete a word. You can usually make the correction in more than one way. Study the examples below.

Incorrect: I can't hardly believe it.

Correct: I can hardly believe it. *or* I can't believe it.

Incorrect: I couldn't never have done it without help.

Correct: I couldn't have done it without help. *or* I could never have done it without help.

Incorrect: Without scarcely any money, the family spent very little on frivolities.

Correct: With scarcely any money, the family spent very little on frivolities.

Sometimes *not* can modify an adjective with a negative prefix. Although this is a negative construction, it is grammatically correct.

The idea is not unappealing. *and* It is not an inconsequential event.

Exercise 1: Rewrite the Sentence

Each of the following sentences contains double negatives. Rewrite each one to eliminate the error. Answers may vary; sample answers provided.

1. Before the Federal Writers' Project in the 1930s, scarcely no writers were making a living. Before the Federal Writers' Project in the 1930s, scarcely any writers were making a living.

2. Without hardly trying, I can name several writers who took advantage of this opportunity. Without trying, I can name several writers who took advantage of this opportunity.

3. I didn't pay no attention to who wrote all those American Guides. I didn't pay attention to who wrote all those American Guides.

4. Didn't nobody agree to write a guidebook about Alaska? Didn't anybody agree to write a guidebook about Alaska?

5. One false claim about the Writers' Project was that they never hired nobody who could write well. One false claim about the Writers' Project was that they never hired anybody who could write well.

Exercise 2: Identify the Sentence Error

One of the underlined words or phrases may contain a grammatical error. If there is one, choose the underlined part that must be changed to make the sentence correct, and fill in the corresponding oval. If the sentence has no error, fill in answer choice Ⓔ.

> **EXAMPLE**
>
> <u>Until</u> today, I didn't <u>have</u> <u>no</u> time for <u>it</u>. <u>No error</u>
>   A   B   C   D   E
>
>   Ⓐ Ⓑ ⓒ Ⓓ Ⓔ
>
> Choice ⓒ is correct because *no* following *didn't* creates a double negative.

1. The Federal <u>Writing</u> Project gave writers the opportunity to <u>have</u> contact with
                     A   B

   other writers they <u>had</u> <u>barely</u> known before. <u>No error</u>
                        C   D   E

                            Ⓐ Ⓑ ⓒ Ⓓ ⬤Ⓔ

2. <u>Hasn't</u> <u>anybody</u> read <u>what</u> Richard Wright <u>contributed</u> to the
      A   B   C   D

   project? <u>No error</u>
               E

                            Ⓐ Ⓑ ⓒ Ⓓ ⬤Ⓔ

3. I hadn't even <u>hardly</u> <u>read</u> two pages <u>before</u> I realized how
             A   B   C

<u>good</u> the book was. <u>No error</u>
 D   E

Ⓐ Ⓑ Ⓒ Ⓓ Ⓔ

4. <u>Even</u> skeptics <u>praised</u> the <u>guidebooks</u> <u>high</u>. <u>No error</u>
   A   B   C   D   E

Ⓐ Ⓑ Ⓒ Ⓓ Ⓔ

5. Despite <u>losing</u> its <u>funding</u>, the project was <u>not</u> <u>unsuccessful</u>. <u>No error</u>
        A   B   C   D   E

Ⓐ Ⓑ Ⓒ Ⓓ Ⓔ

Exercise 3: Improve the Sentence

In each of the following items, all or part of the sentence is underlined. Beneath each sentence are five ways of phrasing the underlined part. Choice (A) is the same as the original; the other four are different. Select the answer choice that best expresses the meaning of the original sentence. Your goal is to produce the most effective sentence, one that is clear and not wordy. Choose (A) if the original sentence is better than any of the other answer choices.

EXAMPLE

<u>Didn't nobody speak out</u> against the detractors of the WPA project?

(A) Didn't nobody speak out
(B) Didn't anybody speak out
(C) Didn't anybody not speak out
(D) Did nobody not speak out
(E) Didn't nobody not speak out

Ⓐ Ⓑ Ⓒ Ⓓ Ⓔ

Choice Ⓑ is correct because it corrects the double negative error without changing the sentence's meaning.

1. The guidebooks were so well written <u>that hardly nobody criticized them</u>.

(A) that hardly nobody criticized them
(B) that nobody hardly criticized them
(C) that scarcely nobody criticized them

(D) that hardly anybody criticized them

(E) that hardly anybody criticized it

Ⓐ Ⓑ Ⓒ **Ⓓ** Ⓔ

2. <u>Many of the writers couldn't scarcely afford not to take the job.</u>

(A) Many of the writers couldn't scarcely afford not to take the job.

(B) Many of the writers couldn't afford not to take the job.

(C) Many of the writers scarcely afforded not to take the job.

(D) Many of the writers couldn't afford to take the job.

(E) Many of the writers couldn't barely afford to take the job.

Ⓐ **Ⓑ** Ⓒ Ⓓ Ⓔ

3. <u>Her prospects were not unimpressive.</u>

(A) Her prospects were not unimpressive.

(B) Her prospects were unimpressive.

(C) Her prospects were not impressive.

(D) Her prospects were nothing if not unimpressive.

(E) Her prospects were not hardly unimpressive.

Ⓐ Ⓑ Ⓒ Ⓓ Ⓔ

4. The WPA guidebook project <u>didn't have no book on Hawaii</u> since Hawaii was not a state at the time.

(A) didn't have no book on Hawaii

(B) didn't have a book on Hawaii

(C) didn't have no books on Hawaii

(D) hadn't had no book on Hawaii

(E) had a book on Hawaii

Ⓐ **Ⓑ** Ⓒ Ⓓ Ⓔ

5. <u>Without hard work, no one can't write a good book.</u>

(A) Without hard work, no one can't write a good book.

(B) Without hard work no one can't write a good book.

(C) With hard work, no one can't write a good book.

(D) Without working hard, no one can't write a good book.

(E) Without hard work, no one can write a good book.

Ⓐ Ⓑ Ⓒ Ⓓ **Ⓔ**

Faulty Idioms

Read the following.

> In the world of astronomy, ideas fall over the wayside and theories blow hot or cold. Every once in a while, scientists slap the jackpot and pull the rug out to below a long-accepted idea. Other times, unexpected revelations throw scientists the curveball and get the ball to roll in an unexpected new direction.

Jupiter and its four Galilean Moons

The passage above does not get the writer's intended message across well because it contains faulty idioms. Idioms are words or expressions, peculiar to a language, whose meanings are accepted and understood by native speakers but cannot be taken literally. Idioms may not be grammatically correct or logical. The use of faulty idioms may confuse readers.

Here is an improved version of the opening passage:

> In the world of astronomy, ideas fall by the wayside and theories blow hot and cold. Every once in a while, scientists hit the jackpot and pull the rug out from under a long-accepted idea. Other times, unexpected revelations throw scientists a curveball and get the ball rolling in an unexpected new direction.

Spotting Faulty Idioms

You are likely to *run across* faulty idioms in multiple-choice questions on a standardized test. To determine whether an idiom or idiomatic expression is being used correctly, listen carefully when you read. If the word or expression sounds awkward, it is probably because it is being used incorrectly. The fault may lie with an error in any part of speech, although errors in preposition choice are likely to be the most common kind.

Look over these examples.

Faulty: The clumsy new lab assistant has all thumbs.

Correct: The clumsy new lab assistant is all thumbs.

Faulty: What kind of behavior gets under your nerves?

Correct: What kind of behavior gets on your nerves?

TEST-TAKING TIP

Because an idiom is a group of words that already has its own meaning but is assigned a new meaning by native speakers, there are no grammatical rules you can use to learn them. To help you become familiar with more idioms, refer to the list of idioms on pages 211–212 of this text.

Exercise 1: Rewrite the Sentence

The following sentences contain faulty idioms. Replace the idioms with the corrected versions.

1. The news of the thrilling discovery brought up the house. brought down the house

2. Finally, after many months of practice, she got the hang on it. hang of it

3. When he tried to pull the fast one, the police were ready for him. pull a fast one

4. "Keep your chin on," my uncle advised when he saw that I was discouraged. keep your chin up

5. "Take it easy," he advised, "let some hair down. It'll do you good to relax." let your hair down

Exercise 2: Identify the Sentence Error

One of the underlined words or phrases may contain a grammatical error. If there is one, choose the underlined part that must be changed to make the sentence correct, and fill in the corresponding oval. If the sentence has no error, fill in answer choice Ⓔ .

> **EXAMPLE**
>
> The <u>new</u> boss begain to <u>throw</u> her <u>weight</u> <u>across</u>. <u>No error</u>
>   A   B   C   D   E
>
>   Ⓐ Ⓑ Ⓒ ⬤ Ⓔ
>
> Choice Ⓓ is correct because the correct idiomatic expression is *throw* (her) *weight around.*

1. The manager <u>played</u> <u>fast</u> and <u>loose</u> <u>by</u> the rules. <u>No error</u>
            A   B   C   D   E

                                   Ⓐ Ⓑ Ⓒ ⬤ Ⓔ

2. Last year the Tigers won, but this year the Lions <u>turned</u> <u>the</u> <u>tables</u> <u>for</u> them.
                                                 A   B   C   D

   <u>No error</u>
    E

                                   Ⓐ Ⓑ Ⓒ ⬤ Ⓔ

3. Can you <u>have</u> <u>a</u> <u>straight</u> <u>face</u> when you hear something very foolish? <u>No error</u>
         A   B   C   D   E

                                   ⬤ Ⓑ Ⓒ Ⓓ Ⓔ

4. After much consultation with her staff, the senator decided to

go ahead and <u>throw</u> her <u>hat</u> <u>into</u> the <u>ring</u>. <u>No error</u>
           A   B   C   D   E

Ⓐ Ⓑ Ⓒ Ⓓ **Ⓔ**

5. The clarinetist didn't know the music, <u>so</u> he had to <u>play</u> <u>in</u> <u>ear</u>. <u>No error</u>
                                   A   B C D   E

Ⓐ Ⓑ **Ⓒ** Ⓓ Ⓔ

Exercise 3: Improve the Sentence

In each of the following items, all or part of the sentence is underlined. Beneath each sentence are five ways of phrasing the underlined part. Choice (A) is the same as the original; the other four are different. Select the answer choice that best expresses the meaning of the original sentence. Your goal is to produce the most effective sentence, one that is clear and not wordy. Choose (A) if the original sentence is better than any of the other answer choices.

EXAMPLE

If you are going to be part of the elite team, you will need to <u>pull on your weight</u>.

(A) pull on your weight
(B) pull your weight
(C) pull all your weight
(D) pull through your weight
(E) hit the nail on the head

Ⓐ **Ⓑ** Ⓒ Ⓓ Ⓔ

Choice **Ⓑ** is correct because the correct idiomatic expression is *pull your weight*, which means "to do as much as others do."

---

1. Chemicals were missing from the science lab; the accused but innocent student was not going to <u>take it facing down</u>.

(A) take it facing down
(B) take it facing up
(C) take it from me
(D) take it lying down
(E) take the cake

Ⓐ Ⓑ Ⓒ **Ⓓ** Ⓔ

2. Does it take much to <u>pull the wool across</u> your eyes?

    (A) pull the wool across

    (B) put the wool across

    (C) pull the wool over

    (D) pull the sheet across

    (E) place the wool over

Ⓐ Ⓑ Ⓒ Ⓓ Ⓔ

3. At first, the astronomer couldn't <u>make heads and tails of it</u>.

    (A) make heads and tails of it

    (B) make heads or tails on it

    (C) make heads or tails of it

    (D) see heads or tails of it

    (E) make heads or tails for it

Ⓐ Ⓑ Ⓒ Ⓓ Ⓔ

4. <u>Come to think on it</u>, although we know precisely how many moons Earth, Mercury, and Venus have, the number of moons for the other planets is still undetermined.

    (A) Come to think on it

    (B) Come to think of it

    (C) Now to think of it

    (D) Coming to think of it

    (E) Coming clean

Ⓐ Ⓑ Ⓒ Ⓓ Ⓔ

5. Tired of delays and quite ready to begin, the director instructed us to <u>get the show to the road</u>.

    (A) get the show to the road

    (B) start the show on the road

    (C) get the show on the road

    (D) bring the show to the road

    (E) get the show up the road

Ⓐ Ⓑ Ⓒ Ⓓ Ⓔ

Pronoun-Antecedent Agreement

Read the following sentence:

> In 1899, Edward Harriman, a wealthy railroad tycoon, invited some of America's foremost scientists to join Edward Harriman on a working trip to Alaska.

As you may have noticed, this sentence needs a pronoun badly. Recall that pronouns take the place of nouns, other pronouns, or groups of words that function as nouns.

Now read the revised version of the opening sentence:

A dog team pulling a sled across a glacier in the shadow of Mt. McKinley

> In 1899, Edward Harriman, a wealthy railroad tycoon, invited some of America's foremost scientists to join him on a working trip to Alaska.

In the second version, the pronoun "him" refers to "Edward Harriman"; "Edward Harriman" is the antecedent of "him." An antecedent is the noun or pronoun to which a pronoun refers. When you write, place pronouns close to their antecedents to avoid confusion. Also, make sure that your pronouns agree with their antecedents in number and in gender.

Agreement in Number

Pronouns must agree with their antecedents in number. This means that if the antecedent is singular, then the pronoun that refers to it must also be singular. If the antecedent may be either masculine or feminine, use "his or her" to refer to it.

- Indefinite pronoun antecedents such as *everyone, everybody, somebody, someone, nobody, no one, one, neither, either,* and *each* are singular and require singular pronouns.

    Incorrect: Everyone on Harriman's Alaskan research trip was a leader in their particular field.

    Correct: Everyone on Harriman's Alaskan research trip was a leader in his or her particular field.

- Indefinite pronoun antecedents such as *several, both, few,* and *many* are plural and require plural pronouns.

    Incorrect: Several on board had his or her own special assignments.

    Correct: Several on board had their own special assignments.

The relationship between compound antecedents and pronouns is the same as that between compound subjects and verbs.

- Singular antecedents linked by *or* or *nor* require singular pronouns.

    Neither John Muir nor John Burroughs thought that he belonged on the same ship with the other scientific all-stars Harriman had recruited.

- Singular antecedents linked by *and* require plural pronouns.

    Wildlife painter Louis Agassiz and photographer Edward Curtis took their places on the Alaskan expedition.

- Plural antecedents linked by *and, or,* or *nor* also require plural pronouns.

    The scientists, writers, and artists stocked a library of 500 books on their ambitious journey.

Keep in mind that a group of words can be a singular subject and therefore serve as a singular antecedent. Use a singular pronoun to refer to it.

    Choosing scientists to join him in Alaska was easy. It took Harriman less than a month to do it.

- When determining whether to use the personal pronoun *me* or *I*, subtract everything from the subject except the personal pronoun, and then read the sentence. This will help you decide which is the correct pronoun to use.

    "My son and (me, I) saw the ship depart Seattle for Skagway."

Now read the sentence with only one of the personal pronouns.

    Incorrect: *Me* saw the ship depart Seattle for Skagway.

    Correct: *I* saw the ship depart Seattle for Skagway.

So, the correct pronoun to use in the sentence is *I*.

    Correct: "My son and I saw the ship depart Seattle for Skagway."

Agreement in Gender

- Nouns and the personal pronouns that refer to them have three genders: female, male, or neuter. Third-person singular pronouns such as *he, she,* and *it* must agree in gender with their antecedents.

    Bird painter Grinnell watched a Native American woman as she skinned a seal.

    When Curtis began photographing Alaska's natives, he was embarking on what would become a lifelong pursuit.

    As the Harriman party's ship steamed north, it encountered the chaotic Klondike gold rush.

Exercise 1: Revise the Paragraphs

The paragraphs that follow contain errors in pronoun-antecedent agreement. Rewrite them to eliminate the mistakes and to make references clear.

John Muir's friendship with Harriman paid off when the naturalist was energetically trying to establish Yosemite Valley as a national park. Harriman lobbied each powerful senator he knew in Washington to convince them to protect the valley. When the bill came up for a vote in Congress, neither the wilderness advocate nor the tycoon could count on getting their way. Each man held their breath. The bill passed in a close vote; all in support of natural parks cheered its success.

Visitors to Yosemite today have a lot to thank Muir and Harriman for, as we reap the benefits of his efforts. When my friends and me hiked its many trails and stood by their cascading waterfalls, we, like many before us, found Yosemite to be an exhilarating, magical place. Choosing this park as a place to spend several spirited days is an easy decision to make. They took us only five minutes to make the choice.

Exercise 2: Identify the Sentence Error

One of the underlined words or phrases may contain a grammatical error. If there is one, choose the underlined part that must be changed to make the sentence correct, and fill in the corresponding oval. If the sentence has no error, fill in answer choice Ⓔ.

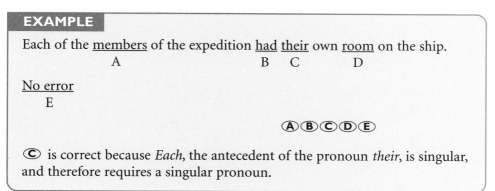

EXAMPLE

Each of the <u>members</u> of the expedition <u>had</u> <u>their</u> own <u>room</u> on the ship.
       A   B   C   D

<u>No error</u>
  E

Ⓐ Ⓑ Ⓒ Ⓓ Ⓔ

Ⓒ is correct because *Each*, the antecedent of the pronoun *their*, is singular, and therefore requires a singular pronoun.

1. When <u>one</u> of the expedition members returned home, <u>he</u> wrote an editorial
       A   B

about what <u>everyone</u> onboard <u>thought</u> about the depleted seal population.
            C   D

<u>No error</u>
    E

Ⓐ Ⓑ Ⓒ Ⓓ Ⓔ

2. After all was said and done, neither Muir <u>nor</u> Burroughs <u>regretted</u> <u>their</u>
                                                  A   B   C

participation in the expedition to <u>explore</u> Alaska. <u>No error</u>
                                    D   E

Ⓐ Ⓑ Ⓒ Ⓓ Ⓔ

3. The <u>expedition</u> visited a fur-seal <u>rookery</u>, and the scientists <u>were astonished</u>
          A   B   C

by <u>them</u>. <u>No error</u>
   D   E

Ⓐ Ⓑ Ⓒ Ⓓ Ⓔ

4. Why did Harriman plan and pay for the expedition? <u>Some</u> said it was because
                                                        A

<u>they</u> also planned to purchase a huge swath of <u>Alaska</u> and then build a railroad
 B   C

through <u>it</u> to Siberia. <u>No error</u>
        D   E

Ⓐ Ⓑ Ⓒ Ⓓ Ⓔ

5. On the way south, the ship stopped at an abandoned Tlingit village that

featured <u>several</u> imposing totem poles, some of <u>them</u> forty feet high. John
          A   B

Muir was appalled when <u>some</u> of the men started to take <u>it</u> down. <u>No error</u>
                        C   D   E

Ⓐ Ⓑ Ⓒ Ⓓ Ⓔ

In each of the following items, all or part of the sentence is underlined. Beneath each sentence are five ways of phrasing the underlined part. Choice (A) is the same as the original; the other four are different. Select the answer choice that best expresses the meaning of the original sentence. Your goal is to produce the most effective sentence, one that is clear and not wordy. Choose (A) if the original sentence is better than any of the other answer choices.

EXAMPLE

When the expedition steamed into Prince William Sound, they had entered what would later become prime cruise-ship territory.

(A) When the expedition steamed into Prince William Sound, they had entered what would later become prime cruise-ship territory.

(B) When the expedition steamed into Prince William Sound, it had entered what would later become prime cruise-ship territory.

(C) When the expedition steamed into Prince William Sound, her had entered what would later become prime cruise-ship territory.

(D) When the expedition steamed into Prince William Sound, she entered what would later become prime cruise-ship territory.

(E) When the expedition steamed into Prince William Sound, we had entered what would later become prime cruise-ship territory.

Ⓐ Ⓑ Ⓒ Ⓓ Ⓔ

Ⓑ is the correct choice because *expedition* is singular and requires a singular pronoun.

---

1. When the ship approached a huge glacier, Harriman asked the captain to find a way around them.

(A) When the ship approached a huge glacier, Harriman asked the captain to find a way around them.

(B) When the ship approached a huge glacier, they asked the captain to find a way around them.

(C) When the ship approached a huge glacier, he asked the captain to find a way around him.

(D) When the ship approached a huge glacier, Harriman asked the captain to find a way around it.

(E) When the ship approached a huge glacier, Harriman asked the captain to find a way around.

Ⓐ Ⓑ Ⓒ Ⓓ Ⓔ

2. Everybody marveled at the glaciers <u>and then went for their sketch pad</u>.

    (A) and then went for their sketch pad

    (B) but then went for their sketch pad

    (C) and then went for his or her sketch pad

    (D) and then went for their sketch pads

    (E) then went for the sketch pads

                               Ⓐ Ⓑ Ⓒ Ⓓ Ⓔ

3. <u>To John Muir's dismay, Harriman shot a bear and then photographed the animal with its massive teeth bared.</u>

    (A) To John Muir's dismay, Harriman shot a bear and then photographed the animal with its massive teeth bared.

    (B) To John Muir's dismay, Harriman shot a bear and then photographed the animal with their massive teeth bared.

    (C) To John Muir's dismay, they shot a bear and then photographed the animal with its massive teeth bared.

    (D) To John Muir's dismay, Harriman shot a bear and then photographed the animals with its massive teeth bared.

    (E) To John Muir's dismay, Harriman shot a bear and then photographed the animal with it's massive teeth bared.

                               Ⓐ Ⓑ Ⓒ Ⓓ Ⓔ

4. <u>Each of Harriman's detractors had their own reason</u> for taking issue with the expedition.

    (A) Each of Harriman's detractors had their own reason

    (B) Each of Harriman's detractors had his or her own reason

    (C) Each of Harriman's detractors had her own reason

    (D) All of Harriman's detractors had their own reason

    (E) Each of Harriman's detractors have their own reason

                               Ⓐ Ⓑ Ⓒ Ⓓ Ⓔ

5. <u>The members of Harriman's family brought along their three maids.</u>

    (A) The members of Harriman's family brought along their three maids.

    (B) Each member of Harriman's family brought along their three maids.

    (C) The members of Harriman's family brought along their maids.

    (D) The members of Harriman's family brought along his three maids.

    (E) The members of Harriman's family brought along three of their maids.

                               Ⓐ Ⓑ Ⓒ Ⓓ Ⓔ

Pronoun Reference and Shift

Read the following sentence.

> When Juan showed the dinosaur egg to his cousin James, he smiled and nodded his head.

Think: Who "smiled and nodded his head"? Was it Juan or James? You cannot be sure because it isn't clear to whom the pronoun *he* refers.

Ambiguous Reference

Children looking at a dinosaur egg

- A pronoun makes an ambiguous reference if it can refer to *more than one* antecedent. When a pronoun has more than one possible antecedent, the meaning of the sentence can be hard to understand.

To fix this kind of problem and clarify the meaning of the sentence, either:

- replace the ambiguous pronoun with a noun, *or*
- revise the sentence entirely.

Here are two ways to make the pronoun reference clear in the opening sentence:

> When Juan showed the dinosaur egg to his cousin James, James smiled and nodded his head.

or

> James smiled and nodded his head when his cousin Juan showed him the dinosaur egg.

Now it is clear that it was *James* who smiled and nodded.

In the examples below, two sentences have been fixed to eliminate ambiguous pronoun reference.

AMBIGUOUS	CLEAR
When Liz e-mailed her mother, she was in Montana looking for dinosaur eggs. *Think:* Who was in Montana looking for dinosaur eggs?	When Liz was in Montana looking for dinosaur eggs, she e-mailed her mother.
When the fossil hunters met the graduate students, they greeted them warmly. *Think:* Who greeted whom warmly?	When the fossil hunters met the graduate students, the students greeted them warmly.

Vague Reference

If an antecedent to a pronoun is only *implied*, or if the pronoun-antecedent link is vague, the meaning of the sentence can be unclear. Watch for vague references commonly made with the pronouns *you*, *it*, and *they*.

To clarify a vague reference, either reword the sentence to make the reference and meaning clear, or replace the pronoun with an appropriate noun, and change the verb, as needed.

Now read the following sentence, which is unclear because it does not provide an antecedent for the pronoun.

> On the arid plains of Argentina, they have found several new dinosaur species.

Think: Who has found several new dinosaur species? It is not clear to whom "they" refers, is it?

To fix this sentence, let's replace the pronoun "they" with a noun:

> On the arid plains of Argentina, paleontologists have found several new dinosaur species.

In the examples below, two sentences have been fixed to eliminate vague pronoun reference.

VAGUE	CLEAR
We'll visit the Museum of Natural History for the new exhibit. It should be fantastic! *Think: What* will be fantastic?	The new exhibit at the Museum of Natural History should be fantastic!
They need volunteers for a Peruvian dig. You do not want to miss this opportunity. *Think: Who* shouldn't miss this opportunity?	They need volunteers for a Peruvian dig. Graduate students in archaeology do not want to miss this opportunity.

The relative pronouns *this*, *that*, and *which* can also create a vague reference if they refer to a general idea instead of a specific noun.

> Not many bones were uncovered at the site, which was disappointing.

Think: What was disappointing—the site, or the lack of discoveries there?

Here are two ways to make clear what "which" refers to in the sentence:

> Not many bones were uncovered at the site. The lack of discoveries was disappointing.

> That not many bones were uncovered at the site was disappointing.

There are two more kinds of pronoun-reference errors to watch out for.

* Pronouns should not be used to refer to a possessive.

> In John Noble Wilford's *The Riddle of the Dinosaur*, he introduces some startling new theories about the demise of those giant beasts.

Think: The pronoun "he" is intended to refer to "Wilford," but only "Wilford's" (a possessive) appears in the sentence.

This revision will make the pronoun reference clear:

> In his book, *The Riddle of the Dinosaur*, John Noble Wilford introduces some startling new theories about the demise of those giant beasts.

* A pronoun that is too far away from its antecedent can cause confusion.

> He left the small bone, which belonged to a raptor, by the nest. When he went back to fetch it, it was gone.

Think: What was gone—the bone or the nest?

To make the pronoun reference clear, place the pronoun closer to its antecedent. Here is one way:

> When he went back to fetch the raptor bone, it was gone. He had left it by the nest.

> **TEST-TAKING TIP**
>
> On standardized tests, make sure that you are able to identify the noun to which a pronoun *clearly and directly refers*. If you are not able to do this, then the sentence most likely contains a pronoun-reference error.

Pronoun Shift

A sentence is unclear when there is an unexpected shift in number or person between a pronoun and its antecedent.

Read the following example, which has a shift in person between the pronoun and its antecedent:

> Paleontologists need practice in the field, and you also need years of classroom work.

To fix the problem, use a pronoun in the same person and number as the antecedent, or revise the sentence so that it is clear. Here are two ways:

> Paleontologists need practice in the field, and they also need years of classroom work.

> Paleontologists need practice in the field, as well as years of classroom work.

Exercise 1: Fix the Sentence

Rewrite each sentence to correct the faulty pronoun reference or shift. Make grammatical corrections as needed. Answers will vary; sample answers provided.

1. When Sandra gave the gift to Becky, she unwrapped it.
   When Sandra gave the gift to Becky, Becky unwrapped it.
2. Fred called his brother after he arrived home.
   After Fred arrived home, he called his brother.
3. We'll go to the excavation site together. It should be very exciting.
   It should be very exciting to go to the excavation site together.
4. Not many pots were unearthed at the site, which was surprising.
   It was surprising that not many pots were unearthed at the site.
5. Jasmine loves anthropology because you learn so much about different cultures.
   Jasmine loves anthropology because she learns so much about different cultures.

Exercise 2: Identify the Sentence Error

One of the underlined words or phrases may contain a grammatical error. If there is one, choose the underlined part that must be changed to make the sentence correct, and fill in the corresponding oval. If the sentence has no error, fill in answer choice Ⓔ.

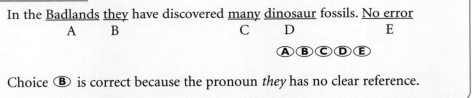

EXAMPLE

In the <u>Badlands</u> <u>they</u> have discovered <u>many</u> <u>dinosaur</u> fossils. <u>No error</u>
     A   B   C   D   E

Ⓐ Ⓑ Ⓒ Ⓓ Ⓔ

Choice Ⓑ is correct because the pronoun *they* has no clear reference.

1. In <u>Johanson's</u> *Lucy's Child*, <u>he</u> <u>writes</u> about the discovery of a <u>human</u> ancestor.
        A   B   C   D

   <u>No error</u>
   E

   Ⓐ Ⓑ Ⓒ Ⓓ Ⓔ

2. During the <u>Johnson</u> <u>administration,</u> <u>they</u> <u>sent</u> soldiers overseas. <u>No error</u>
                    A   B   C D   E

   Ⓐ Ⓑ Ⓒ Ⓓ Ⓔ

3. <u>Dan's</u> <u>professor</u> let <u>him</u> know that <u>she</u> had to stay late and
     A   B   C   D

   work. <u>No error</u>
           E

   Ⓐ Ⓑ Ⓒ Ⓓ Ⓔ

4. Dr. Jones helped the volunteers <u>make</u> <u>their</u> <u>feet</u> <u>wet</u>.
 A B C D

   <u>No error</u>
     E

Ⓐ Ⓑ Ⓒ Ⓓ Ⓔ

5. In the <u>magazine</u> <u>it</u> <u>says</u> that more science teachers <u>are needed</u>. <u>No error</u>
     A   B C   D   E

Ⓐ Ⓑ Ⓒ Ⓓ Ⓔ

Exercise 3: Improve the Sentence

In each of the following items, all or part of the sentence is underlined. Beneath each sentence are five ways of phrasing the underlined part. Choice (A) is the same as the original; the other four are different. Select the answer choice that best expresses the meaning of the original sentence. Your goal is to produce the most effective sentence, one that is clear and not wordy. Choose (A) if the original sentence is better than any of the other answer choices.

> **EXAMPLE**
>
> When the old prospector met the young adventurer, <u>he greeted him warmly</u>.
>
> (A) he greeted him warmly
> (B) the young man greeted him warmly
> (C) they greeted one another warmly
> (D) he will greet them warmly
> (E) you greeted him warmly
>
> Ⓐ Ⓑ Ⓒ Ⓓ Ⓔ
>
> The correct answer is Ⓑ. It is the only choice that makes it clear that it was the young man who greeted the old man warmly.

1. The hiker was inexperienced in frigid weather, <u>which caused him to suffer</u>.

(A) , which caused him to suffer
(B) , which caused them to suffer
(C) . His inexperience caused him to suffer
(D) , that caused him to suffer
(E) , which caused him suffering

Ⓐ Ⓑ Ⓒ Ⓓ Ⓔ

2. In those days, <u>they didn't have electricity</u>.

    (A) they didn't have electricity

    (B) they had electricity

    (C) they didn't have much electricity

    (D) many people didn't have electricity

    (E) they didn't have no electricity

                              Ⓐ Ⓑ Ⓒ **Ⓓ** Ⓔ

3. <u>They liked hiking because it was invigorating</u>.

    (A) They liked hiking because it was invigorating.

    (B) They liked hiking because she thought it was invigorating.

    (C) They liked to hike because he felt it was invigorating.

    (D) They liked to hike because everyone found it invigorating.

    (E) They liked hiking because someone found it invigorating.

                              Ⓐ Ⓑ Ⓒ Ⓓ Ⓔ

4. The reader enjoys poetry because <u>you can learn a lot from poems</u>.

    (A) you can learn a lot from poems

    (B) you can learn a lot from poets

    (C) we can learn a lot from poems

    (D) they can learn a lot from poems

    (E) poetry can be very instructive

                              Ⓐ Ⓑ Ⓒ Ⓓ **Ⓔ**

5. The first time Alex and Peter studied together, <u>he helped him with biology</u>.

    (A) he helped him with biology

    (B) he helped them with biology

    (C) Peter helped Alex with biology

    (D) he helped with biology

    (E) he helped both of them with biology

                              Ⓐ Ⓑ **Ⓒ** Ⓓ Ⓔ

Pronoun Choice: *Who* and *Whom*

Read the following passage, in which each sentence has a mistake.

Teacher and students in class

> The kind of person whom would make a good teacher is one in who students could place their trust. The new Spanish teacher, whom was hired last week, appears to be that kind of person exactly.

As you may have noticed, all of the errors have to do with the use of the pronouns who and whom. Here is an improved version of the passage:

> The kind of person who would make a good teacher is one in whom students could place their trust. The new Spanish teacher, who was hired last week, appears to be that kind of person exactly.

Using *Who* and *Whoever*

Use the subject pronoun **who** (whoever) when it functions *as a subject* or *predicate nominative* in a sentence or clause.

> **Who** will be our Latin teacher? *Think: Who* is the subject.

> **Whoever** the teacher will be, that person will be an improvement over last year's teacher. *Think: Whoever* is the subject.

> **We discussed** who **their first choice was.** *Think: Who* is the predicate nominative.

Using *Whom* and *Whomever*

Use the *object* pronoun **whom** when it functions as the *direct* or *indirect object* or as the *object of the preposition* in a sentence or clause.

> **Whom** did you choose as your teammate? *Think: Whom* is the direct object of *did choose.*

> **For** whom did you buy that tie? *Think: Whom* is the object of the preposition *for.*

> **Whomever** are you looking for? *Think: Whomever* is the direct object of *are looking.*

Another way to help you decide between using *who* and *whom* is by replacing the pronoun in question with *he* or *him*. If *he* sounds right in the sentence, then the subject pronoun *who* is correct. If *him* sounds right, then use the object pronoun *whom*.

> **Who** will be our Latin teacher? **He** will be our Latin teacher.

Exercise 1: Choose the Pronoun

Underline the pronoun in parentheses that correctly completes the sentence.

1. (<u>Who</u>, Whom) were the Neanderthals?

2. If you wished to know more about these relatives of humans, (who, <u>whom</u>) would you ask?

3. Recent findings tell us that Neanderthals, (<u>who</u>, whom) lived in Europe as far back as 500,000 years ago, were more modern than we used to think they were.

4. (<u>Whoever</u>, Whomever) said Neanderthals were unimaginative brutes had it all wrong.

5. Anthropologists have learned much recently about (<u>who</u>, whom) these Neanderthals were.

Exercise 2: Identify the Sentence Error

One of the underlined words or phrases may contain a grammatical error. If there is one, choose the underlined part that must be changed to make the sentence correct, and fill in the corresponding oval. If the sentence has no error, fill in answer choice Ⓔ.

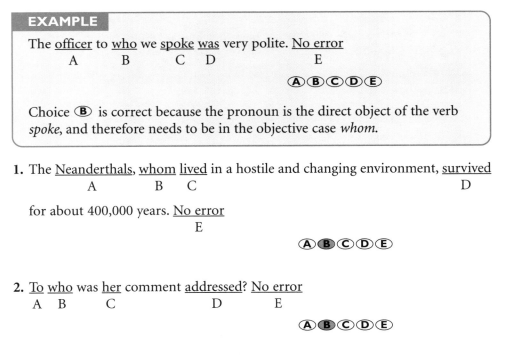

> **EXAMPLE**
>
> The <u>officer</u> to <u>who</u> we <u>spoke</u> <u>was</u> very polite. <u>No error</u>
>   A   B   C   D   E
>
>   Ⓐ Ⓑ Ⓒ Ⓓ Ⓔ
>
> Choice Ⓑ is correct because the pronoun is the direct object of the verb *spoke*, and therefore needs to be in the objective case *whom*.

1. The <u>Neanderthals</u>, <u>whom</u> <u>lived</u> in a hostile and changing environment, <u>survived</u>
          A   B   C   D

   for about 400,000 years. <u>No error</u>
                                 E

                    Ⓐ Ⓑ Ⓒ Ⓓ Ⓔ

2. <u>To</u> <u>who</u> was <u>her</u> comment <u>addressed</u>? <u>No error</u>
    A   B   C   D   E

                    Ⓐ Ⓑ Ⓒ Ⓓ Ⓔ

3. <u>Mary's</u> <u>partner</u> let <u>her</u> know that <u>he</u> had to leave early. <u>No error</u>
   A   B   C   D   E

                Ⓐ Ⓑ Ⓒ Ⓓ Ⓔ

4. <u>Anthropologists</u> are <u>people</u> <u>whom</u> help us understand <u>our</u> world. <u>No error</u>
         A   B   C   D   E

                Ⓐ Ⓑ Ⓒ Ⓓ Ⓔ

5. <u>Whomever</u> said that <u>Neanderthals</u> didn't <u>make</u> tools <u>was</u> wrong. <u>No error</u>
   A   B   C   D   E

                Ⓐ Ⓑ Ⓒ Ⓓ Ⓔ

Exercise 3: Improve the Sentence

In each of the following items, all or part of the sentence is underlined. Beneath each sentence are five ways of phrasing the underlined part. Choice (A) is the same as the original; the other four are different. Select the answer choice that best expresses the meaning of the original sentence. Your goal is to produce the most effective sentence, one that is clear and not wordy. Choose (A) if the original sentence is better than any of the other answer choices.

> **EXAMPLE**
>
> <u>People whom are interested</u> in learning can always find new things to study.
>
> (A) People whom are interested
> (B) People who are interested
> (C) People whoever are interested
> (D) People which are interested
> (E) Whomever are interested
>
>   Ⓐ Ⓑ Ⓒ Ⓓ Ⓔ
>
> Choice Ⓑ is correct because *who* is the subject of *are interested*.

1. <u>To who did you send the postcard?</u>

    (A) To who did you send the postcard?
    (B) To whoever did you send the postcard?
    (C) To who had you sent the postcard?
    (D) To whom did you send the postcard?
    (E) To who did they send the postcard?

                    Ⓐ Ⓑ Ⓒ Ⓓ Ⓔ

2. Whom did Laura choose as her lab partner?

    (A) Whom did Laura choose as her lab partner?

    (B) Who did Laura choose as her lab partner?

    (C) Whoever did Laura choose as her lab partner?

    (D) Whom did Laura choose as their lab partner?

    (E) Who did Laura choose as their lab partner?

                  Ⓐ Ⓑ Ⓒ Ⓓ Ⓔ

3. The Neanderthals, whom lived in small groups, behaved in fundamentally human ways.

    (A) The Neanderthals, whom lived in small groups,

    (B) The Neanderthals, which lived in small groups,

    (C) The Neanderthals, who lived in small groups,

    (D) The Neanderthals, that lived in small groups,

    (E) The Neanderthals, whom all lived in small groups,

                  Ⓐ Ⓑ Ⓒ Ⓓ Ⓔ

4. Whom was the archaeologist who discovered an intact Neanderthal skeleton?

    (A) Whom was the archaeologist who discovered

    (B) Who was the archaeologist who discovered

    (C) Who was the archaeologist whom discovered

    (D) Whom was the archaeologist that discovered

    (E) Whomever was the archaeologist who discovered

                  Ⓐ Ⓑ Ⓒ Ⓓ Ⓔ

5. She was a scientist in who many people placed their faith.

    (A) She was a scientist in who many people placed their faith.

    (B) She was a scientist in whom many people placed her faith.

    (C) She was a scientist in whom many people placed their faith.

    (D) She was a scientist in who you placed your faith.

    (E) She was a scientist in who many people put their faith.

                  Ⓐ Ⓑ Ⓒ Ⓓ Ⓔ

Fragments and Run-Ons

What do the following two groups of words have in common?

> Rapa Nui, or Easter Island, is an isolated island 2,000 miles from the coast of South America, it has captured the attention of historians and anthropologists worldwide.

> Wondered about those massive statues surrounding the island.

Moai on Easter Island

One thing they have in common is that neither is a sentence.

Recall that a **sentence** is a group of words that expresses a complete thought and that, in English, every sentence has two main parts: a complete subject and a complete predicate.

As you can see from the opening examples, groups of words can sometimes look like sentences, but they may not be. Keep in mind that:

- a **complete subject** is a noun, a group of words acting as a noun, or a pronoun, plus any modifiers that describe what or who the sentence is about.
- a **complete predicate** is a verb or verb phrase plus any modifiers and words that complete the meaning of the verb or verb phrase.

TEST-TAKING TIP

For further review and practice identifying sentences and fixing fragments and run-ons, look back at Topic 11 on pages 43–46.

Fixing Fragments

When a group of words fails to express a complete thought but is punctuated as a complete sentence, it is called a **sentence fragment**. Sentence fragments lack subjects, verbs, or both. So, to decide if a group of words *is* a complete sentence, make sure that it has a subject and a verb, and expresses a complete thought.

To fix a fragment:

- Add a subject or verb to complete the thought.

> Wondered about those massive statues surrounding the island.
> *Think:* This fragment has no subject. *Who* wondered about those massive stone statues surrounding the island?

> **Early explorers** wondered about those massive statues surrounding the island.

> And perhaps the statue builders of Peruvian descent. *Think:* This fragment has no verb.

> And perhaps the statue builders **were** of Peruvian descent.

- Attach the fragment to the sentence before or after it, if it makes sense to do so.

  And transport them great distances? *Think:* This fragment has a verb ("transport") but no subject, and does not express a complete thought.

  How did the inhabitants carve the statues and transport them great distances?

- You also can fix fragments by dropping or replacing words.

  Thor Heyerdahl, who suggested that the statue builders came to Easter Island from Peru. *Think:* This fragment has a subject ("Thor Heyerdahl") and a verb ("suggested") but does not express a complete thought.

  Thor Heyerdahl suggested that the statue builders came to Easter Island from Peru.

Fixing Run-Ons

A run-on sentence is made up of two or more sentences masquerading as a single sentence because of incorrect punctuation. Sometimes no punctuation separates the two sentences; sometimes a comma does.

To correct a run-on sentence:

- Separate the two sentences using capitalization and end punctuation.

  Run-on: Rapa Nui, or Easter Island, is an isolated island 2,000 miles from the coast of South America, it has captured the attention of historians and anthropologists worldwide.

  Fixed: Rapa Nui, or Easter Island, is an isolated island 2,000 miles from the coast of South America. It has captured the attention of historians and anthropologists worldwide.

- Use a conjunction, preceded by a comma.

  Run-on: Some have proposed that the island was founded by extra-terrestrials others are convinced that it was once a part of a now-submerged continent.

  Fixed: Some have proposed that the island was founded by extra-terrestrials, but others are convinced that it was once a part of a now-submerged continent.

- Insert a semicolon, or a semicolon along with a transitional word or phrase followed by a comma.

  Run-on: Archaeological evidence indicates that the island was discovered by Polynesians about 1,500–2,000 years ago, scientists have different views on who found it.

  Fixed: Archaeological evidence indicates that the island was discovered by Polynesians about 1,500–2,000 years ago; however, scientists have different views on who found it.

Exercise 1: Fixing Sentence Fragments and Run-Ons

Rewrite each item to make it a complete sentence. Use the strategies presented so far. If a group of words *is* a sentence, leave it as is. Answers may vary; sample answers provided.

1. The islanders having had the only written language in that part of the Pacific.
The islanders had the only written language in that part of the Pacific.

2. Because their stonework resembled that of the Incas. People thought the islanders came from South America.
Because their stonework resembled that of the Incas, people thought the islanders came from South America.

3. Today, there are about 2,000 native people living on Easter Island. And about the same number of Chileans. Today, there are about 2,000 native people and about the same number of Chileans living on Easter Island.

4. Easter Island boasts nearly 1,000 statues some are nearly 30 feet tall and weigh up to 80 tons. Easter Island boasts nearly 1,000 statues; some are nearly 30 feet tall and weigh up to 80 tons.

5. The island's lush palm forests were destroyed, cleared for farming.
Correct as is.

6. Were cleared for transporting the massive stone *Moai*.
Forests were cleared for transporting the massive stone *Moai*.

7. Easter Island, an example of ruinous abuse of natural resources.
Easter Island is an example of ruinous abuse of natural resources.

8. Captain Cook visited the island more than 225 years ago, he speculated on how the statues might have been slowly lifted using scaffolding.
Captain Cook visited the island more than 225 years ago, and he speculated on how the statues might have been slowly lifted using scaffolding.

9. The island possesses a rugged beauty, it is a mix of volcanic cones, lava formations, steep cliffs, and rocky coves.
The island possesses a rugged beauty; it is a mix of volcanic cones, lava formations, steep cliffs, and rocky coves.

10. A once-thriving social order began to decline into bloody civil war.
Correct as is.

11. Contacts with outsiders further decimating the island's declining population.
Contacts with outsiders further decimated the island's declining population.

12. All of the *Moai* were knocked down. By the islanders themselves.
All of the *Moai* were knocked down by the islanders themselves.

13. Many of the statues are now standing again. Recently re-erected by archaeologists.
Many of the statues are now standing again, recently re-erected by archaeologists.

14. Easter Island was named by a Dutch explorer, he first spotted it on Easter of 1722.
Easter Island was named by a Dutch explorer who first spotted it on Easter of 1722.

15. The tiny spit of an island is, even today, the most remote, inhabited place on earth. Correct as is.

16. The first outsiders to see the *Moai* could not understand how the islanders had managed such engineering and artistry, they were perplexed. The first outsiders to see the *Moai* could not understand how the islanders had managed such engineering and artistry. They were perplexed.

17. Easter Island is just 14 miles long, 7 miles wide, and about 1,100 miles from Pitcairn Island, its nearest Polynesian neighbor. Correct as is.

18. In 2000, there was a showing of Easter Islander's crafts at the Metropolitan Museum of Art in New York City it was the first exhibition of the islander's artwork in North America. In 2000, there was a showing of Easter Islander's crafts at the Metropolitan Museum of Art in New York City. It was the first exhibition of the islander's artwork in North America.

19. Visitors to Rapa Nui encountering one of the most unique places on Earth. Visitors to Rapa Nui encounter one of the most unique places on Earth.

20. To get more data about this unique place. Pick up a copy of the *Uncommon Guide to Easter Island.* To get more data about this unique place, pick up a copy of the *Uncommon Guide to Easter Island.*

Exercise 2: Identify the Sentence Error

One of the underlined words or phrases may contain a grammatical error. If there is one, choose the underlined part that must be changed to make the sentence correct, and fill in the corresponding oval. If the sentence has no error, fill in answer choice Ⓔ .

EXAMPLE

Several <u>guesthouses</u> on the island <u>greeting</u> <u>visitors</u>. <u>No error</u>
  A   B   C   D   E

Ⓐ Ⓑ Ⓒ Ⓓ Ⓔ

Choice Ⓒ is correct because the group of words needs a verb to be a complete sentence.

---

1. Visitors <u>say</u> that the locals <u>are</u> friendly, <u>they</u> say that the scenery is <u>spectacular</u>.
        A   B   C   D

<u>No error</u>
 E

Ⓐ Ⓑ Ⓒ Ⓓ Ⓔ

2. The people <u>who</u> we met <u>were</u> <u>particularly</u> <u>welcoming</u>. <u>No error</u>
             A   B   C   D   E

Ⓐ Ⓑ Ⓒ Ⓓ Ⓔ

3. There <u>are</u> several ways <u>to get</u> to the <u>island</u>; few <u>are</u> inexpensive. <u>No error</u>
        A   B   C   D   E

Ⓐ Ⓑ Ⓒ Ⓓ Ⓔ

4. <u>Inhabitants</u> <u>celebrate</u> their heritage with feasts, song, and
    　　　A　　　　　B

<u>by doing</u> <u>traditional</u> dances. <u>No error</u>
    C　　　　D　　　　　　E

Ⓐ Ⓑ Ⓒ Ⓓ Ⓔ

5. <u>Although</u> the island used <u>to be covered</u> <u>with</u> forests and <u>vegetation</u>. <u>No error</u>
    　　A　　　　　　　　　　　　　B　　　　C　　　　　　　　　D　　　　　　E

Ⓐ Ⓑ Ⓒ Ⓓ Ⓔ

Exercise 3: Improve the Sentence

In each of the following items, all or part of the sentence is underlined. Beneath each sentence are five ways of phrasing the underlined part. Choice (A) is the same as the original; the other four are different. Select the answer choice that best expresses the meaning of the original sentence. Your goal is to produce the most effective sentence, one that is clear and not wordy. Choose (A) if the original sentence is better than any of the other answer choices.

EXAMPLE

<u>Easter Island, one of the most isolated places on the planet.</u>

(A) Easter Island, one of the most isolated places on the planet.

(B) Easter Island is one of the most isolated places on the planet.

(C) Easter Island, the most isolated place on the planet.

(D) Easter Island, one of the most isolated places on the planet, far away.

(E) Easter Island becoming one of the most isolated places on the planet.

Ⓐ Ⓑ Ⓒ Ⓓ Ⓔ

Ⓑ is the correct choice because now, with the addition of the verb *is*, the group of words becomes a complete sentence.

---

1. The island boasts a number of <u>rock carvings, the locals</u> produce carved creations using wood, too.

(A) rock carvings, the locals

(B) rock carvings, also the locals

(C) rock carvings, The locals

(D) rock carvings. The locals

(E) rock carvings, because the locals

Ⓐ Ⓑ Ⓒ Ⓓ Ⓔ

2. Easter Island's forests <u>were destroyed, felled for transporting</u> statues and making canoes.

(A) were destroyed, felled for transporting

(B) were destroyed. Felled for transporting

(C) had not been destroyed, felled for transporting

(D) were destroyed; felled for transporting

(E) were destroyed felled for transporting

Ⓐ Ⓑ Ⓒ Ⓓ Ⓔ

3. After hundreds of years of peace, the <u>island falling into a period of extensive warfare</u>, and, eventually, cultural collapse.

(A) island falling into a period of extensive warfare

(B) island falling into a period of violent warfare

(C) island fell into a period of extensive warfare

(D) island fell into a period of extensive warfare;

(E) island had been falling into a period of extensive warfare

Ⓐ Ⓑ **Ⓒ** Ⓓ Ⓔ

4. Contacts with outsiders <u>brought disease and slavery, the island's population sank</u> precipitously as a result.

(A) brought disease and slavery, the island's population sank

(B) brought disease and slavery; the island's population sank

(C) brought disease and slavery therefore the island's population sank

(D) was bringing disease and slavery, the island's population

(E) brought disease and slavery, the island's population was sinking

Ⓐ **Ⓑ** Ⓒ Ⓓ Ⓔ

5. <u>Once Easter Island became a part of Chile, its declining population</u> began to rise again.

(A) Once Easter Island became a part of Chile, its declining population

(B) Once Easter Island became a part of Chile, its quickly declining population

(C) Once Easter Island became a part of Chile; its declining population

(D) Once Easter Island became a part of Chile, its now declined population

(E) Because Easter Island became a part of Chile, its quickly declining population

Ⓐ Ⓑ Ⓒ Ⓓ Ⓔ

Misplaced and Dangling Modifiers

Read the following newspaper headline:

VALUABLE COIN FOUND BY CAB DRIVER WITH TWO HEADS

Now read this one, taken from the travel section:

LOCATED ALONG COAST, TOWN'S CLIMATE IS BALMY

Boats along the St. Thomas coastline

The problem with both headlines has to do with modifiers. The first headline sounds awkward because of a misplaced modifier. It is not clear whether the cab driver or the coin has two heads. The problem with the second headline is that its meaning has been clouded by a dangling modifier. Who or what does the phrase *located along coast* modify?

Read the revised newspaper headlines below:

VALUABLE COIN WITH TWO HEADS FOUND BY CAB DRIVER

Now it is clear that *the coin* has two heads.

TOWN LOCATED ALONG COAST HAS BALMY CLIMATE

Now, *located along coast* clearly modifies *town.*

Spotting and Fixing Misplaced Modifiers

A misplaced modifier is a word, phrase, or clause that is incorrectly placed in a sentence. Because of this, it modifies a word or phrase other than the one it is intended to modify.

- To correct a misplaced modifier, move it as close as possible to the word it is meant to modify, or change words in the sentence to clarify meaning.

Misplaced Modifier: We fed bread crumbs to the pigeons that were stale.
Think: This sentence reads as if the *pigeons* were stale, not the *bread crumbs.*
Fixed: We fed stale bread crumbs to the pigeons.

or

We fed bread crumbs, which were stale, to the pigeons.

- To correct errors commonly made with the placement of the modifying adverb, *only*, place *only* directly before or after the word it modifies.

Misplaced Modifier: The building will only have twenty floors when completed.
Think: This sentence implies that the building will have nothing *other* than twenty floors—such as ceilings, windows, or offices.
Fixed: The building will have only twenty floors when completed.

Spotting and Fixing Dangling Modifiers

A dangling modifier is a word, phrase, or clause that doesn't clearly and logically modify any word or group of words in the sentence. Dangling modifiers can make the meanings of sentences ambiguous, and can confuse readers.

- To correct a dangling modifier, reword the sentence to add a word or words that the modifier can modify.

Dangling Modifier: While hiking on the trail, pebbles got into our boots. *Think:* This sentence reads as if the *pebbles* were doing the hiking.

Fixed: While we were hiking on the trail, pebbles got into our boots.

Dangling Modifier: To comprehend events today, a grasp of world history is essential. *Think:* To *whom* is a grasp of world history essential?

Fixed: To comprehend events today, one must have a grasp of world history.

or

A grasp of world history helps a person to comprehend events today.

Exercise 1: Fixing Misplaced Modifiers

Rewrite each of the following headlines to eliminate the misplaced modifiers.
Answers may vary; sample answers provided.

1. MOVIE STAR BUYS MANSION ALONG WITH HER MOTHER

   MOVIE STAR AND MOTHER BUY MANSION

2. PHILANTHROPIST DIES IN TOWNHOUSE IN WHICH HE WAS BORN AT AGE OF 88

   PHILANTHROPIST, 88, DIES IN TOWNHOUSE OF BIRTH

3. CAR CRASHES INTO FIRE HYDRANT GOING 40 MILES PER HOUR

   GOING 40 MILES PER HOUR, CAR CRASHES INTO FIRE HYDRANT

4. GIRL FINDS INTACT MAMMOTH SKELETON DIGGING UNDER PORCH

   DIGGING UNDER PORCH, GIRL FINDS INTACT MAMMOTH SKELETON

5. MAN DONATES ARTIFACT TO MUSEUM FOUND IN FIELD

   MAN DONATES ARTIFACT FOUND IN FIELD TO MUSEUM

Exercise 2: Fixing Misplaced and Dangling Modifiers

Rewrite each sentence to eliminate all misplaced or dangling modifiers. If the sentence is correct as is, write "correct." Answers may vary; sample answers provided.

1. Passing over the city, the child saw jets in formation.

   The child saw jets in formation passing over the city.

2. Ivan donated his motorcycle to shop class which no longer ran well.

   Ivan donated his motorcycle, which no longer ran well, to shop class.

3. Alone in the house late at night, the lightning scared her.

   Because she was alone in the house late at night, the lightning scared her.

4. Mike only eats vegetables and fish.

   Mike eats only vegetables and fish.

5. Planning to take a snooze, my shoes were kicked onto the floor.

   Planning to take a snooze, I kicked my shoes onto the floor.

6. Carrying grocery bags in both arms, her hat flew off and ended up in her neighbor's yard.

   While she was carrying grocery bags in both arms, her hat flew off and ended up in her neighbor's yard.

7. After driving for hours, Luisa stopped to eat and rest.

   Correct as is.

8. To get ready for the event, and to avoid any last-minute problems, the party preparations started early in the day.

   To get ready for the event, and to avoid any last-minute problems, those responsible for the party preparations started early in the day.

9. If you wish to understand the rules of cricket, watch several matches.

   Correct as is.

10. Driving to town, the slippery road made the trip hazardous.

    Driving to town was hazardous due to the slippery road.

Exercise 3: Identify the Sentence Error

One of the underlined words or phrases may contain a grammatical error. If there is one, choose the underlined part that must be changed to make the sentence correct, and fill in the corresponding oval. If the sentence has no error, fill in oval Ⓔ.

> **EXAMPLE**
>
> The <u>weary</u> politician <u>approached</u> the <u>podium</u> <u>with a long face</u>. <u>No error</u>
>   A   B   C   D   E
>
> Ⓐ Ⓑ Ⓒ Ⓓ Ⓔ
>
> Choice Ⓓ is correct because the phrase *with a long face* should modify *politician*, not *podium*. But that is not the case because the phrase is incorrectly placed in the sentence.

1. <u>A</u> man <u>left</u> a leather <u>briefcase</u> that morning <u>on the train</u>. <u>No error</u>
  A   B   C   D   E

                 Ⓐ Ⓑ Ⓒ **Ⓓ** Ⓔ

2. <u>Luckily</u>, I <u>remembered</u> all the things I <u>had been taught</u> <u>that moment</u>. <u>No error</u>
   A   B   C   D   E

                 Ⓐ Ⓑ Ⓒ **Ⓓ** Ⓔ

3. <u>While</u> <u>painting</u> the garage, Fran <u>slipped</u> <u>on the ladder</u> and fell. <u>No error</u>
    A   B   C   D   E

                 Ⓐ Ⓑ Ⓒ Ⓓ **Ⓔ**

4. Customers <u>say</u> that the fish <u>is</u> fresh<u>, they</u> say that the lobster <u>is cooked</u> to
                   A   B   C   D

perfection. <u>No error</u>
          E

                 Ⓐ Ⓑ **Ⓒ** Ⓓ Ⓔ

5. <u>An</u> <u>increasing</u> number of students are taking <u>foreign language</u> study <u>serious</u>.
    A   B   C   D

<u>No error</u>
  E

                 Ⓐ Ⓑ Ⓒ **Ⓓ** Ⓔ

Exercise 4: Improve the Sentence

In each of the following items, all or part of the sentence is underlined. Beneath each sentence are five ways of phrasing the underlined part. Choice (A) is the same as the original; the other four are different. Select the answer choice that best expresses the meaning of the original sentence. Your goal is to produce the most effective sentence, one that is clear and not wordy. Choose (A) if the original sentence is better than any of the other answer choices.

> **EXAMPLE**
>
> The jacket was given to the winning golfer that was made of green wool.
>
> (A) The jacket was given to the winning golfer that was made of green wool.
> (B) The jacket that was made of green wool was given to the winning golfer.
> (C) The jacket is given to the winning golfer made of green wool.
> (D) The jacket was given to the winning golfer made of green wool.
> (E) Made of green wool, the winning golfer was given a jacket.
>
> (A)(B)(C)(D)(E)
>
> **B** is the correct choice because the phrase *that was made of green wool* is meant to modify *The jacket*, not *the winning golfer*. With its placement immediately following *jacket*, that connection becomes clear.

1. The actor borrowed money to attend the awards ceremony deep in debt.

   (A) The actor borrowed money to attend the awards ceremony deep in debt.
   (B) The actor borrowed money to attend the deep-in-debt awards ceremony.
   (C) The actor borrowed money to attend the awards ceremony, deep in debt.
   (D) The actor, deep in debt, borrowed money to attend the awards ceremony.
   (E) The actor borrowed money, deep in debt, to attend the awards ceremony.

   (A)(B)(C)(D)(E)

2. After an early rain, the graduation proceedings cleared by the afternoon.

   (A) After an early rain, the graduation proceedings cleared by the afternoon.
   (B) The graduation proceedings cleared by the afternoon, after an early rain.
   (C) After an early rain, the weather cleared by the afternoon for the graduation proceedings.
   (D) After an early rain on the graduation proceedings, it cleared by the afternoon.
   (E) The graduation proceedings, after an early rain, cleared by the afternoon.

   (A)(B)(C)(D)(E)

3. <u>To fully understand economics, an understanding of supply and demand is necessary.</u>

(A) To fully understand economics, an understanding of supply and demand is necessary.

(B) To fully understand economics, one must have an understanding of supply and demand.

(C) An understanding of supply and demand is necessary to fully understand economics.

(D) To fully understand economics, one can have an understanding of supply and demand.

(E) To fully understand economics, an understanding of supply and demand is essential.

Ⓐ Ⓑ Ⓒ Ⓓ Ⓔ

4. <u>Annoyed by his constant complaints, the coach got thrown out of the game.</u>

(A) Annoyed by his constant complaints, the coach got thrown out of the game.

(B) Annoyed by their constant complaints, the coach got thrown out of the game.

(C) The coach got thrown out of the game, annoyed by his constant complaints.

(D) Annoyed by the coach's constant complaints, he got thrown out of the game.

(E) Annoyed by the coach's constant complaints, the officials threw him out of the game.

Ⓐ Ⓑ Ⓒ Ⓓ Ⓔ

5. <u>During his acceptance speech, the winning actor credited the other nominees for their outstanding performances.</u>

(A) During his acceptance speech, the winning actor credited the other nominees for their outstanding performances.

(B) During his acceptance speech for outstanding performances, the winning actor credited the other nominees for theirs.

(C) For their outstanding performances during his acceptance speech, the winning actor credited the other nominees.

(D) The winning actor during his acceptance speech credited the other nominees for their outstanding performances.

(E) The winning actor credited the other nominees for their outstanding performances during his acceptance speech.

Ⓐ Ⓑ Ⓒ Ⓓ Ⓔ

Faulty Comparisons

Read the following.

> Andy was very fast.
> Nina was even faster.
> Suki was the fastest of the three.

A sack race competition

Like *fast*, most modifiers can express three degrees of comparison: *positive*, *comparative*, and *superlative*. Use adjectives to make comparisons between one noun or pronoun with another noun or pronoun; use adverbs to make comparisons between verbs.

- Use the comparative degree to compare *two* items. Add *er* to the ending of most one-syllable modifiers to form comparisons in this degree.

- Use the superlative degree to compare *three or more* items. Add *est* to the ending of most one-syllable modifiers to form comparisons in this degree.

POSITIVE	COMPARITIVE	SUPERLATIVE
long	longer	longest
tall	taller	tallest
light	lighter	lightest
soon	sooner	soonest

Forming Degrees of Modifiers Correctly

- Some two-syllable modifiers require *more* and *most* before the positive degree to form the comparative and superlative forms, while others require an *er* or *est* ending.

  earnest, more earnest,   happy, happier, happiest
  most earnest

- For modifiers that have three or more syllables, use *more* and *most* to form the comparative and superlative degrees.

  wonderful, more wonderful,   horrible, more horrible,
  most wonderful   most horrible

- To form the comparative and superlative degrees with adverbs that end in *ly*, use *more* and *most*.

  slowly, more slowly,   gladly, more gladly,
  most slowly   most gladly

- To indicate *decreasing* degrees of comparison, use *less* and *least*.

  strong, less strong,   important, less important,
  least strong   least important

> **TEST-TAKING TIP**
>
> To help you decide if a two-syllable modifier requires *more* or *most* before the positive degree, or an *er* or *est* ending, trust your listening skills. Many times an *er* or *est* ending sounds awkward.

Keep in mind that spelling may change when a comparative or superlative ending is added to a word. For instance, when you add an *er* or *est* ending to the word *crafty*, the *y* changes to an *i*: *craftier, craftiest*.

Some modifiers form their degrees of comparison *irregularly*. Read the examples below.

POSITIVE	COMPARITIVE	SUPERLATIVE
good/well	better	best
bad	worse	worst
little	less	least
many/much	more	most

Spotting and Fixing Faulty Modifiers

- Watch for double comparisons, which are formed when both an *er* or *est* ending and *more* or *most* are added to a modifier.

  Incorrect: The frog-jump competition is the most funniest of the events.

  Correct: The frog jump competition is the funniest of the events.
  Think: Some two-syllable modifiers can take an *er* or *est* ending or *more* or *most*. You could also use *more* or *most* before the positive degree of *funny* to form *most funny*.

- Watch for incomplete comparisons, which sometimes can cause ambiguity.

  Incorrect: Toya likes racing better than Meg.
  Think: This sentence implies that *Toya* likes *racing* better than she likes *Meg*.

  Correct: Toya likes racing better than Meg does.
  Think: Add words to complete the comparison.

  Incorrect: Annual festivals in my hometown are odder than your hometown.
  Think: This sentence incorrectly compares *festivals* to *your hometown*.

  Correct: Annual festivals in my hometown are odder than those in your hometown.

- Watch for faulty parallelism.

  Incorrect: Many teens think that going to plays is not as much fun as movies.

  Correct: Many teens think that going to plays is not as much fun as going to movies.
  Think: Use the same grammatical form to compare parallel ideas.

- Watch for illogical comparisons. Use the words *other* or *else* to compare something with others in the same group.

> **Incorrect:** Steve's pumpkin is larger than any pumpkin at the fair.
> *Think: Steve's pumpkin* cannot be larger than itself.

> **Correct:** Steve's pumpkin is larger than any other pumpkin at the fair.

> **Incorrect:** Hank usually eats more pancakes than anyone in the event.
> *Think:* The word *anyone* includes *Hank*, and he can't eat more pancakes than himself.

> **Correct:** Hank usually eats more pancakes than anyone else in the event.

- Watch for comparisons using as.

> **Incorrect:** He plans to study as hard if not harder than he did last time.

> **Correct:** He plans to study as hard as, if not harder than, he did last time.
> *Think:* You must include the second *as.*

Exercise 1: Correcting Modifiers

Rewrite each sentence to eliminate any faulty modifiers. If the sentence is correct as is, write "correct."

1. I just saw the most largest cantaloupe I have ever seen.
   I just saw the largest cantaloupe I have ever seen.
2. Jerome is a better jumper than anyone in the contest.
   Jerome is a better jumper than anyone else in the contest.
3. Luisa's frog jumped farther than Ben.
   Luisa's frog jumped farther than Ben's.
4. The difficultest decisions were those involving the cucumbers.
   The most difficult decisions were those involving the cucumbers.
5. Sack races drew fewer fans than in-line skating races.
   Sack races drew fewer fans than in-line skating races did.
6. Erin is more interested in horticulture than Evan.
   Erin is more interested in horticulture than Evan is.
7. Because Dave had no expectations of winning, the result was even more surprising. Correct as is.
8. People say that watching ball games on TV is better than to go to them.
   People say that watching ball games on TV is better than going to them.
9. Her nose is longer than Pinocchio.
   Her nose is longer than Pinocchio's.
10. Wearing stovepipe hats is less popular than baseball caps.
    Wearing stovepipe hats is less popular than wearing baseball caps.

Exercise 2: Identify the Sentence Error

One of the underlined words or phrases may contain a grammatical error. If there is one, choose the underlined part that must be changed to make the sentence correct, and fill in the corresponding oval. If the sentence has no error, fill in oval Ⓔ.

1. The <u>funnest</u> part of the <u>entire</u> experience <u>was watching</u> the <u>festive</u> parade.
       A   B   C   D

<u>No error</u>
 E

Ⓐ Ⓑ Ⓒ Ⓓ Ⓔ

2. <u>That</u> was, <u>without</u> question, the <u>biggest</u> grapefruit I <u>had ever</u> seen. <u>No error</u>
  A   B   C   D   E

Ⓐ Ⓑ Ⓒ Ⓓ Ⓔ

3. Alex <u>prepares</u> for the competition <u>more</u> harder than any of the <u>other</u>
        A   B   C

competitors <u>do</u>. <u>No error</u>
       D   E

Ⓐ Ⓑ Ⓒ Ⓓ Ⓔ

4. Anna is the <u>selfisher</u> person of <u>anyone</u> I have ever met, and I have met <u>many</u>
            A   B   C

<u>selfish</u> people over the years. <u>No error</u>
 D   E

Ⓐ Ⓑ Ⓒ Ⓓ Ⓔ

5. <u>Who</u> is <u>most generous</u> with <u>her</u> <u>personal</u> things, Inez or Karin? <u>No error</u>
  A   B   C   D   E

Ⓐ Ⓑ Ⓒ Ⓓ Ⓔ

Exercise 3: Improve the Sentence

In each of the following items, all or part of the sentence is underlined. Beneath each sentence are five ways of phrasing the underlined part. Choice (A) is the same as the original; the other four are different. Select the answer choice that best expresses the meaning of the original sentence. Your goal is to produce the most effective sentence, one that is clear and not wordy. Choose (A) if the original sentence is better than any of the other answer choices.

EXAMPLE

The temperature in Phoenix is usually higher than Boston.

(A) The temperature in Phoenix is usually higher than Boston.
(B) The temperature in Phoenix is usually higher than it is in Boston.
(C) The temperature in Phoenix is usually more higher than in Boston.
(D) The temperature in Phoenix is usually lower than Boston.
(E) The temperature in Phoenix is usually higher than Boston is.

Ⓐ Ⓑ Ⓒ Ⓓ Ⓔ

Ⓑ is the correct choice because now the comparison in the sentence is complete, clear, and logical. Only this version of the sentence compares the temperatures between the two cities without changing the intended meaning of the original sentence.

---

1. Elena, who competes in pumpkin-growing contests, likes attending state fairs more than her younger brothers.

(A) Elena, who competes in pumpkin-growing contests, likes attending state fairs more than her younger brothers.
(B) Elena, who competes in pumpkin-growing contests, likes to attend state fairs more than her younger brothers.
(C) Elena, who competes in pumpkin-growing contests, likes attending state fairs more than she likes her younger brothers.
(D) Elena, who competes in pumpkin-growing contests, likes attending state fairs more than her younger brothers do.
(E) Elena, who competes in pumpkin-growing contests, likes attending state fairs more than her youngest brother.

Ⓐ Ⓑ Ⓒ Ⓓ Ⓔ

2. To learn more about the Buffalo Wallow Chili Cookoff, <u>I had to do more research online than the telephone</u>.

   (A) I had to do more research online than the telephone
   (B) I had to do research online more than the telephone
   (C) I had to do more research online than I did on the telephone
   (D) I had to research online more than using the telephone
   (E) I had to read online more often than telephoning

   Ⓐ Ⓑ Ⓒ Ⓓ Ⓔ

3. <u>Like many farmers in the region, John Johnson's corn crop was smaller than he had expected.</u>

   (A) Like many farmers in the region, John Johnson's corn crop was smaller than he had expected.
   (B) Like many farmers in the region, John Johnson had a smaller corn crop.
   (C) Like many farmers in the region, John Johnson's corn crop was smallest than he had expected.
   (D) Like many farmers in the region, John Johnson had a smaller corn crop than he had expected.
   (E) Like many farmers in the region, John Johnson's corn crop was more small than he had expected.

   Ⓐ Ⓑ Ⓒ Ⓓ Ⓔ

4. In the fishing contest, Jo hopes <u>to do as well, if not better than, the last time</u>.

   (A) to do as well, if not better than, the last time
   (B) to do as well if not more well than the last time
   (C) to do as well if not more better than the last time
   (D) to do as well as, if not better than, the last time
   (E) to do as well, if not better, than the last time

   Ⓐ Ⓑ Ⓒ Ⓓ Ⓔ

5. <u>Sabrina was as surprised as any person was with the outcome.</u>

   (A) Sabrina was as surprised as any person was with the outcome.
   (B) Sabrina was as surprised as anyone was with the outcome.
   (C) Sabrina was as more surprised as any person was with the outcome.
   (D) Sabrina was not as surprised as any person was with the outcome.
   (E) Sabrina was as surprised as any other person was with the outcome.

   Ⓐ Ⓑ Ⓒ Ⓓ Ⓔ

Parallel Construction

Read the following advice, once given by Abraham Lincoln:

> **Better to remain silent and be thought a fool than to speak out and remove all doubt.**

Many find this sentence clever and well put. But suppose our 16th president had put his thought this way:

> **Better to remain silent and be thought a fool than to *be speaking* out and remove all doubt.**

It doesn't sound right anymore, does it? The reason is that the sentence no longer has parallel structure—a repetition of a grammatical form. "To be speaking out" is not parallel with "to remain silent" or "be thought." Although all three are *verbal phrases*, "to be speaking out" contains a verb in the *gerund* form whereas the other two contain verbs in the *infinitive* form only.

Abraham Lincoln (1809–1865)

A sentence that has parallel structure not only has a pleasing rhythm, but it also helps readers to more easily spot similar or related ideas.

Sentences with Articles, Conjunctions, or Prepositions Preceding Ideas in a Series

When you write sentences in which articles (*the, a, an*), prepositions (*on, in, with,* etc.), or conjunctions (*and, or, but,* etc.) precede equal ideas or items in a series, be sure to be consistent. Either repeat the preceding word or phrase before *every* idea, or use it before only the *first* idea in the series.

FAULTY PARALLELISM	REVISED SENTENCE
The officers in the regiment included a colonel, the major, and a lieutenant.	The officers in the regiment included a colonel, a major, and a lieutenant.
The army sought to gain control of the Mississippi River, of the Ohio River, and the Tennessee River.	The army sought to gain control of the Mississippi River, the Ohio River, and the Tennessee River.
The President's party rode to Harrisburg, crossed the Susquehanna River, and it went on to York.	The President's party rode to Harrisburg, crossed the Susquehanna River, and went on to York.
The Confederacy could claim victories at First Manassas, the lopsided victory in Cold Harbor, and at Chancellorsville.	The Confederacy could claim victories at First Manassas, Cold Harbor, and Chancellorsville.

Sentences Containing Compared or Contrasted Ideas

When you write sentences that compare or contrast parallel ideas, be sure to express those ideas using the same grammatical form. For instance, match prepositional phrases with prepositional phrases and indefinite pronouns with indefinite pronouns. Be sure to match verb forms with the same verb forms.

FAULTY PARALLELISM	REVISED SENTENCE
Lincoln was more concerned about losing border state support than for what abolitionists were going to do.	Lincoln was more concerned about losing border state support than about what abolitionists were going to do.
Many great battles were fought in the East, but the West is where some key battles took place.	Many great battles were fought in the East, but some key battles took place in the West.
Moving an army by train was much faster than to move one by foot.	Moving an army by train was much faster than moving one by foot.

Exercise 1: Revise a Paragraph

Some sentences in the paragraph below lack parallel structure. Rewrite the paragraph on the lines below to eliminate the faulty parallelism.

We marched for several long hours through mud, dust, and in sweltering heat. We stopped a few times to eat, rest, and also to let the other regiments keep pace with us. Finally, we reached the bend in the river and the place where we were going to camp for a spell. Most of the men either planned to spend the rest of the day sleeping or writing to their loved ones. I, myself, walked over to the river's edge, was sitting down, and placed my sore, tired feet in the cool water.

We marched for several hours through mud, dust, and sweltering heat. We stopped a

few times to eat, rest, and let the other regiments keep pace with us. Finally, we

reached the bend in the river and the place where we were going to camp for a spell.

Most of the men either planned to spend the rest of the day sleeping or writing to their

loved ones. I, myself, walked over to the river's edge, sat down, and placed my sore,

tired feet in the cool water.

_____

_____

_____

_____

Exercise 2: Identify the Sentence Error

One of the underlined words or phrases may contain a grammatical error. If there is one, choose the underlined part that must be changed to make the sentence correct, and fill in the corresponding oval. If the sentence has no error, fill in oval Ⓔ.

EXAMPLE

For <u>soldiers in camp</u>, <u>singing</u>, <u>letter writing</u>, and <u>to play cards</u> were common
       A   B   C   D
pastimes. <u>No error</u>
       E

Ⓐ Ⓑ Ⓒ Ⓓ Ⓔ

Choice Ⓓ is correct because *to play cards* is not in the same grammatical form as *singing* and *letter writing*. *To play* is an infinitive, whereas *singing* and *letter writing* are in gerund form.

---

1. Historians <u>consider</u> Gettysburg to have been the key battle <u>of the war,</u>
           A   B

<u>maintain</u> that it was a turning point in the contest, and <u>it produced</u> many
  C   D

casualties. <u>No error</u>
        E

Ⓐ Ⓑ Ⓒ ● Ⓔ

2. The noncombatants in the regiment included <u>band members</u>, <u>cooks</u>, <u>wranglers</u>,
                                        A   B   C

assorted aides, and <u>nurses</u>. <u>No error</u>
            D   E

Ⓐ Ⓑ Ⓒ Ⓓ ●

3. <u>Spending</u> countless boring, lonely hours in the camp or <u>marching</u> for hours on
   A   B

end <u>was</u> sometimes harder on soldiers than <u>to face</u> the enemy in battle. <u>No error</u>
   C   D   E

Ⓐ Ⓑ Ⓒ ● Ⓔ

Topic 31: Parallel Construction   **153**

4. <u>Soldiers</u> <u>prefer trains</u> to <u>marching long distances</u> or even <u>riding on horseback</u>.
   A   B   C   D

   <u>No error</u>
   E

                                                     Ⓐ ⬤Ⓒ Ⓓ Ⓔ

5. <u>Although</u> many soldiers <u>died in battle</u>, even <u>most</u> <u>were killed</u> by disease.
   A   B   C   D

   <u>No error</u>
   E

                                                         Ⓐ Ⓑ ⬤Ⓓ Ⓔ

Exercise 3: Improve the Sentence

In each of the following items, all or part of the sentence is underlined. Beneath each sentence are five ways of phrasing the underlined part. Choice (A) is the same as the original; the other four are different. Select the answer choice that best expresses the meaning of the original sentence. Your goal is to produce the most effective sentence, one that is clear and not wordy. Choose (A) if the original sentence is better than any of the other answer choices.

> ### EXAMPLE
>
> <u>The Mississippi River runs through Arkansas, Kentucky, and the state of Illinois.</u>
>
> (A) The Mississippi River runs through Arkansas, Kentucky, and the state of Illinois.
> (B) The Mississippi River runs through Arkansas, Kentucky, and through the state of Illinois.
> (C) The Mississippi River runs through Arkansas, Kentucky, and Illinois.
> (D) The Mississippi River runs through the states of Arkansas, Kentucky, and the state of Illinois.
> (E) The Mississippi River is in Arkansas, Kentucky, and the state of Illinois.
>
>   Ⓐ Ⓑ ⬤Ⓓ Ⓔ
>
> The correct choice is Ⓒ because the given sentence has faulty parallelism. It expresses ideas in a series, and the phrase *the state of* does not agree with the word *through* that starts the series. The word *through* could have been repeated before all three ideas, but since it wasn't repeated before the second idea, it shouldn't be repeated before the third.

1. Harriet Beecher Stowe's novel, *Uncle Tom's Cabin*, requires readers <u>to confront racism, think about theories of race, and to be questioning different feminist ideologies</u>.

   (A) to confront racism, think about theories of race, and to be questioning different feminist ideologies

   (B) to confront racism, to be thinking about theories of race, and to be questioning different feminist ideologies

   (C) to confront racism, think about theories of race, and to question different feminist ideologies

   (D) to confront racism, think about theories of race, and question different feminist ideologies

   (E) to confront racism, to think about theories of race, and be questioning different feminist ideologies

   Ⓐ Ⓑ Ⓒ **Ⓓ** Ⓔ

2. <u>Frederick Douglass escaped from slavery, learned how to read and write, and was speaking out eloquently on behalf of freedom.</u>

   (A) Frederick Douglass escaped from slavery, learned how to read and write, and was speaking out eloquently on behalf of freedom.

   (B) Frederick Douglass escaped from slavery and learned how to read and write, and was speaking out eloquently on behalf of freedom.

   (C) Because Frederick Douglass escaped from slavery, and learned how to read and write, he spoke out eloquently on behalf of freedom.

   (D) Frederick Douglass escaped from slavery, learned how to read and write, and was speaking out on behalf of freedom.

   (E) Frederick Douglass escaped from slavery, learned how to read and write, and spoke out eloquently on behalf of freedom.

   Ⓐ Ⓑ Ⓒ Ⓓ **Ⓔ**

3. Some soldiers were more concerned about glory and honor <u>than about the consequences of their actions</u>.

   (A) than about the consequences of their actions

   (B) than for what the consequences of their actions would be

   (C) than for the consequences of their actions

   (D) than the consequences of their actions

   (E) than the consequences of their actions were

   Ⓐ Ⓑ Ⓒ Ⓓ Ⓔ

4. Harriet Tubman, a freed slave who helped hundreds of others escape to freedom in the North, was more concerned about the runaways' safety than for
   her own.

   (A) Harriet Tubman, a freed slave who helped hundreds of others escape to
       freedom in the North, was more concerned about the runaways' safety
       than for her own.
   (B) Harriet Tubman, a freed slave who helped hundreds of others escape to
       freedom in the North, was more concerned for the runaways' safety than
       she was about her own.
   (C) Harriet Tubman, a freed slave who helped hundreds of others escape to
       freedom in the North, was more concerned about the runaways' safety
       than about for her own.
   (D) Harriet Tubman, a freed slave who helped hundreds of others escape to
       freedom in the North, was more concerned about the runaways' safety
       than about her own.
   (E) Harriet Tubman, a freed slave who helped hundreds of others escape to
       freedom in the North, was more concerned about the runaways' safety
       than she ever could be about her own.

5. Supporting John Brown by secretly giving him money was safer for many
   sympathizers than to support his cause openly.

   (A) Supporting John Brown by secretly giving him money was safer for many
       sympathizers than to support his cause openly.
   (B) Supporting John Brown by secretly giving him money was safer for many
       sympathizers than supporting his cause openly.
   (C) Supporting John Brown by secretly giving him money was safer for many
       sympathizers than to lend their support to his cause openly.
   (D) Supporting John Brown by secretly giving him money was safer for many
       sympathizers than to be openly supporting his cause.
   (E) Supporting John Brown by secretly giving him money was safer for many
       sympathizers than joining with him in all his plans.

Faulty Subordination

Read the following:

> Some did not appreciate the signifi-
> cance of the achievement, although
> the successful completion of the
> transcontinental railroad took place
> with much fanfare at Promontory
> Summit in Utah in 1869.

Golden spike ceremony at Promontory
Summit in Utah

You probably already know that there are two major types of clauses: main (independent) clauses and subordinate clauses. A subordinate clause expresses an idea that is less important than an idea expressed in a main clause of a sentence. Also, because a subordinate clause does not express a complete thought, it cannot form a complete sentence.

A sentence such as the one about the railroad suffers from faulty subordination. The problem is that its main idea is mistakenly placed in a subordinate clause. Here is a more effective version:

> Although some did not appreciate the significance of the achieve-
> ment, the successful completion of the transcontinental railroad took
> place with much fanfare at Promontory Summit in Utah in 1869.

Moving the subordinating conjunction *although* to its appropriate position before the less important idea gives the sentence its intended meaning, and the sentence now conveys an accurate relationship between its two ideas. (For a list of subordinating conjunctions, see page 60.)

Spotting and Fixing Faulty Subordination

You may encounter the following kinds of subordination errors on the multiple-choice section of a standardized test:

**TEST-
TAKING TIP**

Clauses of *equal* rank, or coordinate clauses, are joined by coordinating conjunctions. Faulty coordination happens when *unequal* clauses are joined in this way.

- Misplaced emphasis

  Faulty: When completed, the transcontinental railroad was called the Eighth Wonder of the World, and it was constructed by companies the size of armies.
  Think: Although the two ideas are of unequal importance, using the coordinating conjunction *and* treats them as if they were equally important.

  Fixed: When completed, the transcontinental railroad, constructed by companies the size of armies, was called the Eighth Wonder of the World.

- An incorrect link between ideas

  Faulty: After precautions were taken, there were many casualties.

  Think: The relationship between the two ideas is not clear.

  Fixed: Although precautions were taken, there were many casualties.

- An illogical or unclear relationship between ideas

  Faulty: Because I took an interest in the building of the transcontinental railroad, I am interested in American history during the 1860s.

  Think: This construction is illogical because it subordinates the cause to the effect.

  Fixed: Because I am interested in American history during the 1860s, I took an interest in the building of the transcontinental railroad.

- Too much subordination

  Faulty: Although the politicians looked to take the credit, the transcontinental railroad was conceived by engineers who risked their reputations, funded by investors who risked their fortunes, and built by armies of immigrant workers who, alongside former soldiers who became available because the war had ended, risked their lives doing the backbreaking work the project demanded.

  Fixed: Although the politicians looked to take the credit, the transcontinental railroad was conceived by engineers who risked their reputations, and funded by investors who risked their fortunes. But the actual backbreaking work was completed at great personal risk by immigrants and former soldiers.

Exercise I: Fixing Faulty Subordination

Rewrite each sentence to eliminate any faulty subordination. If the sentence is correct as is, write "correct." Answers may vary; sample answers provided.

1. The surveyor's work was dangerous, although he found it very satisfying.

   Although the surveyor's work was dangerous, he found it very satisfying.

2. Because the engineer took on the job, he enjoyed challenges.

   The engineer took on the job because he enjoyed challenges.

3. Because former Yankees stood alongside former Confederates, the ceremony brought together all Americans.

   Because the ceremony brought together all Americans, former Yankees stood alongside former Confederates.

4. Even though the work started later than had been planned, the job was completed on time.

Correct as is.

5. The lead engineer was seen as a genius and he had no formal training.

The lead engineer was seen as a genius although he had no formal training.

Exercise 2: Identify the Sentence Error

One of the underlined words or phrases may contain a grammatical error. If there is one, choose the underlined part that must be changed to make the sentence correct, and fill in the corresponding oval. If the sentence has no error, fill in oval Ⓔ.

> **EXAMPLE**
>
> <u>Although</u> the country is <u>huge</u>, there <u>is</u> enough land to utilize railroads <u>fully</u>.
>   A   B   C   D
> <u>No error</u>
>   E
>
>   Ⓐ Ⓑ Ⓒ Ⓓ Ⓔ
>
> Choice Ⓐ is correct because the subordinating conjunction *Although* is an illogical choice. It is *because* of the country's great size that railroads can be fully utilized.

1. <u>Because</u> the locomotive <u>was</u> a <u>great</u> success, it <u>cut</u> travel time by days. <u>No error</u>
    A   B   C   D   E

                             Ⓐ Ⓑ Ⓒ Ⓓ Ⓔ

2. <u>Before</u> the advent of the railroad, a person <u>could travel</u> no faster <u>than</u> Julius
    A   B   C

Caesar <u>could</u>. <u>No error</u>
        D   E

                             Ⓐ Ⓑ Ⓒ Ⓓ Ⓔ

3. <u>Whenever they passed</u>, <u>people</u> watched the trains <u>speed</u> by at 60 miles
            A   B   C

per <u>hour</u>. <u>No error</u>
     D   E

                             Ⓐ Ⓑ Ⓒ Ⓓ Ⓔ

4. The telegraph <u>sped</u> up communication <u>dramatically</u> <u>before</u> it was <u>widely</u>
                A   B   C   D

used. <u>No error</u>
     E

Ⓐ Ⓑ **Ⓒ** Ⓓ Ⓔ

5. I <u>noticed</u> that <u>while riding to Reno,</u> the <u>snow</u> made the trail
   A   B   C

hazardous. <u>No error</u>
    D   E

Ⓐ **Ⓑ** Ⓒ Ⓓ Ⓔ

Exercise 3: Improve the Sentence

In each of the following items, all or part of the sentence is underlined. Beneath each sentence are five ways of phrasing the underlined part. Choice (A) is the same as the original; the other four are different. Select the answer choice that best expresses the meaning of the original sentence. Your goal is to produce the most effective sentence, one that is clear and not wordy. Choose (A) if the original sentence is better than any of the other answer choices.

> **EXAMPLE**
>
> <u>The new railroad opened much land for settlement, and it cost a great deal to build.</u>
>
> (A) The new railroad opened much land for settlement, and it cost a great deal to build.
> (B) Although the new railroad cost a great deal to build, it opened much land for settlement.
> (C) The new railroad opened much land for settlement when it cost a great deal to build.
> (D) The new railroad opened much land for settlement while it cost a great deal to build.
> (E) The new railroad opened much land for settlement before it cost a great deal to build.
>
>   Ⓐ Ⓑ Ⓒ Ⓓ Ⓔ
>
> **Ⓑ** is the correct choice because adding *Although* creates a subordinate clause, and produces the correct relationship between ideas. The original item is an example of faulty coordination.

1. <u>Once completed, the transcontinental telegraph line could transmit a message coast to coast in seconds, and it was built alongside the railroad.</u>

    (A) Once completed, the transcontinental telegraph line could transmit a message coast to coast in seconds, and it was built alongside the railroad.

    (B) Once it could transmit a message coast to coast in seconds, the transcontinental telegraph line was completed and built alongside the railroad.

    (C) Once completed, the transcontinental telegraph line could transmit a message coast to coast in seconds, but it was built alongside the railroad.

    (D) Once completed, the transcontinental telegraph line, built alongside the railroad, could transmit a message coast to coast in seconds.

    (E) Because it was built and completed alongside the railroad, the transcontinental telegraph line could transmit a message coast to coast in seconds.

                                     Ⓐ Ⓑ Ⓒ **Ⓓ** Ⓔ

2. <u>When President Grant received a telegram the railroad was completed.</u>

    (A) When President Grant received a telegram the railroad was completed.

    (B) Even though President Grant received a telegram the railroad was completed.

    (C) When the railroad was completed, President Grant received a telegram.

    (D) Although President Grant received a telegram the railroad was completed.

    (E) Because President Grant received a telegram the railroad was completed.

                                       Ⓐ Ⓑ **Ⓒ** Ⓓ Ⓔ

3. <u>When Sherman was notified of the railroad's progress, he promised that he would ride the rails from coast to coast.</u>

    (A) When Sherman was notified of the railroad's progress, he promised that he would ride the rails from coast to coast.

    (B) When Sherman promised that he would ride the rails from coast to coast, he was notified of the railroad's progress.

    (C) While Sherman was notified of the railroad's progress, he promised that he would ride the rails from coast to coast.

(D) Sherman was notified of the railroad's progress and he promised that he would ride the rails from coast to coast.

(E) When General Sherman, formerly a Federal Army commander, was notified of the progress the railroad was making, he promised, afterward, that he would ride the rails from coast to coast whenever the trains were ready for him to do so.

Ⓐ Ⓑ Ⓒ Ⓓ Ⓔ

4. Whenever the railroad was built, it took travelers months and more than $1,000 to go from New York to San Francisco.

(A) Whenever the railroad was built, it took travelers months and more than $1,000 to go from New York to San Francisco.

(B) Before the railroad was built, it took travelers months and more than $1,000 to go from New York to San Francisco.

(C) Although the railroad was built, it took travelers months and more than $1,000 to go from New York to San Francisco.

(D) It took travelers months and more than $1,000 to cross the continent whenever the railroad was built.

(E) It took travelers months and more than $1,000 before the railroad was built to go from New York to San Francisco.

Ⓐ Ⓑ Ⓒ Ⓓ Ⓔ

5. Because a first-class ticket cost $150 in 1869, it went down to $136 a year later.

(A) Because a first-class ticket cost $150 in 1869, it went down to $136 a year later.

(B) Unless a first-class ticket cost $150 in 1869, it went down to $136 a year later.

(C) A first-class ticket cost $150 in 1869, and it went down to $136 a year later.

(D) Before, a first-class ticket cost $150, it went down to $136 a year later.

(E) Although a first-class ticket cost $150 in 1869, it went down to $136 a year later.

Ⓐ Ⓑ Ⓒ Ⓓ Ⓔ

Revising Sentences in Paragraphs

This is the first of three topics that address the *Improving Paragraphs* section of the test. The passages you will come across on a standardized test are followed by multiple-choice questions addressing basically three kinds of issues: revising sentences, combining sentences, and overall essay organization and development. Many of the questions relating to revising and combining sentences will also ask you to choose the revision that makes the best improvement within the context of the paragraph or essay.

Preparing to Revise Sentences in Paragraphs

The questions in the *Improving Paragraphs* section that ask you to revise sentences address many of the same usage issues as the questions in the *Identifying Sentence Errors* and the *Improving Sentences* sections of the test. Therefore, as you work through the items in this topic, feel free to look back at Topics 20–32.

As you read the passage, watch for the following kinds of sentence errors:

- Faulty subject-verb agreement
- Wrong verb form or tense
- Faulty pronoun-antecedent agreement
- Faulty comparisons
- Confusion between adjectives and adverbs
- Misplaced or dangling modifiers
- Redundancy or wordiness
- Wrong word choice (i.e., *accept* vs. *except*)
- Wrong pronoun choice
- Double negatives
- Faulty parallel construction
- Faulty subordination/coordination

In the *Improving Paragraphs* section, each set of answer choices may include more than one grammatically correct revision. Be sure to pick the alternative that fixes the sentence in need of repair, but does not change the intended meaning of that sentence or of the paragraph in which it appears.

Strategies for Revising Sentences in Paragraphs

- Read the passage quickly, but carefully enough to get a good sense of what it is about.
- Read each question stem closely to make sure you understand what it asks you to do.
- When you reread the sentence that the question addresses, make sure also to reread the portions of the essay immediately before and after it to understand the context within which the sentence appears.
- Try to determine what the answer is before you read the choices.
- Be sure to read choice (A); it *does not* always repeat the original, although it may sometimes be "(As it is now)."

Directions: The passage that follows is an early draft of an essay. Some parts need to be rewritten. Read the passage carefully and answer the questions that follow. Choose the answer that most clearly and effectively expresses the writer's intended meaning. In making your decisions, follow the conventions of standard English. After you have chosen your answer, fill in the corresponding oval.

[1] If I had ever needed convincing, the interstate crash that killed a family from our neighborhood has done the job: One thing that must change in America, right away, is how we drive. [2] If common sense alone doesn't convince us to address the issue of road safety, then the facts should. [3] And one key fact is this: The single largest cause of death in our country are car accidents. [4] It's high time we did something to change that gloomy statistic.

[5] For starters, we simply must have better and safer drivers on our roads. [6] To accomplish this, we need to create tougher written tests and driving tests. [7] We should also retest drivers several times during their lifetimes to make sure that their knowledge is up to date and that their vision and reflexes remain good enough to keep our roads safe. [8] When a person's skills have eroded with age, they should not be behind a steering wheel. [9] Similarly, tougher written tests will keep the weak, dangerous drivers off the road until they are truly ready, if they ever are. [10] Just because someone turns sixteen doesn't never mean that he or she should be allowed to step on the gas and endanger us all. [11] What, I ask, is the argument against putting only good drivers on the road?

[12] The second thing we need to do right away is to take a careful look at and enforce the rules of the road, and change any that contribute to the safety problem. [13] One thing we should change immediately is speed limits. [14] Studies regularly show that with lower speed limits the number of accidents decreases. [15] Another thing I would change is the rule that allows drivers to make right turns on red lights. [16] Changing this rule would also cut back on the number of accidents. [17] To discourage those who will break the no-right-turn-on-red rule, I would raise the fines for both infractions dramatically. [18] And I would put more police officers on the road to issue expensive tickets to those drivers who do break the rules. [19] I would instruct them to have a "Go ahead, make my day" attitude when they leave the station house each day. [20] Although this approach may be unpopular, it would help to motivate people to obey the rules more closely, which would in turn help to cut back on accidents.

[21] But making all these changes is only part of a real, meaningful solution to our driving safety problems. [22] Another, perhaps more important part, is to cut back on the number of cars on the road. [23] More than anything else, creating more and better public transportation is the best solution to this problem. [24] Statistics and common sense show that this is the most reasonable thing to do. [25] What, I ask you, is the argument against having more and better public transportation?

1. Which of the following is the best revision of sentence 3?
And one key fact is this: The single largest cause of death in our country are car accidents.

   (A) And one key fact is this: The single, largest cause of death in our country are car accidents.

   (B) And one key fact is this; The single largest cause of death in our country is car accidents.

   (C) And one key fact is this: The single largest cause of death in our country is car accidents.

   (D) And one key fact is this: The single largest cause of death in our country are a car accident.

   (E) And one key fact is this, the single largest cause of death in our country are car accidents.

   Ⓐ Ⓑ Ⓒ Ⓓ Ⓔ

2. Which is the best revision of the underlined portion of sentence 8?
When a person's skills have eroded with age, they should not be behind a steering wheel.

   (A) they shouldn't be behind a steering wheel

   (B) behind a steering wheel is where he or she should not be

   (C) he or she should not be in a car

   (D) he or she should not be behind a steering wheel

   (E) they should not be in front of a steering wheel

   Ⓐ Ⓑ Ⓒ Ⓓ Ⓔ

3. Which is the best revision of the underlined portion of sentence 10?
Just because someone turns sixteen doesn't never mean that he or she should be allowed to step on the gas and endanger us all.

   (A) doesn't never mean that he

   (B) doesn't mean that he or she

   (C) doesn't hardly ever mean that he or she

   (D) doesn't mean that they

   (E) means that he or she

   Ⓐ Ⓑ Ⓒ Ⓓ Ⓔ

4. In the context of the third paragraph, which is the best revision of the under-lined portion of sentence 17?

To discourage <u>those who will break the no-right-turn-on-red rule</u>, I would raise the fines for both infractions dramatically.

(A) speeders as well as those who might break the no-right-turn-on-red rule

(B) those who might break the no-right-turn-on-red rule

(C) them who might break the no-right-turn-on-red rule

(D) speeders and those that broke the no-right-turn-on-red rule

(E) those who might break the new no-right-turn-on-red rule

Ⓐ Ⓑ Ⓒ Ⓓ Ⓔ

5. Which best replaces the word *them* in sentence 19?

(A) speeders

(B) tickets

(C) fines

(D) dangerous drivers

(E) the officers

Ⓐ Ⓑ Ⓒ Ⓓ Ⓔ

6. In the context of the last paragraph, which of the following sentences is most in need of further support and development?

(A) sentence 21

(B) sentence 22

(C) sentence 23

(D) sentence 24

(E) sentence 25

Ⓐ Ⓑ Ⓒ Ⓓ Ⓔ

Combining Sentences in Paragraphs

This is the second of the three topics that address the *Improving Paragraphs* section of the test. In this topic, some of the questions following the passage will ask you to revise by combining sentences. As in Topic 33, you can expect to come across questions that ask you to choose the revision that makes the best improvement within the *context* of the paragraph or essay.

Preparing to Combine Sentences in Paragraphs

The questions in the *Improving Paragraphs* section that ask you to combine sentences address some of the same issues as the *Identifying Sentence Errors* and the *Improving Sentences* sections of the test do. As you work through the items in this topic, feel free to look back at Topics 20–32 as well as Topics 8–17 in this textbook.

As you read the passage, watch, in particular, for the following kinds of errors:

- Run-on sentences
- Wordy sentences
- Sentence fragments
- Choppy sentences

As in Topic 33, each set of answer choices may include more than one grammatically correct revision. Be sure to pick the alternative that does not change the intended meaning of the sentence or sentences in need of revision.

Strategies for Combining Sentences in Paragraphs

- Read the passage quickly, but carefully enough to get a good sense of what it is about.
- "Listen" for any errors.
- Read each question stem closely to make sure you understand what it asks you to do.
- When you reread the sentence or sentences that the question addresses, also make sure to reread the surrounding text—the text that comes immediately before and after—in order to understand the context.
- When answering questions in this section, try to determine what the answer is before you read the choices.
- Go back and refer to the passage as often as necessary to help you answer each question.
- Be sure to read choice (A); it *does not* always repeat the original, although it may sometimes be "(As it is now)."

Directions: The passage that follows is an early draft of an essay. Some parts need to be rewritten. Read the passage carefully and answer the questions that follow. Choose the answer that most clearly and effectively expresses the writer's intended meaning. In making your decisions, follow the conventions of standard English. After you have chosen your answer, fill in the corresponding oval.

[1] The Minoan civilization, named by a British archaeologist for legendary King Minos, flourished for approximately 1,500 years during the Bronze Age. [2] Minoan culture was the first high civilization of Europe. [3] Minoans developed an early form of writing. [4] They also used their maritime skills to found colonies. [5] They used them to develop a trade empire. [6] But, suddenly, at the height of its power and glory, the Minoan civilization collapsed.

[7] For decades, scholars have debated the cause of the collapse. [8] Many have thought that the fall was caused by the enormous eruption of the Thera volcano more than 3,000 years ago. [9] Thera, known today as Santorini, is only about 70 miles from what once was Minoan Crete. [10] It was reasonable to hold its powerful explosion accountable for the rapid fall. [11] Then, in the late 1980s, a team of Dutch scientists dealt that theory a blow. [12] Their studies resulting in evidence that the eruption had taken place 150 years earlier than had been thought, which would mean that it occurred 200 years earlier than the date usually cited for the Minoan fall. [13] Armed with this new data, they proposed that the natural disaster occurred too early to be the cause of the demise of the Minoans, any link between the eruption and the decline, they said, is far-fetched at best.

[14] It is far-fetched no longer. [15] According to recent findings, the Thera upheaval was many times larger than had been previously thought, larger even than the 1883 Krakatoa eruption that killed more than 36,000 people. [16] Based on the new evidence, scientists now say that the repercussions from the Thera explosion were felt throughout the entire eastern Mediterranean region. [17] They say that the explosions lasted longer, and were more widespread than originally thought, citing as evidence ash from Thera found in the Nile delta and at the bottom of the Black Sea. [18] The violent eruption, which sent dense clouds of volcanic ash over the region, crippled cities and fleets, and created climate changes that ruined crops and sowed political instability. [19] The scholars assert that the eruption not only had immediate consequences for Minoan Crete, but long-term ones, too. [20] Archaeological findings that show changes in Cretan artistic output, as well as in food production, support the idea of political upheaval. [21] When, in 1450 B.C., Mycenaean invaders from mainland Greece took control of Crete, the Minoan age was over. [22] The catastrophic eruption on Thera was the likely catalyst.

1. Which is the best way to revise and combine sentences 4 and 5?
They also used their maritime skills to found colonies. They used them to develop a trade empire.

(A) They also used their maritime skills to found colonies and a developed trade empire.

(B) They also used their maritime skills not only to found colonies, but also to found trade empires.

(C) They also used their maritime skills to found colonies and develop a trade empire.

(D) They also used their maritime skills to found a colony and trade empires.

(E) They also used their maritime skills to found colonies in addition to a trade empire.

2. Which is the best way to revise and combine sentences 9 and 10?
Thera, known today as Santorini, is only about 70 miles from what once was Minoan Crete. It was reasonable to hold its powerful explosion accountable for the rapid fall.

(A) Thera, known today as Santorini, is only about 70 miles from what once was Minoan Crete and it was reasonable to hold its powerful explosion accountable for the rapid fall.

(B) Because Thera, known today as Santorini, is only about 70 miles from what once was Minoan Crete, it was reasonable to hold its powerful explosion accountable for the rapid fall.

(C) Thera, known today as Santorini, is only about 70 miles from what once was Minoan Crete, but it was reasonable to hold its powerful explosion accountable for the rapid fall.

(D) Although Thera is only about 70 miles from what once was Minoan Crete, it was reasonable to hold its powerful explosion accountable for the rapid fall.

(E) Thera is known today as Santorini, and it is only about 70 miles from what once was Minoan Crete, and that is very close by, and its explosion was very powerful, and it was reasonable to hold it accountable for Crete's rapid fall.

Ⓐ Ⓑ Ⓒ Ⓓ Ⓔ

3. Which is the best way to revise the underlined portion of sentence 12?
Their studies <u>resulting in evidence that the eruption had taken place 150 years earlier than had been thought, which would mean that it occurred</u> 200 years earlier than the date usually cited for the Minoan fall.

(A) resulted in evidence. The eruption had taken place 150 years earlier,

(B) resulting in evidence that the eruption was 150 years earlier than was thought, which would mean that it occurred

(C) resulted in evidence that the eruption had taken place 150 years earlier than had been thought. That would mean that they occurred

(D) resulted in evidence that the eruption had taken place 150 years earlier than had been thought, which would mean that it occurred

(E) resulting in evidence that the eruption had taken place 150 years earlier than had been thought. This new information put the event

4. Which is the best way to revise the underlined portion of sentence 13?
Armed with this new data, they proposed that the natural disaster occurred too early to be the cause of the demise of the Minoans, any link between the eruption and the decline, they said, is far-fetched at best.

(A) of the Minoans whereas any link between

(B) of the Minoans; whereas any link between

(C) of the Minoans. Nevertheless, any link between

(D) of the Minoans any link between

(E) of the Minoans. Therefore, any link between

Ⓐ Ⓑ Ⓒ Ⓓ Ⓔ

5. Which is the best way to revise sentences 19 and 20 in order to combine them?
The scholars assert that the eruption not only had immediate consequences for Minoan Crete, but long-term ones, too. Archaeological findings that show changes in Cretan artistic output, as well as in food production, support the idea of political upheaval.

(A) too, therefore, archaeological findings that show changes in Cretan artistic output and food production, support the idea of political upheaval.

(B) too, because archaeological findings that show changes in Cretan artistic output and food production, support the idea of political upheaval.

(C) too; they cite archaeological findings that show political upheaval as well as changes in Cretan artistic output and food production.

(D) too, finding archaeology that show changes in Cretan artistic output, as well as in food production, and support the idea of political upheaval.

(E) too; Archaeological findings that show changes in Cretan artistic output, as well as in food production, support the idea of political upheaval.

Ⓐ Ⓑ Ⓒ Ⓓ Ⓔ

Organizing and Developing Paragraphs

This is the last of the three topics that address the *Improving Paragraphs* section of the test. All of the questions following the passage in this topic address broad organizational or developmental concerns.

Focusing on Paragraph Organization and Development

The questions in the *Improving Paragraphs* section that ask you to focus on paragraph organization or development address some of the same issues that the *Writing Better Essays* and the *Writing Better Paragraphs* sections of this textbook do. Therefore, as you work through the items in this topic, feel free to look back at Topics 5–10.

As you read the passage, watch, in particular, for the following kinds of issues:

- Paragraph unity
- Main idea and supporting details
- Functions of sentences
- Use and placement of topic sentences

- Coherence and transitions
- Paragraph structure
- Functions of paragraphs
- How essays open and close

Although more than one answer choice may be grammatically correct, be sure to pick the alternative that doesn't change the intended meaning of the sentences or paragraph in which it appears.

Paragraph Organization and Development

- Read the passage quickly, but carefully enough to get a good sense of what it is about.
- Read each question stem closely to make sure you understand what it asks you to do.
- When you reread the paragraph or sentences that the question addresses, also make sure to reread the surrounding text—the text that comes immediately before and after—in order to understand the context.
- For questions that address the entire essay, skim the passage again, as needed, to refamiliarize yourself with its content and structure.
- When answering questions in this section, try to determine what the answer is before you read the choices.
- Be sure to read choice (A); it *does not* always repeat the original, although it may sometimes be "(As it is now)."

Directions: The passage that follows is an early draft of an essay. Some parts need to be rewritten. Read the passage carefully and answer the questions that follow. Choose the answer that most clearly and effectively expresses the writer's intended meaning. In making your decisions, follow the conventions of standard English. After you have chosen your answer, fill in the corresponding oval.

[1] *Although some think that "the light at the end of the tunnel" is only that of an oncoming train, I don't see it that way.* [2] *Yes, sometimes it does seem that bad news is everywhere and that the future holds more of the same.* [3] *And, yes, sometimes it does appear that there is more wrong with the world than is right with it.* [4] *But these are only appearances; I know that if we let appearances alone guide us, they will defeat us.* [5] *It is important to remain confident that the future is a bright one and to act on that optimism.*

[6] *We always need to believe that adversity can bring out the best in us as long as we remain hopeful.* [7] *I know this to be true.* [8] *When my mother lost her job, for example, it scared us at first.* [9] *But we hung together as a family and saw ourselves through the setback.* [10] *Mom was home more and we talked more, even about her plans for her job search.* [11] *We did more things together, too, and became closer as a family.* [12] *And Mom, on her own, took on small jobs and made new connections that could help her to find the job she wanted.* [13] *For our family, good things evolved from bad news.* [14] *Although losing her job and the money it brought in was certainly a bad thing, we survived, even thrived.* [15] *In the face of troubles, we gained the realization that in our family, there was more to cheer about than to cry about.* [16] *I'm certain many other families have similar amazing stories to tell.*

[17] *I'm sure that George Washington struggled to keep his chin up during the rough winter at Valley Forge before rallying his troops to victory.* [18] *Abraham Lincoln had many sleepless nights watching the great sacrifice Americans were making to keep the country together.* [19] *I'm certain, too, that Dr. Martin Luther King, Jr., along with those who marched and demonstrated with him, kept his head high even though he had doubts about where all his hard work would lead.* [20] *Well, it led to civil rights for millions of Americans!*

[21] *All of these great leaders understood that despite the difficulties they faced, they needed to keep on going because what they knew to be right was worth the struggle.* [22] *They, and many others like them, saw the future as a distant, flickering light, not as a train bearing down on them.* [23] *Their view then should be ours today, because although it may not always seem so, hopefulness results in success.* [24] *After all, since "the future is ours to make," let's make it the best it can be!*

1. Which sentence best states the main idea of paragraph 1?

(A) sentence 1

(B) sentence 2

(C) sentence 3

(D) sentence 4

(E) sentence 5

Ⓐ Ⓑ Ⓒ Ⓓ Ⓔ

2. Sentences 6 and 7 function together to

(A) describe today's troubles.

(B) defend adversity.

(C) support the idea that the future is bright.

(D) introduce the idea that the writer has learned something from a personal experience.

(E) summarize the main points in the first paragraph.

Ⓐ Ⓑ Ⓒ Ⓓ Ⓔ

3. Which of the following sentences would best improve the third paragraph if it were inserted before sentence 17?

(A) You all have heard of George Washington, Abraham Lincoln, and Martin Luther King, Jr.

(B) From studying history, I also know that optimism, even in the most trying circumstances, reaps rich benefits.

(C) I know, too, that many American Presidents and other leaders have had much in common.

(D) I'm certain that many Presidents have had similar experiences to mine.

(E) Unlike families, who struggle just to keep up with day-to-day issues, great leaders must always look ahead and plan for the future.

Ⓐ Ⓑ Ⓒ Ⓓ Ⓔ

4. Which of the following is the best way to revise and combine sentences 17 and 18?

(A) I'm sure that George Washington struggled to keep his chin up during the rough winter at Valley Forge before rallying his troops to victory, while Abraham Lincoln must have had many sleepless nights watching the great sacrifice Americans were making to keep the country together.

(B) I'm sure that George Washington struggled to keep his chin up during the rough winter at Valley Forge before rallying his troops to victory, and that Abraham Lincoln must have had many sleepless nights watching the great sacrifice Americans were making to keep the country together.

(C) I'm sure that George Washington struggled to keep his chin up during the rough winter at Valley Forge before rallying his troops to victory, but that Abraham Lincoln must have had many sleepless nights watching the great sacrifice Americans were making to keep the country together.

(D) I'm sure that George Washington struggled to keep his chin up during the rough winter at Valley Forge before rallying his troops to victory, Abraham Lincoln must have had many sleepless nights watching the great sacrifice Americans were making to keep the country together.

(E) I'm sure that George Washington struggled to keep his chin up during the rough winter at Valley Forge before rallying his troops to victory; Abraham Lincoln, on the other hand, must have had many sleepless nights watching the great sacrifice Americans were making to keep the country together.

5. Including a paragraph on which of the following would strengthen the writer's argument the most?

(A) the effects of doing nothing constructive during tough times

(B) the most intractable causes of anger and disaffection in the world today

(C) examples of actions by governments, leaders, or groups today that are not likely to make for a brighter future

(D) examples of how other households coped under difficult circumstances

(E) quotations from Washington, Lincoln, or Martin Luther King, Jr.

Ⓐ Ⓑ Ⓒ Ⓓ Ⓔ

6. All of the following strategies are used by the writer of the passage EXCEPT

(A) drawing conclusions from past events

(B) drawing upon personal experiences

(C) presenting counterarguments

(D) suggesting alternative viewpoints of the future

(E) providing examples in support of a position

Ⓐ Ⓑ Ⓒ Ⓓ Ⓔ

Practice Tests

The following two practice tests are meant to help familiarize you with the general format and time constraints you will encounter when you take a college admissions standardized test. However, although the two practice tests that follow are very similar in length and format to current, widely used college admissions standardized tests, they are not identical to them.

The aspects that are different and that should be noted here are:

- The pages of *Writing for Standardized Tests* are smaller than those of actual college admissions standardized tests.

- On current standardized tests, you are provided with a separate answer sheet on which to write your essay and to answer the multiple-choice items (you will answer the multiple-choice items by darkening the oval that corresponds to the correct answer for each). However, in *Writing for Standardized Tests*, you are not provided with a separate answer sheet; the answer ovals appear on the same page as the multiple-choice items. You are asked to write your essay on a separate sheet of paper.

- The number of multiple-choice items and time allotted to answer them may vary between current, widely used standardized tests, but in these two practice tests you should aim to complete 53 items within 35 minutes.

Time—25 Minutes (1 question)

You have 25 minutes to write an essay on the topic below.

DO NOT WRITE AN ESSAY THAT ADDRESSES ANY OTHER TOPIC. AN ESSAY ON A DIFFERENT TOPIC WILL NOT BE ACCEPTED.

Plan and write an essay on the assigned topic. Present your thoughts clearly and effectively. Include specific examples to support your views. The quality of your essay is more important than its length, but to express your ideas on the topic adequately, you will probably want to write more than one paragraph. Keep your writing to a reasonable size and avoid wide margins. Be sure to make your hand-writing legible.

Consider the following statement. Then write an essay as directed.

> **"My definition of a free society is a society where it is safe to be unpopular."**

Assignment: Write an essay in which you agree or disagree with the statement above, using examples from history, current events, science, art, music, or your own experience to support your position.

WRITE YOUR ESSAY ON A SEPARATE SHEET OF PAPER.

Part B

Time—35 Minutes (53 questions)

Each of the following sentences may contain an error in grammar, usage, diction (word choice), or idiom. Some of the sentences are correct as written. None contains more than one error. The error, if there is one, is underlined and lettered. Assume that the parts of the sentence not underlined are correct. Read each sentence carefully, and if there is an error, choose the underlined part that must be changed to make the sentence correct, and fill in the corresponding oval. If the sentence has no error, fill in oval E. In selecting answers, follow the requirements of standard written English.

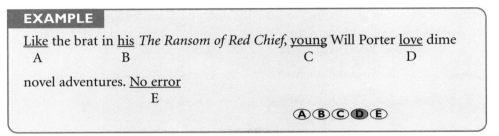

1. <u>Either</u> *The Godfather* <u>or</u> *The Godfather II* <u>are</u> <u>playing</u> at the theater tonight.
    A   B   C   D

   <u>No error</u>
    E

                         Ⓐ Ⓑ ⬤ Ⓓ Ⓔ

2. <u>Whomever</u> thinks <u>he or she</u> has seen a large tree will think <u>differently</u> after
    A   B   C

   a visit to Yosemite National <u>Park</u>. <u>No error</u>
                           D   E

                         ⬤ Ⓑ Ⓒ Ⓓ Ⓔ

3. <u>No</u> member <u>of the team</u> favored leaving <u>their</u> gear in the abandoned cave
    A   B   C

   while the bandits were still <u>on the loose</u>. <u>No error</u>
                            D   E

                         Ⓐ Ⓑ ⬤ Ⓓ Ⓔ

4. Because <u>it</u> had just <u>rained</u> and the trail was muddy, our shoes
          A   B

<u>had been</u> wet and <u>covered</u> with mud. <u>No error</u>
   C   D   E

Ⓐ Ⓑ Ⓒ Ⓓ Ⓔ

5. The climbers slowly made <u>their</u> <u>assent</u> up the <u>steep</u> eastern slope <u>of the peak</u>.
                               A   B   C   D

<u>No error</u>
 E

Ⓐ Ⓑ Ⓒ Ⓓ Ⓔ

6. Joseph Ellicott's masterful eighteenth-century clock, <u>recently</u> donated to the
                                                   A

museum, <u>has</u> more embellishments <u>than</u> <u>any clock</u> there. <u>No error</u>
      B   C   D   E

Ⓐ Ⓑ Ⓒ Ⓓ Ⓔ

7. <u>Neither</u> danger <u>nor</u> rainstorms <u>stops</u> the troupe from keeping <u>its</u> regular schedule.
    A   B   C   D

<u>No error</u>
 E

Ⓐ Ⓑ Ⓒ Ⓓ Ⓔ

8. I couldn't <u>hardly</u> believe it when I <u>received</u> my test results<u>; they</u> were much
             A   B   C

higher than I <u>had imagined</u> they would be. <u>No error</u>
             D   E

Ⓐ Ⓑ Ⓒ Ⓓ Ⓔ

9. For a decade, work crews <u>have been constructing</u> a subway in Athens<u>, they</u>
                                  A   B

<u>unexpectedly</u> unearthed a <u>trove</u> of treasures in the process. <u>No error</u>
    C   D   E

Ⓐ Ⓑ Ⓒ Ⓓ Ⓔ

10. Today, fifty years after her death, Frida Kahlo's artwork appears on calendars,
     A   B

pins, greeting cards, posters, and it appears on paper dolls, too. No error
                             C   D   E

Ⓐ Ⓑ **Ⓒ** Ⓓ Ⓔ

11. I have broke my right ankle twice while playing in a football game.
           A   B   C   D

No error
E

Ⓐ Ⓑ Ⓒ Ⓓ Ⓔ

12. Choosing the perfect setting for her novel was hard for the writer, who took
     A   B   C

several months to do it. No error
               D   E

Ⓐ Ⓑ Ⓒ Ⓓ **Ⓔ**

13. Whoever said that escape via the Underground Railroad was a piece of cake
     A   B

had better reconsider his or her view, unless riding for hours in a sealed crate
C

is an experience that person would find appealing. No error
                       D   E

Ⓐ Ⓑ Ⓒ Ⓓ **Ⓔ**

14. Although I didn't catch in at first, I soon began to see the point the teacher
     A   B   C

was trying so hard to make. No error
   D   E

Ⓐ **Ⓑ** Ⓒ Ⓓ Ⓔ

15. The product comes in three sizes: small, medium, and one that is large.
                     A   B   C   D

No error
E

Ⓐ Ⓑ Ⓒ **Ⓓ** Ⓔ

16. Everybody in the <u>small</u> frontier town <u>appreciate</u> the bawdy
    A   B

jokes as <u>well</u> as the sensible ideas of the rough new <u>arrival</u> from Kentucky.
    C   D

<u>No error</u>
    E

Ⓐ Ⓑ Ⓒ Ⓓ Ⓔ

17. I <u>first</u> read a novel by Hemingway, <u>which</u> I <u>thoroughly</u> enjoyed, <u>near</u> twenty
    A   B   C   D

years ago. <u>No error</u>
              E

Ⓐ Ⓑ Ⓒ Ⓓ Ⓔ

18. Novelists <u>need</u> a quiet place to work on <u>their</u> craft, and <u>you</u> also need a home
              A   B   C

library of <u>reference</u> materials. <u>No error</u>
              D   E

Ⓐ Ⓑ Ⓒ Ⓓ Ⓔ

19. I <u>can't help</u> <u>being impressed</u> by the <u>competitive spirit</u> the participants in the
      A   B   C

Special Olympics <u>display</u>. <u>No error</u>
                      D   E

Ⓐ Ⓑ Ⓒ Ⓓ Ⓔ

20. Several of the people <u>who</u> have seen the exhibit <u>agrees</u> that the <u>most</u>
                        A   B   C

interesting thing about it, by far, is <u>its</u> novelty. <u>No error</u>
                                        D   E

Ⓐ Ⓑ Ⓒ Ⓓ Ⓔ

In each of the following items, all or part of the sentence is underlined. Beneath each sentence are five ways of phrasing the underlined part. Choice (A) is the same as the original; the other four are different. Select the answer choice that best expresses the meaning of the original sentence. Your goal is to produce the most effective sentence, one that is clear and not wordy. Choose (A) if the original sentence is better than any of the other answer choices.

EXAMPLE

It was a bazaar occurrence, to say the least, when the lightning hit that same tree in our yard again.

(A) It was a bazaar occurrence,

(B) It was a bizarre occurrence,

(C) It has been a bazaar occurrence,

(D) It was a typical occurrence,

(E) It was a very bazaar occurrence,

Ⓐ Ⓑ Ⓒ Ⓓ Ⓔ

---

21. It can get pretty hot in Tucson and in Phoenix, but neither city get as hot as Yuma gets.

(A) get as hot as Yuma gets

(B) get as hot as Yuma

(C) get as hot as Yuma does

(D) gets as hot as Yuma gets

(E) gets as hot as Yuma, the hottest of Arizona cities, gets, which is quite hot

Ⓐ Ⓑ Ⓒ Ⓓ Ⓔ

22. The Brooklyn Bridge was built across the East River to link Brooklyn and Manhattan, it was the tallest structure in the city.

(A) The Brooklyn Bridge was built across the East River to link Brooklyn and Manhattan, it was the tallest structure in the city.

(B) The Brooklyn Bridge was built across the East River to link Brooklyn and Manhattan, so it was the tallest structure in the city.

(C) The Brooklyn Bridge was built across the East River to link Brooklyn and Manhattan and it was the tallest structure in the city.

(D) The Brooklyn Bridge was built across the East River to link Brooklyn and Manhattan, but it was the tallest structure in the city.

(E) When the Brooklyn Bridge was built across the East River to link Brooklyn and Manhattan, it was the tallest structure in the city.

Ⓐ Ⓑ Ⓒ Ⓓ Ⓔ

23. The gifted young athlete made the jump from high school basketball straight to the National Basketball Association, <u>and he was not yet up to the task of competing successfully at that high level</u>.

(A) , and he was not yet up to the task of competing successfully at that high level

(B) , for he was not yet up to the task of competing successfully at that high level

(C) . He was not yet up to the task of competing successfully at that high level

(D) , because he was not yet up to the task of competing successfully at that high level

(E) , but he was not yet up to the task of competing successfully at that high level

Ⓐ Ⓑ Ⓒ Ⓓ Ⓔ

24. Not only do other solar systems exist within our galaxy, but the planets in them may be <u>as common as the stars itself</u>.

(A) as common as the stars itself

(B) as common as all stars

(C) as common as the stars themselves

(D) more common than stars

(E) as common as stars, which themselves are quite common

Ⓐ Ⓑ Ⓒ Ⓓ Ⓔ

25. <u>We donated our old television to the local public school which no longer had a clear picture.</u>

(A) We donated our old television to the local public school which no longer had a clear picture.

(B) We donated our old television, which no longer had a clear picture, to the local public school.

(C) We donated our old television which no longer had a clear picture to the local public school.

(D) We donated to the local public school, which no longer had a clear picture, our new television.

(E) We donated our old television to the local public school that no longer had a clear picture.

Ⓐ Ⓑ Ⓒ Ⓓ Ⓔ

26. Like many exhibitors at the crafts fair, Julie's sales this year were higher than she had expected.

(A) Like many exhibitors at the crafts fair, Julie's sales this year were higher than she had expected.

(B) Like many exhibitors at the crafts fair, Julie's sales this year were higher than she expected.

(C) Like many of this year's exhibitors at the crafts fair, Julie's sales were more than she had expected.

(D) Like many exhibitors at the crafts fair this year, Julie made more sales than she had expected.

(E) Like the sales of many exhibitors at the crafts fair, Julie's sales this year were higher than she had expected.

Ⓐ Ⓑ Ⓒ ⦿ Ⓔ

27. When the understudy was introduced to the famous lead actress, she smiled warmly and offered her hand.

(A) When the understudy was introduced to the famous lead actress, she smiled warmly and offered her hand.

(B) When the understudy was introduced to the famous lead actress, the stage star smiled warmly and offered her hand.

(C) The understudy was introduced to the famous lead actress. She smiled warmly and offered her hand.

(D) She smiled warmly and offered her hand when the understudy was introduced to the famous lead actress.

(E) When the understudy was introduced to the famous lead actress, she smiled with warmth and offered her hand.

Ⓐ ⦿ Ⓒ Ⓓ Ⓔ

28. Since its invention 300 years ago in Italy by Bartolomeo Cristofori a keeper of musical instruments for the Medici family the piano has become indispensable.

(A) Since its invention 300 years ago in Italy by Bartolomeo Cristofori a keeper of musical instruments for the Medici family the piano has become indispensable.

(B) Since its invention, 300 years ago, in Italy, by Bartolomeo Cristofori, a keeper of musical instruments for the Medici family, the piano has become indispensable.

(C) Since its invention 300 years ago in Italy by Bartolomeo Cristofori a keeper of musical instruments for the Medici family, the piano has become indispensable.

(D) Since its invention 300 years ago in Italy by Bartolomeo Cristofori, a keeper of musical instruments for the Medici family, the piano has become indispensable.

(E) Since its invention 300 years ago in Italy by Bartolomeo Cristofori a keeper of musical instruments for the Medici family the piano is a must.

Ⓐ Ⓑ Ⓒ 🅓 Ⓔ

29. Although the contest appeared to be one-sided at first, <u>the candidates were running neck by neck by the end</u>.

(A) the candidates were running neck by neck by the end.

(B) the candidates were running neck and neck by the end.

(C) the candidates ran neck to neck by the end.

(D) the candidates were neck in neck by the end.

(E) the candidates were running neck by neck to the end.

Ⓐ 🅑 Ⓒ Ⓓ Ⓔ

30. Like Mr. Potter in *It's a Wonderful Life,* <u>the fellow reacted greedy when he discovered</u> that a pile of cash had been unexpectedly dropped in his lap.

(A) the fellow reacted greedy when he discovered

(B) the fellow reacted greedy with the discovery

(C) the fellow reacted greedily when he discovered

(D) the fellow was greedy upon the discovery

(E) the fellow reacted greedily when you discovered

Ⓐ Ⓑ 🅒 Ⓓ Ⓔ

31. <u>We would of spent more time in Pierce, but there were other ghost towns on our itinerary and time was of the essence.</u>

(A) We would of spent more time in Pierce, but there were other ghost towns on our itinerary and time was of the essence.

(B) We would of spent more time in Pierce, and there were other ghost towns on our itinerary, and we were running out of time.

(C) We would have spent more time in Pierce, but there were other ghost towns on our itinerary had time not been of the essence.

(D) We could of spent more time in Pierce, but there were other ghost towns on our itinerary and time was of the essence.

(E) We would have spent more time in Pierce, but there were other ghost towns on our itinerary and time was of the essence.

Ⓐ Ⓑ Ⓒ Ⓓ 🅔

32. Our writing teacher, who loves Russian literature, told us that <u>you can learn a lot by reading the works of the great Russian novelists</u>.

    (A) you can learn a lot by reading the works of the great Russian novelists

    (B) you can learn a lot by reading the work of the great Russian novelists

    (C) writers can learn a lot by reading the works of the great Russian novelists

    (D) you can learn a great deal about writing by reading the works of the great Russian novelists

    (E) writing students should read the works of the great Russian novelists

                       Ⓐ Ⓑ Ⓒ Ⓓ Ⓔ

33. Astronomers, by employing the Doppler effect to measure minute shifts in light waves from a wobbling star<u>, have discovered twenty-eight extrasolar planets.</u>

    (A) , have discovered twenty-eight extrasolar planets.

    (B) , has discovered twenty-eight extrasolar planets.

    (C) have discovered twenty-eight extra solarplanets.

    (D) have, to date, discovered twenty-eight extra solarplanets.

    (E) , will have discovered twenty-eight extrasolar planets.

                       Ⓐ Ⓑ Ⓒ Ⓓ Ⓔ

34. <u>Contacts with European fishermen decimating the local Native American groups, it left a widowed coast which greeted the Pilgrims when they arrived in the early 17th century.</u>

    (A) Contacts with European fishermen decimating the local Native American groups, it left a widowed coast which greeted the Pilgrims when they arrived in the early 17th century.

    (B) Contacts with European fishermen decimating the local Native American groups and left a widowed coast, which greeted the Pilgrims when they arrived in the early 17th century.

    (C) Contacts with European fishermen decimated the local Native American groups. A widowed coast greeted the Pilgrims when they arrived in the early 17th century.

    (D) Contacts with European fishermen decimating the local Native American groups. A widowed coast greeted the Pilgrims when they arrived in the early 17th century.

    (E) Contacts with European fishermen decimated the local Native American groups, a widowed coast greeted the Pilgrims when they arrived in the early 17th century.

                       Ⓐ Ⓑ Ⓒ Ⓓ Ⓔ

35. <u>Annoyed by his bad behavior, the unruly student got suspended from school.</u>

(A) Annoyed by his bad behavior, the unruly student got suspended from school.

(B) Annoyed by his bad behavior, the unruly administrators got the student suspended from school.

(C) Unruly students, annoyed by his bad behavior, suspended him from school.

(D) Annoyed by his bad behavior, administrators suspended the unruly student from school.

(E) Annoyed by his bad behavior, the unruly student had been suspended from school.

Ⓐ Ⓑ Ⓒ Ⓓ Ⓔ

36. When she arrived home after being away on vacation for a week<u>, she was stinged by the news that her pet was ill</u>.

(A) , she was stinged by the news that her pet was ill

(B) , she was stung by the news that her pet was ill

(C) she was stung by the news that her pet was ill

(D) , she was stinged by the knowledge that her pet was ill

(E) , she is stinged by the news that her pet was ill

Ⓐ Ⓑ Ⓒ Ⓓ Ⓔ

37. We were pleased to learn that the local newspaper is going to <u>come out with a monthly real estate supplement on a regular basis</u>.

(A) come out with a monthly real estate supplement on a regular basis

(B) come out with a monthly real estate supplement regularly

(C) regularly come out with a monthly real estate supplement

(D) be coming out with a monthly real estate supplement on a regular basis

(E) come out with a monthly real estate supplement

Ⓐ Ⓑ Ⓒ Ⓓ Ⓔ

Directions: The passage that follows is an early draft of an essay. Some parts need to be rewritten. Read the passage carefully and answer the questions that follow. Choose the answer that most clearly and effectively expresses the writer's intended meaning. In making your decisions, follow the conventions of standard English. After you have chosen your answer, fill in the corresponding oval.

[1] The enormous rise in the number of people speaking English is one of the main reasons for the increasing vibrancy of the language, not for its deterioration as some people claim. [2] Immigrants to the United States and other English-speaking countries have always made welcome contributions to their countries, and the words and phrases they have brought with them have enriched English speech, too.

[3] English is always changing, it is changing for the better. [4] When people from western European countries settled in the United States, for example, they gave us terms such as <u>blond</u>, <u>chef</u>, <u>attorney</u>, <u>mayor</u>, and <u>nuance</u>, as well as <u>hamburger</u>, <u>frankfurter</u>, <u>sauerkraut</u>, <u>wanderlust</u>, <u>wagon</u>, <u>yacht</u>, <u>pickle</u>, <u>pasta</u>, <u>spaghetti</u>, and <u>mascara</u>. [5] And whenever we ride in a <u>limousine</u>, wear <u>denim</u>, put on <u>cologne</u>, or enjoy the fragrance of <u>magnolia</u> or <u>wisteria</u>, we can thank the immigrants who brought those terms to the United States. [6] Who would argue that these additions have detracted from the English we speak?

[7] In recent years, immigrants to the United States have put their stamp to the English language. [8] We should be grateful for African words such as <u>banana</u> and <u>zombie</u>, and for East Indian words such as <u>loot</u> and <u>shampoo</u>. [9] I certainly am thankful for the Chinese words <u>soy</u> and <u>tofu</u>, as these foods have helped to improve my eating habits. [10] So, too, have <u>potatoes</u> and <u>tortillas</u>, two Spanish additions from this side of the Atlantic.

[11] English is a living language and new English speakers breathe life into it day by day. [12] Each new immigrant group arriving in an English-speaking land not only adds welcome new words to the language, but also enriches the cultural life for all. [13] A difference from the past is that among the new words and expressions that are being absorbed into the English language today, fewer and fewer of them owe their origins to Greek or Latin. [14] Not to mention Old English roots. [15] I say that people who bemoan the worsening of English should say "sayonara" to their worries about its demise and, instead, cuddle up on a sofa in their pajamas, eat a pastrami sandwich on a bagel, wash it down with coffee, and then listen to a mesmerizing virtuoso cellist or pianist on the radio.

38. Which of the following is the best revision of the underlined portion of sentence 2?

Immigrants to the United States and other English-speaking countries have always made <u>welcome contributions to their countries, and the words and phrases</u> *they have brought with them have enriched English speech, too.*

(A) welcome contributions to those countries; and the words and phrases

(B) welcome contributions to their countries. The words and phrases

(C) welcome contributions to those countries, and the words and phrases

(D) welcome contributions to their countries: The words and phrases

(E) welcome contributions to their own countries, and the words and phrases

Ⓐ Ⓑ Ⓒ Ⓓ Ⓔ

39. Which of the following is the best revision of sentence 3?

English is always changing, it is changing for the better.

(A) English is always changing, but it is changing for the better.

(B) English is always changing, and it is changing for the better.

(C) English is changing. It is always changing for the better.

(D) English is always changing because it is changing for the better.

(E) English is always changing; it is changing for the better.

Ⓐ Ⓑ Ⓒ Ⓓ Ⓔ

40. Which best replaces the underlined phrase in sentence 7?

In recent years, immigrants to the United States have <u>put their stamp to</u> *the English language.*

(A) given their stamp to

(B) had no effect on

(C) put a stamp on

(D) stamped on

(E) put their stamp on

Ⓐ Ⓑ Ⓒ Ⓓ Ⓔ

41. Which is the best way to revise and combine sentences 13 and 14?
A difference from the past is that among the new words and expressions that are being absorbed into the English language today, fewer and fewer of them owe their origins to Greek or Latin. Not to mention Old English roots.

(A) (As it is now)

(B) A difference from the past is that among the new words and expressions that are being absorbed into the English language today, fewer and fewer of them will owe their origins to Greek or Latin, not to mention Old English roots.

(C) A difference from the past is that among the new words and expressions that are being absorbed into the English language today, fewer and fewer of them owe their origins to Greek, Latin, or Old English roots.

(D) A difference from the past is that among the new words and expressions that are being absorbed into the English language today, fewer and fewer of them owes their origins to Greek, Latin, or Old English roots.

(E) A difference from the past is that among the new words and expressions that are being absorbed into the English language today, fewer and fewer of them owe their origins to Greek or Latin; not to mention Old English roots.

Ⓐ Ⓑ Ⓒ Ⓓ Ⓔ

42. Which sentence best states the main idea of paragraph 4?

(A) sentence 11

(B) sentence 12

(C) sentence 13

(D) sentence 14

(E) sentence 15

Ⓐ Ⓑ Ⓒ Ⓓ Ⓔ

43. All of the following strategies are used by the writer of the passage EXCEPT

(A) drawing conclusions from events

(B) recognizing and acknowledging patterns

(C) drawing upon personal experiences

(D) presenting counterarguments

(E) providing examples in support of a position

Ⓐ Ⓑ Ⓒ Ⓓ Ⓔ

Each of the following sentences may contain an error in grammar, usage, diction (word choice), or idiom. Some of the sentences are correct as written. None contains more than one error. The error, if there is one, is underlined and lettered. Assume that the parts of the sentence not underlined are correct. Read each sentence carefully, and if there is an error, choose the underlined part that must be changed to make the sentence correct, and fill in the corresponding oval. If the sentence has no error, fill in oval E. In selecting answers, follow the requirements of standard written English.

EXAMPLE

<u>Like</u> the brat in <u>his</u> *The Ransom of Red Chief,* <u>young</u> Will Porter <u>love</u> dime
A　　　　　　B　　　　　　　　　　　　　C　　　　　　　D

novel adventures. <u>No error</u>
　　　　　　　　　　E

Ⓐ Ⓑ Ⓒ Ⓓ Ⓔ

---

44. Hasn't <u>nobody</u> <u>seen</u> the <u>architects'</u> thrilling plans for the new <u>skyscraper?</u>
　　　　　A　　B　　　　C　　　　　　　　　　　　　　　　　D

<u>No error</u>
E

Ⓐ Ⓑ Ⓒ Ⓓ Ⓔ

45. Each <u>of the members</u> of the mysterious and secretive league <u>agreed</u> to keep
　　　　　A　　　　　　　　　　　　　　　　　　　　　　　　　B

<u>his</u> true identity to <u>themselves.</u> <u>No error</u>
C　　　　　　　　D　　　　E

Ⓐ Ⓑ Ⓒ Ⓓ Ⓔ

46. How many minutes <u>lapsed</u> between the time we <u>arrived</u> on the island and the
　　　　　　　　　　A　　　　　　　　　　　B

time we finally <u>settled</u> into <u>our</u> hotel room? <u>No error</u>
　　　　　　　C　　　　D　　　　　　　E

Ⓐ Ⓑ Ⓒ Ⓓ Ⓔ

47. I <u>nearly</u> <u>fell for it</u> when my opponent tried to <u>pull the wool in</u> my eyes, but
　　A　　　B　　　　　　　　　　　　　　　　C

I <u>kept my wits about me.</u> <u>No error</u>
　　D　　　　　　　　E

Ⓐ Ⓑ Ⓒ Ⓓ Ⓔ

48. Visitors to our nation's capital seeing the newly completed World War II
     A   B   C   D

Memorial. No error
           E

Ⓐ Ⓑ Ⓒ Ⓓ Ⓔ

49. I painted the family of deer as they are peacefully eating in the meadow,
                    A   B

completely unaware of my presence a mere stone's throw away. No error
                      C   D   E

Ⓐ Ⓑ Ⓒ Ⓓ Ⓔ

50. We attended the museum opening together; it was very exciting.
       A   B   C   D

No error
E

Ⓐ Ⓑ Ⓒ Ⓓ Ⓔ

51. It was just five minutes before curtain, yet only one-third of the audience
         A   B   C

have arrived. No error
 D   E

Ⓐ Ⓑ Ⓒ Ⓓ Ⓔ

52. I felt badly because I was out of town and therefore unable to help my brother
        A   B   C

move into his new apartment. No error
  D   E

Ⓐ Ⓑ Ⓒ Ⓓ Ⓔ

53. All the critics agree: The more boring part of the movie, by far, is the middle
               A   B   C   D

third. No error
    E

Ⓐ Ⓑ Ⓒ Ⓓ Ⓔ

Part A

Time—25 Minutes (1 question)

You have 25 minutes to write an essay on the topic below.

DO NOT WRITE AN ESSAY THAT ADDRESSES ANY OTHER TOPIC. AN ESSAY ON A DIFFERENT TOPIC WILL NOT BE ACCEPTED.

Plan and write an essay on the assigned topic. Present your thoughts clearly and effectively. Include specific examples to support your views. The quality of your essay is more important than its length, but to express your ideas on the topic adequately, you will probably want to write more than one paragraph. Keep your writing to a reasonable size and avoid wide margins. Be sure to make your handwriting legible.

Consider the following statement. Then write an essay as directed.

Walt Disney once said, "Fancy being remembered around the world for the invention of a mouse." If I had to choose one thing for which to be remembered, that one thing would be _____.

Assignment: Write an essay to complete the statement above. Use examples from history, current events, literature, or your personal experience to support your position.

WRITE YOUR ESSAY ON A SEPARATE SHEET OF PAPER.

Part B

Time—35 Minutes (53 questions)

Each of the following sentences may contain an error in grammar, usage, diction (word choice), or idiom. Some of the sentences are correct as written. None contains more than one error. The error, if there is one, is underlined and lettered. Assume that the parts of the sentence not underlined are correct. Read each sentence carefully, and if there is an error, choose the underlined part that must be changed to make the sentence correct, and fill in the corresponding oval. If the sentence has no error, fill in oval E. In selecting answers, follow the requirements of standard written English.

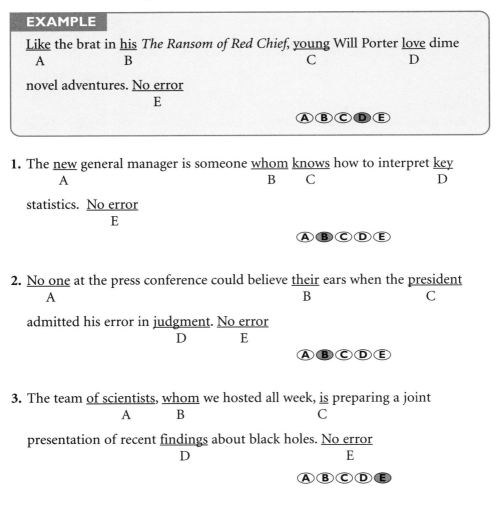

EXAMPLE

<u>Like</u> the brat in <u>his</u> *The Ransom of Red Chief,* <u>young</u> Will Porter <u>love</u> dime
  A   B   C   D

novel adventures. <u>No error</u>
           E

Ⓐ Ⓑ Ⓒ ⬤ Ⓔ

1. The <u>new</u> general manager is someone <u>whom</u> <u>knows</u> how to interpret <u>key</u>
     A   B   C   D

statistics. <u>No error</u>
          E

Ⓐ ⬤ Ⓒ Ⓓ Ⓔ

2. <u>No one</u> at the press conference could believe <u>their</u> ears when the <u>president</u>
    A   B   C

admitted his error in <u>judgment</u>. <u>No error</u>
                         D   E

Ⓐ ⬤ Ⓒ Ⓓ Ⓔ

3. The team <u>of scientists</u>, <u>whom</u> we hosted all week, <u>is</u> preparing a joint
              A   B   C

presentation of recent <u>findings</u> about black holes. <u>No error</u>
                     D   E

Ⓐ Ⓑ Ⓒ Ⓓ ⬤

4. The family <u>that</u> lives in the apartment upstairs <u>from</u> us
           A   B

<u>immigrated</u> from <u>Eastern</u> Europe. <u>No error</u>
   C   D   E

ⒶⒷ●ⒹⒺ

5. The tree, once a <u>mere</u> sapling, <u>had grew</u> to a <u>height</u> of <u>forty-two</u> feet.
                  A   B   C   D

<u>No error</u>
  E

Ⓐ●ⒸⒹⒺ

6. The <u>most</u> trickiest part of trout <u>fishing</u> is not <u>casting; it</u> is tying <u>flies</u>.
    A   B   C   D

<u>No error</u>
  E

●ⒷⒸⒹⒺ

7. My uncle can name all the different <u>kinds</u> of aircraft<u>, even</u> enemy aircraft
                                    A   B

<u>flown</u> in WWII, without <u>hardly</u> trying. <u>No error</u>
  C   D   E

ⒶⒷⒸ●Ⓔ

8. <u>Neither</u> Spokane nor Walla Walla <u>get</u> as much rain <u>as</u> Seattle <u>does</u>.
    A   B   C   D

<u>No error</u>
  E

Ⓐ●ⒸⒹⒺ

9. Last year, archaeologists <u>were excavating</u> a site in <u>Rome, to their</u> surprise and
                              A   B

<u>delight, they</u> discovered a <u>long-buried</u> fresco in the process. <u>No error</u>
   C   D   E

Ⓐ●ⒸⒹⒺ

10. In the Rockies, avalanches pose a serious threat, forest fires are another
         A   B   C   D

    danger. No error
            E

    Ⓐ Ⓑ Ⓒ Ⓓ Ⓔ

11. The great ocean liner will have sank remarkably quickly after it hit the huge
                          A   B   C   D

    iceberg. No error
             E

    Ⓐ Ⓑ Ⓒ Ⓓ Ⓔ

12. Choosing the perfect dress for the prom was hard for Elena, who visited
    A   B   C

    several stores in her search. No error
                     D   E

    Ⓐ Ⓑ Ⓒ Ⓓ Ⓔ

13. Whomever said that building the canal was a walk in the park ought to think
    A   B   C

    about it again; the experience was a brutal one for everyone involved. No error
                    D   E

    Ⓐ Ⓑ Ⓒ Ⓓ Ⓔ

14. When the students got to the museum, the teacher took them aside to quickly
                         A   B

    call attention of the fact that no eating is allowed there. No error
    C   D   E

    Ⓐ Ⓑ Ⓒ Ⓓ Ⓔ

15. Three mountain ranges with good skiing are the Rockies, Alps, and the
                          A   B   C

    Wasatch Range. No error
    D   E

    Ⓐ Ⓑ Ⓒ Ⓓ Ⓔ

16. The <u>inspired</u> cooking of many young<u>, creative</u> chefs <u>has been</u>
        A   B   C

<u>well</u> received across the country. <u>No error</u>
 D   E

Ⓐ Ⓑ Ⓒ Ⓓ ⬤

17. Few <u>in the government</u> <u>expects</u> the new colonial settlement <u>to pay</u> dividends
           A   B   C

<u>within</u> the first few years. <u>No error</u>
 D   E

Ⓐ ⬤ Ⓒ Ⓓ Ⓔ

18. Massage therapists <u>need</u> a license to practice <u>their</u> profession, and <u>you</u> also
                   A   B   C

need to buy equipment <u>to set up</u> an office. <u>No error</u>
                    D   E

Ⓐ Ⓑ ⬤ Ⓓ Ⓔ

19. I could <u>hardly</u> believe my eyes when I saw my favorite actor get up from <u>his</u>
        A   B

seat in the restaurant, <u>look in my direction</u>, and <u>nod</u> in greeting. <u>No error</u>
                            C   D   E

Ⓐ Ⓑ Ⓒ Ⓓ ⬤

20. As a member <u>of the student council,</u> <u>it is important to focus</u> on what <u>is</u> <u>best</u>
                          A   B   C D

for all students. <u>No error</u>
               E

Ⓐ ⬤ Ⓒ Ⓓ Ⓔ

In each of the following items, all or part of the sentence is underlined. Beneath each sentence are five ways of phrasing the underlined part. Choice (A) is the same as the original; the other four are different. Select the answer choice that best expresses the meaning of the original sentence. Your goal is to produce the most effective sentence, one that is clear and not wordy. Choose (A) if the original sentence is better than any of the other answer choices.

EXAMPLE

It was a bazaar occurrence, to say the least, when the lightning hit that same tree in our yard again.

(A) It was a bazaar occurrence,

(B) It was a bizarre occurrence,

(C) It has been a bazaar occurrence,

(D) It was a typical occurrence,

(E) It was a very bazaar occurrence,

(A) (B) (C) (D) (E)

---

21. A ring of four lakes, all with beaches and camping facilities, surround the capital city.

   (A) A ring of four lakes, all with beaches and camping facilities, surround the capital city.

   (B) A ring of four lakes, all with beaches and camping facilities, is surrounding the capital city.

   (C) A ring of four lakes, all with beaches and camping facilities, surrounds the capital city.

   (D) A ring of four lakes, all with beaches and camping facilities, go around the capital city.

   (E) A ring of four lakes, all with beaches and camping facilities, wrap around the capital city.

(A) (B) (C) (D) (E)

---

22. Iceberg wranglers lasso giant bergs, they do so to protect vulnerable oil rigs.

   (A) Iceberg wranglers lasso giant bergs, they do so to protect vulnerable oil rigs.

   (B) Iceberg wranglers lasso giant bergs; they do so to protect vulnerable oil rigs.

   (C) Iceberg wranglers lasso giant bergs, but they do so to protect vulnerable oil rigs.

   (D) Iceberg wranglers lasso giant bergs because they protect vulnerable oil rigs.

   (E) Iceberg wranglers lasso giant bergs because of protecting vulnerable oil rigs.

(A) (B) (C) (D) (E)

23. <u>Because the Alamo holds a special place in the minds of many Americans, it exemplifies courage in the face of overwhelming odds.</u>

(A) Because the Alamo holds a special place in the minds of many Americans, it exemplifies courage in the face of overwhelming odds.

(B) After the Alamo holds a special place in the minds of many Americans, it exemplifies courage in the face of overwhelming odds.

(C) The Alamo exemplifies courage in the face of overwhelming odds because it holds a special place in the minds of many Americans.

(D) The Alamo holds a special place in the minds of many Americans, it exemplifies courage in the face of overwhelming odds.

(E) The Alamo holds a special place in the minds of many Americans because it exemplifies courage in the face of overwhelming odds.

Ⓐ Ⓑ Ⓒ Ⓓ **Ⓔ**

24. Off and on, Meriwether Lewis kept a journal in which he recorded <u>what he saw and learned during their journey</u>.

(A) what he saw and learned during their journey

(B) what they saw and learned during his journey

(C) what he saw and learned while on their journey

(D) what he saw and learned during his journey

(E) what he saw and learned on their journey

Ⓐ Ⓑ Ⓒ **Ⓓ** Ⓔ

25. <u>The excited fan sold the home run baseball to a collector that he caught.</u>

(A) The excited fan sold the home run baseball to a collector that he caught.

(B) The excited fan sold the home run baseball that he caught to a collector.

(C) A collector caught the excitement from the fan who sold the home run baseball to him.

(D) The excited fan had sold the home run baseball to a collector that he had caught.

(E) The excited fan, who caught the home run baseball, sold the home run baseball to a collector.

Ⓐ **Ⓑ** Ⓒ Ⓓ Ⓔ

26. <u>Reba generally spends more time on her homework assignments than her friends.</u>

(A) Reba generally spends more time on her homework assignments than her friends.

(B) Reba generally spends more time on her homework assignments than on her friends.

(C) Reba usually spends more time on her homework assignments than her friends.

(D) Reba generally spends more time on her homework assignments than her friends do.

(E) Reba generally spends more time on her homework assignments than any of her friends.

Ⓐ Ⓑ Ⓒ ⬤Ⓓ Ⓔ

27. <u>When the doctor entered the young boy's room early that evening, he began to explain what his problem was.</u>

(A) When the doctor entered the young boy's room early that evening, he began to explain what his problem was.

(B) When the doctor entered the young boy's room early that evening, he began to explain his problem.

(C) When the doctor entered the young boy's room early that evening, he began to explain what the problem was.

(D) After the doctor entered the young boy's room early that evening, he began to explain to him what the problem was.

(E) When the doctor entered the young boy's room early that evening, the boy began to explain what his problem was.

Ⓐ Ⓑ Ⓒ Ⓓ ⬤Ⓔ

28. <u>Trying to get the raft out to sea, the powerful waves made the already difficult task seem nearly impossible.</u>

(A) Trying to get the raft out to sea, the powerful waves made the already difficult task seem nearly impossible.

(B) Trying to get the raft out to sea, the already powerful waves made the difficult task seem nearly impossible.

(C) The powerful waves seemed to make the already difficult task of trying to get the raft out to sea nearly impossible.

(D) The powerful waves made the already difficult task of trying to get the raft out to sea seem nearly impossible.

(E) While trying to get the raft out to sea, the powerful waves made the already difficult task seem nearly impossible.

Ⓐ Ⓑ Ⓒ 🅓 Ⓔ

29. Although the airplane was late in taking off, the pilot confidently promised that we would be able <u>to make up on lost time</u> during the long flight.

(A) to make up on lost time

(B) to make up by lost time

(C) to make up for lost time

(D) to make up with lost time

(E) to make up in lost time

Ⓐ Ⓑ 🅒 Ⓓ Ⓔ

30. The loose-lipped newcomer <u>became nervously when it appeared that</u> his antics were finally beginning to irritate the short-tempered gunslinger.

(A) became nervously when it appeared that

(B) became unsurely when it appeared that

(C) became nervous when it appeared that

(D) became anxiously when it appeared that

(E) seemed to act nervous when it appeared to all those in attendance as if

Ⓐ Ⓑ 🅒 Ⓓ Ⓔ

31. <u>Of all the foods in the world, the one that tastes more terrible is overcooked liver, even when it's smothered in onions.</u>

(A) Of all the foods in the world, the one that tastes more terrible is overcooked liver, even when it's smothered in onions.

(B) Of all the foods in the world, one that tastes terribly is overcooked liver, even when it's smothered in onions.

(C) Of all the foods in the world, the one that tastes the more terrible is overcooked liver, even when its smothered in onions.

(D) Of all the foods in the world, the one that tastes the most terribly is overcooked liver, even when it's smothered in onions.

(E) Of all the foods in the world, the one that tastes the most terrible is overcooked liver, even when it's smothered in onions.

Ⓐ Ⓑ Ⓒ Ⓓ 🅔

32. Back then, they didn't have cell phones; in fact, they didn't even have telephones.

    (A) Back then, they didn't have cell phones; in fact, they didn't even have telephones.

    (B) Back then, they didn't have cell phones. In fact, they didn't even have telephones.

    (C) Back then, they didn't have cell phones; in fact, people didn't even have telephones.

    (D) Back then, people didn't have cell phones; in fact, they didn't even have telephones.

    (E) Back then, when they didn't have cell phones, they didn't, in fact, even have telephones.

    Ⓐ Ⓑ Ⓒ **Ⓓ** Ⓔ

33. Statisticians, by examining a variety of batting statistics, have provided coaches with new and better ways of evaluating a player's value to his team.

    (A) statistics, have provided coaches with new and better ways of evaluating a player's value to his team.

    (B) statistics have provided coaches with new and better ways of evaluating a players' value to his team.

    (C) statistics, has provided coaches with new and better ways of evaluating a player's value to his team.

    (D) statistics, have provided coaches with new and better ways of evaluating a player's value to their team.

    (E) statistics. They have provided coaches with new and better ways of evaluating a player's value to his team.

    Ⓐ Ⓑ Ⓒ Ⓓ Ⓔ

34. Once a remote, sleepy island, Vieques, located off the coast of Puerto Rico, which is now quickly becoming a magnet for sun seekers from all over the globe.

    (A) Once a remote, sleepy island, Vieques, located off the coast of Puerto Rico, which is now quickly becoming a magnet for sun seekers from all over the globe.

    (B) Once a remote, sleepy island, Vieques, located off the coast of Puerto Rico, Vieques which is now quickly becomes a magnet for sun seekers from all over the globe.

    (C) Once a remote, sleepy island, Vieques, located off the coast of Puerto Rico, is now quickly becoming a magnet for sun seekers from all over the globe.

(D) Once a remote, sleepy island, Vieques, which is located off the coast of Puerto Rico, now quickly becomes a magnet for sun seekers from all over the globe.

(E) Once a remote, sleepy island, Vieques, located off the coast of Puerto Rico, that is now becoming a magnet for sun seekers from all over the globe.

Ⓐ Ⓑ Ⓒ Ⓓ Ⓔ

35. <u>When it opens, the new hotel will only have room for twenty-five guests.</u>

(A) When it opens, the new hotel will only have room for twenty-five guests.
(B) When it opens, the new hotel will have room for twenty-five guests.
(C) When it opens, the new hotel will have only room for twenty-five guests.
(D) When it opens, the new hotel will have room for only twenty-five guests.
(E) When it opens, the new hotel will have room only for twenty-five guests.

Ⓐ Ⓑ Ⓒ Ⓓ Ⓔ

36. Following the awards ceremony, <u>participants will have gone</u> to one of several parties.

(A) participants will have gone
(B) participants will go
(C) participants have gone
(D) participants had been going
(E) participants will have been going

Ⓐ Ⓑ Ⓒ Ⓓ Ⓔ

37. Visitors to Banff and Jasper National Parks in Alberta, Canada, get many opportunities to <u>gaze at the views of magnificent scenery they see</u>.

(A) gaze at the views of magnificent scenery they see
(B) gaze at the magnificent scenery of views they see
(C) gaze at the views they see
(D) gaze at the views of magnificent scenery
(E) gaze at magnificent scenery

Ⓐ Ⓑ Ⓒ Ⓓ Ⓔ

Directions: The passage that follows is an early draft of an essay. Some parts need to be rewritten. Read the passage carefully and answer the questions that follow. Choose the answer that most clearly and effectively expresses the writer's intended meaning. In making your decisions, follow the conventions of standard English. After you have chosen your answer, fill in the corresponding oval.

[1] I agree that it takes a great event to make a person great. [2] Examples from history that support this view are plentiful. [3] One surefire place to find instances of how events brought out the best in people are in history books of the American presidency.

[4] When we try to decide which president was the greatest, we find that one theme is common to all: [5] Each leader faced huge challenges during his life or term that changed him forever and brought out his greatness. [6] Let's start at the beginning. [7] George Washington's reputation as a great leader emerged from the unique challenges he faced as commander of a ragtag army during an uphill fight. [8] By the time Washington became the unanimous choice as the young nation's first president, the steadfastness, courage, and compassion he had displayed during wartime crises had transformed him from a prosperous Virginia planter to a commander of the Continental Army, and prepared him for the difficult responsibilities ahead.

[9] Since Washington's time, several major events have brought out the true character of other presidents. [10] John Kennedy's reputation was much improved by the Cuban missile crisis that rocked the country. [11] His firm stance during that emergency showed the world that he had the "right stuff" for leadership and it solidified his reputation as a great leader. [12] It took the calamity of the Great Depression and the disaster of World War II to firmly establish Franklin Roosevelt's reputation as a strong and creative leader.

[13] But perhaps the best example of how "events make the man" comes in the person of Abraham Lincoln. [14] Lincoln, a relative newcomer to national politics, established himself as perhaps the greatest of our presidents for his unwavering sense of right and wrong, and his commitment to preserving the union in the face of the greatest American catastrophe of the 19th century—the bloody Civil War. [15] Before and even during the war, Lincoln was seen by many as ignorant, weak, and wavering; he was treated with disdain by politicians and generals alike. [16] In fact, it looked for a time as if he was not going to serve a second term. [17] But by the time the war began to wind down, Lincoln had achieved the exalted status by which he is regarded today.

[18] The four presidents mentioned above are seen by most today as great leaders. [19] But it is a good bet to say that without the crises they faced, these men may not have had the opportunity to show the world what they were truly made of. [20] And they are but four among many whose lives have been shaped by their times. [21] Therefore, I wholeheartedly agree with the notion that "events make the man."

38. Which of the following is the best revision of the underlined portion of sentence 3?

One surefire place to find instances of how events brought out the best in people <u>are in history books of the American presidency</u>.

(A) (As it is now)

(B) is in the American presidency

(C) is in history books of the American presidency

(D) will be in history books of the American presidency

(E) was in history books of the American presidency

Ⓐ Ⓑ **Ⓒ** Ⓓ Ⓔ

39. In context, what is the best way to deal with sentence 6?

(A) Leave it as it is.

(B) Use "where" at the end of sentence 6 to link it with sentence 7.

(C) Change sentence 6 to "To begin with," and link it with sentence 7.

(D) Use "because" at the end of sentence 6 to link it with sentence 7.

(E) Place it after sentence 7.

Ⓐ Ⓑ Ⓒ Ⓓ Ⓔ

40. Which of the following best replaces the word "improved" in sentence 10?

(A) fixed

(B) bettered

(C) furthered

(D) diminished

(E) enhanced

Ⓐ Ⓑ Ⓒ Ⓓ **Ⓔ**

41. In context, which is the best way to deal with sentence 12?

(A) Insert "On the other hand," at the beginning of the sentence.

(B) Insert "But" at the beginning of the sentence.

(C) Insert "Similarly," at the beginning of the sentence.

(D) Insert "Frankly," at the beginning of the sentence.

(E) Insert "like Washington" at the end of the sentence.

Ⓐ Ⓑ Ⓒ Ⓓ Ⓔ

42. Which sentence best states the main idea of paragraph 4?

(A) sentence 13

(B) sentence 14

(C) sentence 15

(D) sentence 16

(E) sentence 17

Ⓐ Ⓑ Ⓒ Ⓓ Ⓔ

43. All of the following strategies are used by the writer of the passage EXCEPT

(A) drawing conclusions from historical events

(B) recognizing and acknowledging patterns of behavior

(C) presenting an opposing point of view

(D) offering a personal viewpoint

(E) providing specific details in support of a position

Ⓐ Ⓑ Ⓒ Ⓓ Ⓔ

Each of the following sentences may contain an error in grammar, usage, diction (word choice), or idiom. Some of the sentences are correct as written. None contains more than one error. The error, if there is one, is underlined and lettered. Assume that the parts of the sentence not underlined are correct. Read each sentence carefully, and if there is an error, choose the underlined part that must be changed to make the sentence correct, and fill in the corresponding oval. If the sentence has no error, fill in oval E. In selecting answers, follow the requirements of standard written English.

EXAMPLE

<u>Like</u> the brat in <u>his</u> *The Ransom of Red Chief,* <u>young</u> Will Porter <u>love</u> dime
 A   B   C   D

novel adventures. <u>No error</u>
                          E

Ⓐ Ⓑ Ⓒ Ⓓ Ⓔ

44. <u>Has</u> <u>anybody</u> in America <u>not</u> <u>seen</u> the *Lord of the Rings* trilogy?
        A   B   C   D

<u>No error</u>
    E

Ⓐ Ⓑ Ⓒ Ⓓ Ⓔ

45. Each <u>of the members</u> of the voyage reached for <u>their</u> camera when the boat
              A   B

sailed <u>past</u> the spent volcano and entered the narrow <u>strait</u>. <u>No error</u>
        C   D   E

Ⓐ Ⓑ Ⓒ Ⓓ Ⓔ

46. When the general arrived at the <u>scene</u>, he directed his commanders to <u>have</u>
                                   A   B

troops immediately <u>cease</u> the <u>enemy's</u> makeshift fort. <u>No error</u>
                    C   D   E

Ⓐ Ⓑ Ⓒ Ⓓ Ⓔ

47. Our new teacher did not <u>beat over the bush</u>; she <u>warned</u> us that we <u>were</u>
                              A   B   C

<u>dangerously</u> unprepared for the upcoming test. <u>No error</u>
    D   E

Ⓐ Ⓑ Ⓒ Ⓓ Ⓔ

48. The new musical opened to <u>rave</u> reviews<u>, critics</u> predicted that <u>it</u> would set the

A   B   C

bar high for the <u>season's</u> other new shows. <u>No error</u>

D   E

Ⓐ Ⓑ Ⓒ Ⓓ Ⓔ

49. The <u>morning</u> mist obscured our view of the valley and <u>makes</u> us unable <u>to see</u>

A   B   C

the falls that were <u>not half a mile away</u> from where we stood. <u>No error</u>

D   E

Ⓐ Ⓑ Ⓒ Ⓓ Ⓔ

50. I bumped <u>into</u> an old friend at the parade; <u>it</u> was an <u>unexpected</u> treat for

A   B   C

<u>both</u> of us. <u>No error</u>

D   E

Ⓐ Ⓑ Ⓒ Ⓓ Ⓔ

51. The food critic, <u>who</u> <u>has feasted</u> on culinary delights from one end of the

A   B

world to the other<u>, nonetheless</u> claims that spaghetti and meatballs <u>remain</u> his

C   D

favorite food. <u>No error</u>

E

Ⓐ Ⓑ Ⓒ Ⓓ Ⓔ

52. <u>Not wishing</u> <u>to disturb</u> the rare jay perched <u>only ten paces away</u>, the woman

A   B   C

with the camera walked <u>slow and steady</u>. <u>No error</u>

D   E

Ⓐ Ⓑ Ⓒ Ⓓ Ⓔ

53. More and more Americans<u>, particularly in the South,</u> <u>are in agreement</u> that

A   B

<u>going to car races</u> is more fun <u>than baseball games</u>. <u>No error</u>

C   D   E

Ⓐ Ⓑ Ⓒ Ⓓ Ⓔ

Commonly Confused Words

You will have to pay attention to word choice both on the essay part and on the multiple-choice part of a standardized test. When you write your essay, you want to make sure that you use words that mean what you intend them to mean. When you take the multiple-choice part of the test, you need to be able to identify words that are either grammatically incorrect or simply misused.

Below is a list of some of the many pairs or groups of words in the English language that are easily confused. Some of the words are often confused because although they have different meanings, they sound the same. Others are confused because they have related meanings even though they sound different.

Study the following list to remember the distinctions between these commonly confused words.

accept (v.): to take what is offered or to agree
except (prep.): leaving out or excluding

all ready (adj.): totally ready
already (adv.): by this time; even now

all together (pron., adj.): everyone or every thing in one place
altogether (adv.): entirely

allusion (n.): an implied or indirect reference
illusion (n.): mistaken vision

ascent (n.): the act of rising or climbing upward
assent (v.): to agree to something

breadth (n.): distance from side to side
breath (n.): air inhaled or exhaled
breathe (v.): to inhale and exhale

cease (v.): to come to an end
seize (v.): to take possession of

continual (n.): repeated, happening again and again
continuous (adj.): uninterrupted

credible (adj.): believable
creditable (adj.): deserving of praise

descent (n.): a downward inclination
dissent (n., v.): disagreement, to disagree

device (n.): something contrived
devise (v.): to plan

disburse (v.): to pay out
disperse (v.): to scatter

disinterested (adj.): impartial
uninterested (adj.): not interested

elapse (v.): to pass
lapse (v.): to become void

elusive (adj.): hard to catch or comprehend
illusive (adj.): misleading, deceptive

emigrate (v.): to leave one's country or place of residence to live elsewhere
immigrate (v.): to come into a country for the purpose of living there

eminent (adj.): well known, standing out
imminent (adj.): ready to take place

expand (v.): to open up or increase in size
expend (v.): to spend or pay out

farther (adj.): more distant or more advanced
further (adj.): extending beyond a point; moreover

formally (adv.): with rigid ceremony
formerly (adv.): at an earlier time

human (adj.): relating to mankind
humane (adv.): kind, compassionate

hypercritical (adj.): very critical
hypocritical (adj.): pretending to be virtuous

incredible (adj.): too extraordinary to be believed
incredulous (adj.): skeptical

infer (v.): to derive as a conclusion from facts or premises
imply (v.): to suggest meaning indirectly

lay (v.): set something down, to place something
lie (v.): to recline

lend (v.): to give for a time
loan (n.): received to use for a time

magnate (n.): a person of rank, power, influence, or distinction, often in large industry
magnet (n.): iron bar with power to attract iron

moral (n., adj.): ethic, lesson
morale (n.): mental and emotional condition

perpetrate (v.): to be guilty of; to commit
perpetuate (n.): to cause to last indefinitely

perquisite (n.): a privilege or profit in addition to salary
prerequisite (n.): a preliminary requirement

personal (adj.): private
personnel (n.): a body of people, usually employed in some organization

precede (v.): to go before
proceed (v.): to advance

preposition (n.): a part of speech
proposition (n.): a proposal or suggestion

pretend (v.): to make believe
portend (v.): to give an omen or anticipatory sign

respectively (adv.): in order indicated
respectfully (adv.): in a respectful manner

restive (adj.): stubbornly resisting control
restless (adj.): unquiet, constantly moving

than (conj.): used in comparison
then (adv.): at that time; next in order of time

veracious (adj.): truthful, honest
voracious (adj.): having a huge appetite, ravenous, gluttonous

Idioms

Recall that idioms are common expressions whose meanings are accepted and understood by speakers of a language, although none of the expressions can be taken literally, nor are they guaranteed to be grammatically correct or logical. On the essay part of the test, including colorful idiomatic expressions effectively and in moderation can *spice up* your writing; on the multiple-choice part however, you will need to be able to spot faulty idioms.

Below is a chart that defines a selection of idioms. To help you to understand them, a sentence with each idiom has been provided for you.

Study these pages to make sure you understand the meanings of the idioms below.

IDIOM	SENTENCE WITH IDIOM
catch a cold: become sick with a cold	Even though he was taking vitamins, Ed **caught a cold**.
on the last leg: the final stage of a trip	Sarah was glad to be **on the last leg** of her long trip.
up his sleeve: keep secretly ready for the right time	We could tell from the mischievous expression on Sid's face that he had something **up his sleeve**.
get the red carpet treatment: to receive lavish treatment	We **got the red carpet treatment** after winning the award.
not my cup of tea: not something you enjoy	I like folk music, but country-western music is simply **not my cup of tea**.
dawn on: to become clear	After long consideration, the perfect solution finally **dawned on** me.
stick one's neck out: to do something dangerous, usually on someone else's behalf	When my colleague was blamed for the error, I **stuck my neck out** for her and ended up angering our boss.
a lemon: something that is defective	Despite the good reputation that brand of vacuum cleaners has, the one I bought turned out to be **a lemon**.
to make ends meet: to earn enough to pay one's bills	The poor, young couple struggled **to make ends meet**.
skate on thin ice: to take a chance or risk disapproval	I was **skating on thin ice** when I forgot to take out the trash again.
as plain as the nose on your face: something that is obvious	The solution to the puzzle is **as plain as the nose on your face**.

IDIOM	SENTENCE WITH IDIOM
on the loose: free to go; not stopped by anything or anyone	When I got home, my dog was **on the loose**, having escaped her cage due to a faulty lock.
catch on: to understand or learn about something	At first this job may seem difficult, but you will **catch on** before you know it.
fall for: to believe something meant to trick you; to begin to like something a lot	He is such a good storyteller that I almost always **fall for** his tall tales.
keep one's wits about one: to remain calm and composed in a troublesome or dangerous situation	She is a good person to have around during an emergency; she really **keeps her wits about her**.
drive a hard bargain: to make a deal that is to your advantage	The dealer **drove a hard bargain**, so I did not get a particularly good price.
pull the wool over one's eyes: to trick someone into thinking good things about you; to deceive	He **pulled the wool over my eyes**, and I ended up trusting him when I shouldn't have.
beat around the bush: to talk without giving a clear answer; avoiding the point	When I asked him how my grandmother was doing, he **beat around the bush**.
steal the spotlight: to attract attention away from what everyone should be paying attention to	The lead actor was good, but the young actress who played his niece **stole the spotlight**.
put away: to eat or drink a lot	She may look small, but she can **put away** a whole pizza.
get the ball rolling: to start something	The meeting began slowly, but once we **got the ball rolling**, everyone started to participate.
cough up the money: to pay for something reluctantly	My uncle finally **coughed up the money** for a bus ticket and visited us here.
pay through the nose: to pay a lot of money for something	The play is great, but you have to **pay through the nose** for tickets.
shell out: to pay or spend	I had to **shell out** a hefty sum to pay for the renovations.
neck and neck: equal or almost equal in a race or contest	By the end, the contestants were running **neck and neck**.

Test-Taking Tips

Study the pointers below to help you prepare for the writing section of a standardized test:

- Review the various direction lines for test items.

- Practice writing persuasive essays.

- Familiarize yourself with the different formats of the multiple-choice items that will appear on the test. Make sure you know the different types of skills you will be tested on.

- Get regular exercise and eat a healthy diet. (Although this is always good advice, it is particularly important for the time leading up to the exam, as you want to be sure to be physically and mentally sharp on the day of the test.)

- Do not study right up until bedtime each night. Relax instead, before you go to sleep.

- Try to cut back on the time you spend studying for the test as the exam time approaches. In fact, try to do something relaxing on the day before the test.

- Put all other matters out of your mind and get plenty of rest the night before the test. You want to avoid stress as much as you can.

- Think positive thoughts; picture yourself being successful on the test.

Below is a list of pointers to help you on the day you take the test.

- Read any new instructions carefully, but skip any with which you are familiar.

- Eat a healthy breakfast that morning.

- Make sure you know where the testing site is and how to get there well before the test date. You will have enough on your mind that day; don't leave these details for the last minute.

- Wear comfortable clothing to the exam. If you wear layers, you can adjust to any temperature in the room.

- Be sure to take two or three sharpened pencils with erasers to the testing site. Be sure, too, to bring along your admission papers and your photo ID.

- Get to the testing site on time! And bring a positive, confident attitude.

- Pick a seat away from any possible distractions. For instance, stay away from the door or the proctor's desk.

- Work purposefully, but carefully. Pay no attention to the other test takers.

- Pay attention to your breathing. If you are holding your breath because you are tense, that can get in the way of clear thinking. Breathe steadily. You are in a long-distance race, not a sprint.

- When you write your essay, write as neatly as you can. In addition, keep your writing as small as you can manage legibly, and avoid wide margins.

- For the multiple-choice items, be sure to read the entire question and all answer choices before you mark anything on your answer sheet. Remember that you do not need to read choice (A) on *Improving Sentences* items, as it is always a repeat of the original sentence.

- If you change your mind about an answer, be sure to erase your mark completely before marking your new choice.

- Know when to make a guess and to move on.

- Try to answer all questions, but if you can't answer one, write down the item number on your scrap paper, and move on. Come back to it later.

- Check your answer sheet periodically to make sure that you are filling in the item numbers that match the item numbers on the test. This is a particularly important step to follow if you have skipped any questions.

- Erase any stray marks on your answer sheet. Make notes only on the scrap paper or the test booklet.

- Use *every* minute given. If you finish early, take the remaining time to check your work.

- Double-check your answers, particularly for those items with which you struggled.

Student Self Evaluation

Use these pages as a personal study guide to help you practice and prepare for the test. In the outline provided, record your key concerns, ideas, questions, and comments on any of the writing or grammar topics addressed in the text. Use your notes to identify areas that you need to improve upon.

PREWRITING STEPS: Do I need to review the prewriting steps?

_____

_____

_____

_____

_____

WRITING BETTER ESSAYS: Do I understand what makes a good essay?

_____

_____

_____

_____

_____

WRITING BETTER PARAGRAPHS: Do I understand what makes a good paragraph?

_____

_____

_____

_____

_____

WRITING BETTER SENTENCES: Do I understand what makes a good sentence?

_____

_____

_____

_____

_____

POLISHING YOUR ESSAY: Do I understand how to make improvements and corrections to my essay?

_____

_____

_____

_____

_____

IDENTIFYING SENTENCE ERRORS AND IMPROVING SENTENCES: Do I need to review any of topics 20–32?

_____

_____

_____

_____

_____

IMPROVING PARAGRAPHS: Do I need to review any of topics 33–35?

_____

_____

_____

_____

_____

TEST TAKING: Do I need to review any important test-taking tips?

_____

_____

_____

_____

_____

A

active voice, 63
adjective(s), 103–104
   degrees of comparison in, 145–146
   predicate, 103
   proper, 103
   versus adverb, 104
adverb(s), 103–104
   degrees of comparison in, 145–146
   versus adjective, 104
agreement
   pronoun-antecedent, 117–118
   subject-verb, 91–92
antecedent, 117
   compound, 118

C

clauses
   dependent (subordinate), 48, 157–158
   independent (main), 48
clichés, 53
coherence, 37–39
colon(s), 66
combining sentences, 59–60
comma, 65–66
commonly confused words, 209–210
comparisons, 145–147
   avoiding double, 146
   avoiding illogical, 147
   avoiding incomplete, 146
   degrees of, 145–146
complete predicate defined, 43, 133
complete sentence defined, 43, 133
complete subject defined, 43, 133
complex sentence, 48
compound sentence, 48
compound subject, 91
compound-complex sentence, 48
conclusion in essays, 26–27
conjunctions
   coordinating, 59, 151
   subordinating, 60
connotation, 30

D

dangling modifier, 139–140
definite article, 103
degrees of comparison, 145–146
dependent clause (subordinate), 48
details
   elaborating with supporting, 33–34
   sensory, 30
diction, 29
direct object, 129
double negatives, 109

E

editing (making changes), 69–70
editorial marks, 70
elaboration, 33–34
essay
   conclusion in, 26–27
   introduction in, 22, 25–26
   thesis statement in, 21–22
   topic sentence in, 41
examples
   in persuasive writing, 13–14, 33–34

F

figurative language, 30
fragments defined, 43, 133
   correcting, 43–44, 133–134
future perfect tense, 97
future tense, 97

H

hyperbole, 30

I

idea web, 33–34, 78
idioms, 53, 113, 211–212
importance, transitional words and expressions to show order of, 38–39
indefinite articles, 103
indefinite pronouns, 92, 117–118, 152
independent (main) clauses, 48
indirect object, 129
intervening phrase, 92